Diversity in Mind and in Action

Diversity in Mind and in Action

Volume 2

Disparities and Competence: Service Delivery, Education, and Employment Contexts

EDITED BY JEAN LAU CHIN

Foreword by Joseph E. Trimble

Praeger Perspectives
Race and Ethnicity in Psychology

PRAEGER
An Imprint of ABC-CLIO, LLC

A B C CLIO

Santa Barbara, California • Denver, Colorado • Oxford, England

Library of Congress Cataloging-in-Publication Data

Diversity in mind and in action / edited by Jean Lau Chin ; foreword by Joseph E. Trimble.
    p. cm. — (Praeger perspectives race and ethnicity in psychology)
    Includes bibliographical references and index.
    ISBN 978-0-313-34709-2 (v. 1 : alk. paper) : (978-0-313-34710-8 (e-book) — ISBN 978-0-313-34711-5 (v. 2 : alk. paper) : (978-0-313-34712-2 (e-book) — ISBN 978-0-313-34713-9 (v. 3 : alk. paper) : (978-0-313-34714-6 (e-book) — ISBN 978-0-313-34707-8 (set) : (978-0-313-34708-5 (set e-book)
    1. Prejudices—United States. 2. Intercultural communication—United States. 3. Minorities—Mental health services—Social aspects. 4. Psychiatry, Transcultural—United States. 5. Minorities—Employment—United States. 6. Minorities—Education—United States. I. Chin, Jean Lau.
HM1091.D58 2009
305—dc22   2009000516

13 12 11 10 09   1 2 3 4 5

This book is also available on the World Wide Web as an eBook.
Visit www.abc-clio.com for details.

ABC-CLIO, LLC
130 Cremona Drive, P.O. Box 1911
Santa Barbara, California 93116-1911

This book is printed on acid-free paper (∞)
Manufactured in the United States of America

Contents

Foreword

Within and without the sombre veil of color vast social forces have been at work—efforts for human betterment, movements toward disintegration and despair, tragedies and comedies in social and economic life, and a swaying and lifting and sinking of human hearts which have made this land a land of mingled sorrow and joy, of change and excitement and unrest.

W.E.B. DuBois (1903, p. 129)

The poignant, profound, and haunting words of the eminent African American scholar, W.E.B. DuBois, set the tone for the contents of these volumes with their emphasis on diversity in mind and action. Indeed, the lives of countless immigrants and those of the indigenous peoples of the Americas are filled with the "swaying and sinking of human hearts" that continue to move to and fro as the populations in the Western Hemisphere swell in number. An afternoon stroll down the busy sidewalks of major cities in North America gives attention to the multitudes of people from different nationalities and ethnocultural populations; the principal elements of diversity in all of its forms rise up when one hears the sounds and tones of various languages, becomes aware of distinctive clothing styles and dress patterns, and observes the manner in which couples stroll along arm-in-arm. The multiplicity of differences is more apparent now than it has ever been. The differences have always been there, but they were suppressed. Often, when diverse groups appeared out in the open, they drew sneers, derision, sarcasm, attacks on the dignity of the people, exclusion, harsh commentary, and outright offensive injustices.

The spectacle created by rapid sociocultural changes is no more evident than in educational institutions. In some school districts around the

United States, for example, there are countless foreign languages and dialects spoken in the homes of the youth. In the southwestern quadrant of the country, Spanish is the lingua franca in homes, communities, religious institutions, and the workplace, but not necessarily in the school systems. Similarly, Canada endorses French and English as the two primary languages of the country. Diversity, as represented by the expression and declaration of one's ethnocultural allegiance and affiliations, is no longer concealed; it's out in the open.

Survey results from the 2000 U.S. Census Bureau, for example, indicate that countless Americans opted to identify an ancestral nationality or ethnic group as significant for them. One of the survey questions in the 2000 form asks, "What is this person's ancestry or ethnic origin?" Eighty percent of the respondents specified their ancestry; 58 percent provided a single ancestry and 22 percent provided multiple ancestries (U.S. Census Bureau, 2004). The specific ancestral or ethnic groups listed reveal an interesting and illuminating pattern, as 42.8 million considered themselves to be of German ancestral background; this figure represents over 15 percent of the total responses. Groups mentioned with over 15 million reporting included Irish (30.5 million), African American (24.9 million), English (24.5 million), American (20.2 million), Mexican (18.4 million), and Italian (15.6 million). Overall, the census item generated some 92 different ancestries with 100,000 or more people belonging to them; furthermore, it generated some 500 different ancestral listings. Additionally, an inspection of the ancestral demographic distributions by U.S. county provided by the Census Bureau shows heavy concentrations of national groups in certain areas of the country; a quick glance at Minnesota, Wisconsin, and the Dakotas shows pockets of people of Nordic and German descent. County maps in Florida, Texas, New Mexico, Arizona, and California show heavy concentrations of descendants from the Caribbean, Mexico, and Central and South America.

There are other powerful influences among the populations of North America that emerge from interethnic marriages and childbearing. In the 2000 census, for example, the Census Bureau asked citizens to indicate their multiethnic affiliation by asking them to check more than one so-called racial category if this was applicable; results from the survey showed that, on average, 2.4 percent of the U.S. population identified with two or more racial groups. Use of the new multiracial item created debates and problems for all who rely on use of census outcomes. The addition of the multiracial category presents difficult tabulation and reporting problems for health care professionals, economists, demographers, social and behavioral scientists and others who use racial categories for their work. Prewitt (2002) pointed out that the addition of the multiracial category represents a "turning point in the measurement of race . . . and . . . the arrival of a multiple-race option in the census classification will so blur racial distinctions in the political and legal spheres and perhaps also in the public consciousness that race classification will gradually disappear" (p. 360).

People from similar ethnocultural heritages tend to cluster in communities; this clustering is most evident when groups migrate to North America and gravitate to an area where people reside who share a common identity, cultural lifeways, values and beliefs, that are unique from the mainstream culture. This resettlement suggests a strong sense of identity and the need for affiliation. The path to like-minded communities also implies that one will find a haven from discrimination and social ostracism, as well as a place where one can feel comfortable expressing one's traditional lifeways and thoughtways. Degrees of subjective self-identity influence the extent to which one seeks social support from peers to validate and substantiate this identity; it's a reciprocal and often negotiated progression, accompanied with rules and acceptable sources of evidence such as language use, family birthrights, physiognomic features, interaction styles, and so on. Social validation brings comfort and reinforcement of one's personal identity. Personal well being is also strengthened and, along with it, the hope that daily life will be free from the suppression of traditions, customs, and beliefs.

But as the landscape changes and culture and diversity become more obvious, people insensitive to these issues must learn to accommodate differences and understand the strengths that differences and diversity provide to society as a whole; history books and chapters tell gripping and chilling stories about what happens when insensible bigots refuse to accommodate differences and, in the process, exert and ultimately abuse their power. Change must occur if we are to avoid any further intergroup and interpersonal conflict. And one of the ways proactive change can occur is through an emphasis on the development of multicultural competence, as suggested in several chapters in these volumes. While there are numerous ways to achieve and define cultural competence, no doubt there is much greater agreement about recognizing instances of multicultural incompetence. The fallout and the untoward consequences of cultural incompetence are unprecedented in the annals of the history of our planet; the emotional, psychological, physical, ecological, and economic costs are extraordinary and often beyond comprehension. Advocating and encouraging cultural competency in every aspect of life can avoid cultural incompetence; many of the chapters in these volumes provide thoughtful guidance and orientation on this topic.

In reading the chapters in the volumes, we should be mindful of the psychosocial complexities of the melting pot theory and the strong influence of individualism in North America. In one of the classic statements on personhood in non-Western cultures, Clifford Geertz (1973), an American cultural anthropologist, reminds us that: "The Western conception of the person as a bounded, unique, more or less integrated motivational and cognitive universe, a dynamic center of awareness, emotion, judgment, and action, organized into a distinctive whole and set contrastively—both against other such wholes and against social and natural background—is however incorrigible it may seem to us, a rather peculiar idea within the context of the world's cultures" (p. 34). His observation is worthy of serious consideration and contemplation as we forge and promote intergroup relationships deriving from respectfulness and civility.

The collection of thoughtful and coherent chapters in the *Diversity in Mind and in Action* collection provides a discourse on an extensive range of topics in the rapidly emerging field of multiculturalism in the social and behavioral sciences, as well as in other academic disciplines. Readers may not agree with some of the concepts, proposals, and arguments. But there may be countless others who have waited for the contents of the volumes to come along to provide them with support and direction. Volumes like these are set out to encourage debate and discussion, especially about the growing multicultural populations of North America where, eventually, no single ethnocultural group will be dominant.

Editor Jean Lau Chin and her hand-picked collection of competent and often inspiring authors are to be heartily congratulated for their stimulating and thought-provoking contributions. Many of the contributions are based on first-hand experiences, while others provide a blend of empirical research findings with practical applications. Examples abound describing the effects of cultural incompetence; their blend with wonderful and insightful examples of how to deal with them add an important dimension to the field. Above all else, however, is the hope provided by the content and flow of the volumes and chapters that intergroup and interethnic relations will improve to eliminate discrimination, prejudice, hatred, incivilities, and the vile and venomous hatred they provoke.

Joseph E. Trimble, PhD
Professor of Psychology
Western Washington University
Bellingham, WA 98225
September 28, 2008

REFERENCES

Du Bois, W. E. B. (1903). *The souls of black folk.* Chicago: A. C. McClurg.
Geertz, C. (1973). *The interpretation of cultures: Selected essays.* New York: Basic Books.
Prewitt, K. (2002). Race in the 2000 census: A turning point. In J. Perlmann & M. C. Waters (Eds.), *The new race question: How the census counts multiracial individuals* (pp. 354–360). New York: Russell Sage Foundation.
U.S. Census Bureau. (2004). *Ancestry: 2000.* Washington, DC: U.S. Department of Commerce, Economic and Statistics Administration.

Preface

This new three-volume set is part of the Praeger Series on Race, Ethnicity, and Psychology. A previous set, *The Psychology of Prejudice and Discrimination*, also edited by Dr. Chin, was named a 2005 Choice Outstanding Academic Title (Chin, 2005b).

Diversity is a hot and contemporary issue. While the successes of the Civil Rights Movement and Women's Movement in the twentieth century led to transformations in U.S. society, diversity remains an issue in the twenty-first century as it becomes even more important for diverse people and communities to live and work together for the common good and mutual survival. Diversity has also become a global issue as advances in technology, transportation, and the Internet have narrowed our borders and made our boundaries more permeable. Internationally, many countries now share the common experiences and problems of increased mobility among its citizens and a more diverse population. We must now address the contemporary issues of diversity and move beyond the melting-pot myth of the twentieth century and the segregationist policies that legislated different paths for people based on their skin color. We are talking about tolerance and cultural competence, and these traits start in our minds. We are saying that *diversity matters!* We must *act* to create equitable work and living environments, and *advocate* to change that which perpetuates the intolerance of difference and diversity.

Diversity is complex. Whereas promoting diversity once meant simply meeting the needs of immigrants and ethnic minorities, and welcoming new and different racial/ethnic groups into our communities and institutions, promoting diversity now means much more. We must address the differences between new immigrants and those racial/ethnic minority

groups born and bred in the United States. We must expand our definitions of diversity to include not only race and ethnicity, but also gender,
sexual orientation, religion, and disability. Moreover, it has become clear
that our identities do not manifest themselves in isolation, and we must
understand the complexity of how they interact. Our attention to diversity must also grapple with the issues of multiculturalism, both within the
United States and in a global society.

Diversity must also be placed in a historical context. The melting-pot
myth in America reflects a time in which the dominant group in the
United States was white and middle class; those in positions of power
were white men; the social ideal was to call on a nation to unite. Technology, terrorism, and continued immigration changed all that. We have
become increasingly global and diverse. Even our labeling of groups has
evolved, and must be placed in a historical context. It is more difficult to
label African Americans, Latin Americans, Asian Americans, and American Indians, the four historical groups of color, as minority groups. The
individual labels changed through the preference to avoid the stigma of
marginalization and racism inherent in the labels of "Negro," "Oriental,"
and "Indian."

Diversity is both a state of mind and a stance of action. How we conduct
ourselves as responsible citizens, and how we practice as ethical professionals amid a diverse population, community, and society is central in
this conversation. This volume set, *Diversity in Mind and in Action*, intends
to address just that. How do we grapple with inequity in our institutions
and workplaces? How do we honor our multiple identities? How do we
confront the adverse consequences of privilege and power that favor
some groups while oppressing others? How do we transform the bias in
our minds and actions that lead to disparities and incompetence in the
delivery of services? How do we recognize the narrowness of our borders
and our interdependence within a global society?

This set organizes each volume by major themes related to diversity
and multiculturalism that beset today's society. Volume 1 addresses the
themes of identity and how individuals and groups identify with one
another based on race, ethnicity, country of origin, gender, sexual orientation, and religion, often cutting across geographic boundaries and professional affiliations. Volume 2 addresses disparities in health and mental
health, and how our care delivery systems are often biased in providing
differential access to care for different groups. Diversity as a matter of ethics and cultural competence is the theme. The climate and contexts of our
educational institutions and workplaces in which diverse groups learn,
work, and live will be discussed, as well as diversity and leadership. Diversity matters! Volume 3 discusses the themes of social justice, power,
and oppression, which are associated with racism, classism, and social
privilege. Social, political, and psychological challenges face us as we seek
strategies and solutions to create social institutions that honor diversity,

and are the training grounds for diverse citizens living together with differences of perspectives, origins, and persuasions. This is social change and advocacy. It is a contemporary view of diversity amid a historical context.

Contributors to this set provide a framework not only for understanding diversity, but also for acting together in transforming our society and its institutions to create equity for diverse groups. All volumes are anchored in a global perspective, attend to issues of difference, and contribute to a *vision for diversity in mind and action*—a vision to honor diversity, and of a society where all groups can co-exist while respecting differences; where our institutions will no longer be biased against any one group over another, and will be culturally competent in serving their diverse needs.

Key Questions at the end of each volume are intended to make the set useful for training by educators and professionals, as well as for further inquiry by a broader audience addressing diversity in contemporary society. Each chapter author has contributed a key question to promote discussion and challenge thinking based on the theme and key issue or main focus of the chapter. These have been compiled as a table at the end of each volume to be used as exercises.

ACKNOWLEDGMENTS

I would like to acknowledge my family, and especially my mother, an immigrant from Nanking, China, from whom I gained valuable insights about our journey in life. I documented her narrative in *Learning from My Mother's Voice* (Chin, 2005a) and learned important lessons, with her as my mentor, about the importance of resiliency and endurance. These serve as lifelong lessons for us to continue that struggle and goal toward inclusion and equity and of valuing the differences that make us human and humane.

I am also grateful to my graduate assistants who contributed to this volume set including Gideon Kim, Kirsten Petersen, and especially Jessica Shimberg, who toiled together to bring together the contributions of this diverse groups of authors.

Jean Lau Chin

REFERENCES

Chin, J. L. (2005a). *Learning from my mother's voice: Family legend and the Chinese American experience.* New York: Teacher's College Press.

Chin, J. L. (Ed.). (2005b). *The psychology of prejudice and discrimination.* Westport, CT: Praeger Publishers.

Introduction to Volume 2: Disparities and Competence: Service Delivery, Education, and Employment Contexts

Disparities and *competence* are two terms that have been central to the service delivery of health and mental health in the last few decades. A historical view of these terms is informative to our understanding of diversity today. The U.S. Department of Health and Human Services, Health Resources Services Administration (2001) defines health disparities as population-specific differences in the presence of disease, health outcomes, or access to health care. In the United States, health disparities are well documented among minority populations such as African Americans, Native Americans, Asian Americans, and Latinos. When compared to whites, these minority groups have higher incidence of chronic diseases, higher mortality, and poorer health outcomes. The cancer incidence rate among African Americans is 10 percent higher than among whites. Adult African Americans and Latinos have twice the risk as whites of developing diabetes. Compared to whites, chronic Hepatitis B infection is more common among Asian Americans with carrier rates of 10 to 13 percent, making them more prone to contracting liver cancer.

Several landmark reports brought the issue of racial health disparities to the national forefront in the United States. The *Report of the Secretary's Task Force on Black and Minority Health* (Heckler, 1985) documented significant disparities in the burden of illness and mortality experienced by blacks and other minority groups in the U.S. population. The report precipitated national attention to racial and ethnic disparities in six health areas: cancer, cardiovascular disease, chemical dependency, diabetes, homicides and unintentional injuries, and infant mortality. It documented how blacks and Latinos faced inequities in access, utilization, and quality of care, which adversely influenced their health status. For Asian

Americans and Native Americans, significant findings of health disparities was masked by their low incidence within the population; as this and
other studies demonstrated, they were often either omitted from studies
or findings were spurious.

Despite the emphasis on quality in the U.S. health care delivery system,
research findings and policy reports have consistently demonstrated the
existence of disparities among racial and ethnic minority groups, compared to whites, in health status and health care. Minority Americans
have poorer health outcomes, compared to whites, from preventable and
treatable conditions such as cardiovascular disease, diabetes, asthma, and
cancer. The Institute of Medicine's report, *Unequal Treatment* (Smedley,
Stith, & Nelson, 2002), remains the preeminent study of the issue of racial
and ethnic disparities in health care in the United States. Reports by the
Commonwealth Fund (Collins et al., 2002; McDonough et al., 2004) and
the Kaiser Family Foundation confirmed these findings, which pervade
both physical and mental health, and concluded that strategies to eliminate the disparities must be culturally competent and address access, utilization, and quality of care.

Two other studies brought national attention to the issue of health disparities and the history of bias in the delivery of health care to minority
Americans—the legendary Tuskegee syphilis study (Katz, Russell, Kegeles, & Kressin, 2006) and the Schulman (1999) study. The Tuskegee syphilis study, conducted between 1932 and 1972 in Tuskegee, Alabama, was
a project in which 399 poor and mostly illiterate African American share-
croppers were studied to observe the natural progression of the disease if
left untreated. The fact that penicillin, discovered in 1941 to treat syphilis,
was withheld for more than 30 years raised ethical concerns and bias based
on race and socioeconomic status. The study has had more ramifications
on standards of care, ethical responsibility, and mistrust among African
Americans of the health care system and research than any of its kind.

Another social science research study receiving almost as much attention was the study by Kevin Schulman et al. (1999), which reported large
differences in physicians' responses to identical heart disease symptoms
presented by black and white actors portraying patients. The 720
physician-subjects who participated in the study referred lower proportions
of African American patients than white patients, matched for age and sex,
for cardiac catheterization, a costly, state-of-the-art diagnostic measure.
This occurred even after the researchers controlled for physicians' subjective impressions of disease likelihood and severity. While this study was
quickly criticized for methodological errors that exaggerated racial disparities, the *New England Journal of Medicine*, in which the article appeared,
took the extraordinary step of issuing a partial retraction. Nevertheless,
the publication of the Schulman study did more than any other single
event to put the matter of racial disparities in health care on the American
public policy agenda. While hundreds of prior publications had reported

evidence of racial disparities in life expectancy, morbidity from various illnesses, access to health insurance and services, and clinical management of disease, the Schulman study's use of African American and white actors with identical medical scripts was convincing of a pervasive picture of racial bias, uncomplicated by the effects of educational background, economic status, or other social cues. The intense national media attention, and subsequent congressional appropriations report targeting the Schulman study as alarming, led to funding for an Institute of Medicine (IOM) inquiry and the ensuing *Unequal Treatment* report on racial bias in American medicine. Other public and private sector initiatives targeting racial bias in American health care as a topic of research and intervention followed.

Why were these studies so dramatic? The Schulman study reflected the unconscious bias operating among physicians in diagnosing and recommending treatment based on race, while the Tuskegee experiment reflected the overt bias and ethical violations in withholding treatment from blacks for the benefit of science. These studies speak to the importance of ethics and social responsibility in addressing the needs of diverse populations. Conscious and overt discrimination has diminished in the twenty-first century by virtue of legislation and changes in social attitudes that uphold affirmative action, antidiscrimination and promote diversity, and yet there remain covert attitudes and behaviors that continue to disadvantage communities of color and diverse groups with regard to access, utilization, and quality of care in today's U.S. health care system.

These racial disparities in health reflect not only inequities and biases in our health care system, but also the deficit model being used to assess health status and health behaviors among racial and ethnic minorities. Our care delivery systems continue to provide differential and inadequate access to care for groups of color (see U.S. Public Health Service, 2001). Though it uses a comparative paradigm, the disparities model does not identify significant health issues among minority groups that are not issues for white Americans. For example, the incidence of stomach, liver, and esophageal cancer among Asian Americans is disproportionately high, but it is not a prevalent cancer site among whites. The 10 to 15 percent incidence of Hepatitis B carriers among Asian Americans compared to the 1 percent incidence in the general population places Asian Americans at high risk for cirrhosis and primary liver cancer. Yet, it was not included as a major morbidity indicator on these reports.

These racial and ethnic differences in incidence of disease, response to treatment and access to care suggest that racial and ethnic-specific indicators, which are not comparative in nature, are needed to address the issues of health for diverse communities.

Sensitivity to cultural factors, biological, psychological and social is needed. For example, racial and ethnic differences found in regard to pharmacologic responses require adjustments in medication dosage levels and routes of administration (Chen, 2006). Asian Americans, for example, metabolize some medications poorly (e.g., somcytochrome 2C19 found in diazepam used in diabetes), or show higher concentrations after a single dose (e.g., cytochrome P450 found in antidepressants and antipsychotics). Consequently, compared to Caucasians, they respond to lower dosages and will also develop toxicity and side effects at lower dosages.

Diversity is a matter of ethics and cultural competence. Cultural competence is a solution to eliminating disparities in health status and health care. Culturally competent care is both ethical and quality care (Chin, 1999). The concept of cultural competence arose out of disappointment with attempts at cultural sensitivity training in the 1960s, which failed to produce a more competent service delivery system serving diverse populations. We then turned to an emphasis on skills and competence needed for treating diverse populations—presumably something all providers could learn (Cross, 1989)—and developing a system able to differentiate diverse needs from what was normative.

Cultural competence, therefore, defined an ideal and an aspiration for how providers could develop the skills and how systems could evolve to become culturally competent in serving diverse populations. In addressing the deficiency and inattention to culture by providers and systems of care, it was hoped to dispel the issues of bias within our systems of care and eliminate disparities in our racial and ethnic minority populations.

This concept of cultural competence, however, has come under criticism in the twenty-first century, a generation after its inception. While cultural competence was initially proposed as an aspirational goal that is never complete, subsequent attributions to the term confused it with measureable outcomes; dissenters have argued that no one is ever completely competent when operating outside one's culture. Despite significant reform in our care delivery system and attention to health status following the reports and studies cited above, the term *health disparities* has also been problematic. First, the disparities approach uses a comparative paradigm to compare minority health status against the white majority as the norm. Second, the health indicators relevant to and tracked for the overall population failed, at times, to track key variables significant to diverse populations. For example, cancer sites untracked because of a low incidence among whites, were more significant and highly prevalent among Asian Americans, such as liver and esophageal cancer (Chin, 2000).

As we talk about diversity today in the twenty-first century, we need some paradigmatic shifts. Globalization and diversity have taken center stage well beyond their initial conceptualizations. We now can claim that culture is not just held by racial and ethnic minority groups, but by all individuals and groups. Diversity no longer characterizes those in the minority or those who are different. We now see culture as characterizing work and social environments, geographic areas and neighborhoods, and all affinity groups, including religion, disability, age, gender, and so on. We now characterize our society and country as diverse, and the pursuit of diversity in our institutions as worthy—that is, in our communities, workplace, education and health care institutions. We also recognize how our society and our countries are becoming increasingly global; now, globalization is frequently viewed as the social responsibility to ensure that students and citizens are prepared to live and work within a global society.

However, there are many who believe that we need to be mindful of not diluting the original intent of cultural competence—that is, to address the unmet needs, differential access, and marginalized status of diverse and underrepresented groups. Our goal now is how to frame these differences as different routes to common ends or as alternative perspectives for understanding behavior using strength-based models for attending to diversity. These are both in our minds and in our actions.

Several chapters in Volume 2 address issues of disparities and competence and the care delivery system within the United States. The influence of culture on access, utilization, and quality is pervasive. Cultural competence is paramount to ethical and quality care. We must transform our care delivery system and liberate our paradigms care so that the needs of diverse groups are competently met. Cultural competence is a matter of ethics and quality.

The point is that *diversity matters*, not only in our service delivery systems, but also in the climate and contexts in which diverse groups learn, work, and live; it is critical that we create social institutions that honor and promote diversity. Our schools and workplaces are the training grounds for diverse citizens living together amidst differences in perspectives, places of origin, and persuasions.

Despite significant gains made through affirmative action and antidiscrimination policies in our workplace and educational systems, disparities remain, as do obstacles to career advancement among racial and ethnic minority groups, women, and other marginalized groups. Whereas the twentieth century used the metaphor of the glass ceiling to symbolize the rigid and impermeable barrier keeping women and racial and ethnic minorities from entering the higher echelons of these institutions, Eagly and Carli (2007) have posed a new metaphor to capture the environment of the twenty-first century—the labyrinth to connote the numerous barriers that women and racial and ethnic minorities must navigate on their road to leadership. Although white men still predominate as leaders, the increasing representation of women and of racial and ethnic minorities in the United States is unmistakable. For example, among chief executives of all U.S. organizations in 2007, 26 percent were women, 4 percent black, 4 percent Asian, and 5 percent Hispanic (U.S. Bureau of Labor Statistics, 2008).

Diversity is about just that: equality and access. We cannot pride ourselves on our diversity in our country, community, or institutions if there remain barriers to access for marginalized groups and there are inequalities with differential rewards for privileged groups—whether this is based on social class, racial and ethnic minority group status, age, gender, sexual orientation, ability status, or any of the other -isms apparent in our society today. Workforce and workplace diversity are goals to mirror the demographic changes occurring in U.S. society.

While the twentieth century has seen more women and more racial and ethnic minorities reach positions of leadership in the United States, the goals of diversity are not just about numbers. Diversity is not simply affirmative action or equitable treatment. It is about living and working with diverse groups; it is about affirming diverse leadership styles and perspectives for achieving common goals. As the twenty-first century increasingly seeks globalization—through the growth of multinational companies and enterprise, through the interdependence of nations in economics, trade, and resources, through the rapid communication and travel of its citizens across national and virtual borders—it becomes increasingly important to promote diversity in our education and workplace environments.

Yet, our training models and work environments are ill-equipped to promote the tolerance of difference, to teach the inter-communication skills needed to live and work among diverse groups, and to achieve effective models for leading, managing, and educating diverse communities. Managing Diversity, Valuing Differences, Valuing Diversity—whatever the name of the initiative may be, corporate America is slowly waking up to the fact that the changing employee demographics outlined in the landmark Hudson Institute report *Workforce 2000: Work and Workers for the 21st Century* is already a reality. This groundbreaking 1987 report forecasted widespread shortages of skilled labor and pointed out that between the years 1985 and 2000, 85 percent of the entrants in the workforce will be women, minorities and immigrants. The report also said that older workers and disabled employees will require more of their employer's attention (Judy & D'Amico, 1997).

In the twentieth century, we witnessed the development of training programs for diversity, valuing differences, and cultural competence whose intent was to promote tolerance across different groups. We saw it in the mushrooming of gender and ethnic studies on college campuses during the 1960s. The goals of such training often focused on self-awareness, providing information of the history of and contributions of diverse groups, and to eliminate biases associated with racial/ethnic minority groups—generally using a majority-minority group perspective.

The original intent was presumably that these diverse groups represented minorities having to face a dominant culture; we needed to help them adjust. The reality now is quite different; we need a paradigm shift that promotes diversity as enriching the lives of all who participate. It is not an obligation of the privileged or tokenism toward the marginalized. While we focused on affirmative action or getting a seat at the table during the twentieth century in our diversity goals, we largely ignored the fact that women and racial and ethnic minority groups were inadequately rep-resented in the higher echelons of our institutions. They made headlines when they did. We largely ignored that the world was changing as we became increasingly interdependent and global. It is time now to address diversity in preparing our leaders of tomorrow and in our recognition of local, national, and international contexts. As we create diverse environ-ments in our workplaces and educational institutions, we empower all to share in a just and humane society.

The chapters in Volume 2 promote the notion that diversity matters in our lives, in our work, and in our institutions—to prepare students for responsible citizenry and to enable our citizens to live and work to-gether in a just and humane society. Our education and training should focus not only on the diversity in our populations, but also on the dif-ferent contexts and different ways of acquiring skills and knowledge. Existing pedagogy in many institutions have been dominated by West-ern thinking; other cultures have been successful in their use of other methods for learning and scholarly inquiry. An examination of critical reflection and transformational learning links to Confucian humanism and principles of learning, for example, is necessary to question the meanings and assumptions of one's surroundings and values (Wang & King, 2006). This is a critical point because Asian modes of learning are often described by Westerners as rote memory. Perhaps an examina-tion of objective versus subjective modes of inquiry, of active listening versus active participation, of empirical versus narrative methods of research using a strength-based approach might be instructive. While inclusiveness is a goal of diversity, often a secondary benefit is that it promotes increased flexibility of thinking, enhanced creativity, and innovation.

Diversity "in mind and in action" means examining what we do and how we think as we develop the goals and policies of our institutions—*climate, composition,* and *content* are the terms to promote the tolerance of difference and to enable us to live, work, and play together as equal citizens, in peace and with respect for one another. Some of these chap-ters illustrate the skills and training models that enable us to do just that across different contexts and different communities. Diversity matters because it enables all to achieve their potential. We need to do what matters! We need to promote a society that recognizes the ben-efits of a diverse workforce and trains its citizens to become tolerant of differences.

REFERENCES

Chen, M. L. (2006). Ethnic or *racial differences* revisited: impact of dosage regimen and dosage form on pharmacokinetics and pharmacodynamics. *Clinical Pharmacokinetics, 45*(10), 957–964.

Chin, J. L. (1999). *Cultural competence and health care in Massachusetts: Where are we? Where should we be?* (Issue Brief No.5). Waltham, MA: Massachusetts Health Policy Forum, Brandeis University.

Chin, J. L. (2000). Culturally competent health care. *Public Health Reports, 115,* 29–38.

Collins, K., Hughes, D., Doty, M., Ives, B., Edwards, J., & Tenney, K. (2002). *Diverse communities, common concerns: Assessing health care quality for minority Americans.* Boston, MA: The Commonwealth Fund.

Cross, T., Bazron, B., Dennis, K. W., & Issacs, M. R. (1989). *Towards culturally competent systems of care.* Washington, DC: Georgetown University Child Development Center.

Eagly, A. H., & Carli, L. L. (2007). *Through the labyrinth: The truth about how women become leaders.* Boston, MA: Harvard Business School Press.

Heckler, M. M. (Ed.). (1985). *Report of the secretary's task force on black and minority health: Crosscutting issues in minority health* (Vol. 2). Washington, DC: U.S. Department of Health and Human Services.

Judy, R. W., & D'Amico, C. (1997). Workforce 2020: Work and workers in the 21st century. Indianapolis, IN: Hudson Institute.

Katz, R. V., Russell, S. L., Kegeles, S. S., & Kressin, N. R. (2006). The Tuskegee legacy project: Willingness of minorities to participate in biomedical research. *Journal of Health Care of the Poor and Underserved, 17*(4), 698–715.

McDonough, J., Gibbs, B., Scott-Harris, J., Kronebusch, K., Navarro, A., & Taylor, K. A. (2004). *State policy agenda to eliminate racial and ethnic health disparities.* New York: The Commonwealth Fund.

Schulman, K. A., Berlin, J. A., Harless, W., Kerner, J. F., Sistrunk, S., Gersh, B. J., et al. (1999). The effect of race and sex on physicians' recommendations for cardiac catheterization. *The New England Journal of Medicine, 340*(8), 618–625.

Smedley, B., Stith, A., & Nelson, A. (2002). *Unequal treatment: Confronting racial and ethnic disparities in health care.* New York: Institute of Medicine.

U.S. Bureau of Labor Statistics. (2008). *Household data, annual averages: Employed persons by detailed occupation, sex, race, and Hispanic or Latino ethnicity.* Retrieved March 17, 2008, from http://www.bls.gov/cps/cpsaat11.pdf.

U.S. Department of Health and Human Services, Health Resources Services Administration. (2001). *Eliminating health disparities in the United States.* Washington, DC: Author.

U.S. Public Health Service, Office of the Surgeon General. (2001). *Mental health: Culture, race, and ethnicity–A supplement to mental health: A report of the Surgeon General.* Washington, DC: Author.

Wang, V. C. X., & King, K. P. (2006). *Understanding Mezirow's theory of reflectivity from Confucian perspectives: A model and perspective.* Radical Pedagogy Web site. Retrieved September 30, 2008, from http://radicalpedagogy.icaap.org/content/issue8_1/wang.html.

CHAPTER 1

Empowerment through Inclusion: Education and Employment

Rosie Phillips Bingham

Can a society be truly prosperous, powerful, and peaceful with an "us and them" social agenda? Can our educational institutions produce citizens who are able to advance in a global society if students are able to exist in segregated groups? Is it possible for a workforce to increase a society's prosperity while maintaining segregated groups? Will peace have a chance if the structure of society promotes homogeneous settings? Can we achieve diversity in mind and in action if we allow group hegemony? Can the United States remain a strong, competitive force in a global society if it does not use all of the talents of all of its peoples? I believe that "no" is the answer to all of these questions and that inclusion is the way for us to reach the ideals on which our American society was founded.

In the United States we have talked about equality and desegregation for at least two hundred years. At its core, the United States was founded on principles of freedom and equality, though the country has not lived up to its ideals. At various points throughout U.S. history, different groups in the country have felt oppressed and discriminated against. These groups have even fought with each other about which one is more oppressed.

Such a fight threatened to develop during the 2005 National Multicultural Conference and Summit (NMCS) held in Los Angeles, California. The NMCS was inaugurated in 1999 as a forum to discuss cutting-edge multicultural research, education, and practice (Sue, Bingham, Porche-Burke, & Vasquez, 1999). The conference was cohosted and supported by a number of divisions within the American Psychological Association (APA). Groups of different races, ethnicities, sexual orientations, genders, physical and mental abilities, religions, and so on, had come to view the summit as a "safe" place to present papers and exchange ideas. The 2005 NMCS challenged this notion of safety.

A highly controversial session on sexual orientation conversion was, perhaps inadvertently, presented at the 2005 summit. At the concluding town hall meeting there appeared to be a growing fight and schism between bisexual, gay, lesbian, and transgendered groups and racial/ethnic minorities. As the words escalated, Derald Wing Sue (2005) cautioned the meeting that there seemed to be a fight brewing about which group had the most "blood on the floor." Which group was most oppressed? Which had been most victimized? The groups seemed to turn on each other and away from the idea of trying to build a united and diverse society that espoused social justice principles.

The fight threatened to derail a conference empowered by the principle of inclusion. Founded on principles of inclusion, the NMCS had grown from about 550 participants in 1999 to nearly 1,200 in 2005 and had, in the process, empowered itself enough to attract presidents of and contenders to the presidency of the American Psychological Association. If the groups separated because of their differences, then what would become of the conference and this aggregate of people who explored cutting-edge multicultural research, training, and practice?

The same question can be asked of U.S. society and, indeed, of all societies in the world. If we separate, then what? The United States has often seemed to struggle with issues of inclusion and segregation; oppressor and oppressed; freedom and slavery; us and them. These struggles beg the question of "us and them."

Sometimes it appears that even as we live in our country, our United States, racial and ethnic groups are totally separate from each other and that each is content with that arrangement. At other times it seems like the groups are separate and yet come in contact with each other. My position is that we must find a way to merge the "us and them" so that we can be stronger as a society. I arrived at my position by posing this question: Structurally, is it more sound to have a system that is divided or one that embraces all? Even Lincoln (1858) said, "A house divided cannot stand." As we ponder the issue of diversity in education and employment we might wonder if the notion of inclusion leads to empowerment. We might also wonder about the relationship between inclusion, empowerment, education and employment, and why we should care about it.

In this chapter it will be argued that for the United States to be truly competitive in a global society, it must intentionally include and empower all races and ethnicities and, indeed, all groups subjected to discrimination because of characteristics such as sexual orientation, religion, gender, race, ethnicity, ability status, and class. The focus will be on race and ethnicity, and it will entail my reviewing a brief history of some events that demonstrate a history of oppression and providing some demographics that support the claim of discrimination and point to progress in overcoming discrimination. How discrimination and microaggressions are disempowering and how they can blur the image of progress, exclude categories of people, and negatively impact the health and prosperity of society will be discussed. A discussion of the need for U.S. society to empower every group in order to remain a strong partner in global society and what psychology can do to help will conclude the chapter.

BRIEF HISTORY

When we look at examples from the history of various minority groups in the United States, it is clear that each group has suffered or left "blood on the floor." When the Mayflower reached the soil of North America there were approximately 10 million Native Americans living on the continent. Instead of becoming a blended nation, immigrants and Native Indians fought wars that ended with Native Americans living mainly on reservations. Today Native Americans number only about 2.5 million and have high school graduation rates that are reported to be only about 64 percent (NativeAmericans.com, 2008). If one does not graduate from high school, prosperity and health become nearly impossible.

African Americans reached the soils of North America sometimes as free persons but more often as slaves. The United States fought a bitter civil war over the slavery issue, a war in which over 1.5 million lost their lives. The union remained in tact, but society was left segregated. Segregation was sanctioned by the Supreme Court in 1896, when *Plessey v. Ferguson* declared that African Americans could gain an education equal to that of white Americans even if they attended segregated public schools. The work of Kenneth and Mamie Clark (Clark, 1950; Clark & Clark, 1940) demonstrated the devastation wrought in the minds and souls of young black children by such a philosophy. In 1954 the Supreme Court decision in *Brown v. Board of Education Topeka* ended the separate but equal scheme, but did it end the "blood on the floor" for African Americans? Current educational statistics indicate the answer is positive but not definitive.

Asian Americans were subjected to a similar "us and them" mentality during some of their early experiences in the United States. The Chinese were major contributors to the completion of the transcontinental railroad, which changed the industrial complexion of this country in the nineteenth century. Fear of job loss among white Americans caused the forty-seventh Congress of the United States to pass the Chinese Exclusion Act of 1882. The preamble of the act states that "in the opinion of the Government of the United States the coming of Chinese laborers to this country endangers the good order of certain localities," going on to deny the Chinese the ability to work in certain areas. The act was abolished in 1943. The Chinese thus experienced "blood on the floor."

Asian discrimination was not limited to the Chinese. The Alien Land Law of 1913 was strengthened in 1943 to prevent customary Japanese farming. Several localities in California used the law to seize Japanese-owned farm lands, and numerous Japanese Americans were incarcerated during World War II. Some of these Japanese had not only been born and raised in the United States, they had never been outside of the country; they had never been to Japan but were now torn from their homes and forced to reside in camps because of their ethnic heritage. The United States paid for reparations for this very shameful act.

The dawn of the twenty-first century gave birth to a movement to build a wall between the United States and Mexico in the continuing theme of "us and them." The battle on this front was cloaked in words of fear and anger that illegal immigrants were taking jobs from Americans, being a burden on the social welfare system and increasing crime. Of course, the theme, reminiscent of the fear exhibited in the preamble to the Chinese Exclusion Act, that sounded the loudest was one of job loss.

Unlike the 1800s and the Chinese, the economy of the United States in 2008 is much more a part of a global society and is now more dependent on international exchanges, including trade with Mexico and other Latin American countries. Thus, when there is a "them" attitude toward Latinos within the United States, and those attitudes turn into actions, citizens in the United States, Mexico and other countries suffer. For example, farm jobs that Mexicans have done in the United States go unfilled, thus increasing product costs to all Americans. The money that Mexicans send home to help place-bound relatives is no longer available, so those families suffer. Perhaps equal to the economic problem is the psychological harm created when a group of people legally in the country hears words that say loudly and clearly: "You are not wanted here."

The move to build a wall along the U.S.-Mexican border could even be having an impact on the high school graduation success of Latinos legally in the United States. While I am aware of no such studies, a question could be posed about the contribution of calls for walls to the success of Latinos in education and employment. With a high school drop out rate that hovers between 40 and 50 percent, Hispanics have one of the lowest high school completion rates of any racial/ethnic group in the United States. A form of exclusion such as this leaves the group vulnerable to a lack of real economic power and subsequent detrimental health problems. In the words of undergraduate student Susana Hernandez (2007), "Their children were born in the U.S., so am I really a Mexicana? I was raised in a society that saw me as a waste of time and money" (p. 18). Hispanics have "blood on the floor."

Clearly racial/ethnic groups are not the only groups in U.S. society that fall into the "us and them" paradigm. The riot at Stonewall Inn in 1969 was a fight by lesbian and gay individuals and their supporters to end discrimination based on sexual orientation. Moreover, the consequences of the September 11, 2001, attacks pushed society to try to discriminate between Muslins and Arabs who might be terrorists and those who were not. As a result, many American Muslims and Arabs felt the psychological sting of discriminatory actions and attitudes. Fear-influenced measures were not limited to these groups, however. As the United States moved to make itself safer, passengers were checked more thoroughly at airports. Before computers began to randomly search suspected individuals at airport security check points, numerous African Americans reported that they were "randomly" selected for searches nearly 100 percent of the time. It happened to me just as often. (In fact, my white colleagues were amazed by the results when they traveled with me and were never searched along with me.) The United States also closed its borders to more international students, resulting in far fewer students matriculating at U.S. schools, especially in science, technology, engineering and mathematics (STEM). Many graduate schools saw declines in enrollment and several industries were hard-pressed to fill certain job categories (Brown & Neubig, 2006; Kayyali, 2006; Redd, Neubig, & Mahler, 2007). Exclusion can have far-reaching effects. Exclusionary attitudes toward racial and ethnic minorities have been a part of U.S. history for centuries and continue today. A look at trends provides clear data that supports this notion.

EDUCATION AND INCOME

In 1983 Coladaric reported a staggering high school drop out rate for Native Americans in one Montana high school. While Native Americans made up 90 percent of the student body, 60 percent of them did not finish high school. The students mainly reported psychological reasons for their lack of success. Among the reasons given were that teachers did not care about them and the disagreements that they had with teachers. They were also concerned that the curriculum did not reflect Indian values or culture. A cursory review of the history of Native Americans or American Indians reveals behaviors that suggest some truth to the students' statements. The United States has a long history of assimilation through education with American Indians. Often such assimilation meant removal from their homes to boarding schools where a European American curriculum and environment prevailed (Pavel et al., 1998). Writes Todd Wilcox (2007): "I am from a history of the Long Walk, government policy, cultural assimilation, relocation, boarding school education, and broken promises" (p. 3). In a collection of essays by Borrego and Manning, Wilcox (2007) spoke about how Native American history still lingers with him today. The question is how to effectively maintain a diverse society and still empower all individuals so that they can be successful.

The high school drop out problem among Native Americans is replicated in cities across the United States for black and Hispanic groups. An April 2008 report from the Editorial Projects in Education Research Center indicated that high school graduation rates for American Indians were 49.3 percent, blacks were 53.4 percent and Hispanics were 57.8 percent.

And the rates for whites and Asians were 76.2 percent and 80.2 percent respectively. If Hechman and LaFontain (2007) are correct that the nation's high school drop out rate is an indication of the nation's current and future economic health, then society has a major problem because large sections of the population will not be able to participate in the economic recovery that is needed in the United States.

Furthermore, Rehyner (1993) maintained that high school graduation rates are a predictor of college-going rates. And, similar to the high school completion trend, college completion rates reflect a continuing difference along race/ethnicity lines. In a New England study of college graduation rates, Asian and Pacific Islanders lead with a 74 percent completion rate, while American Indians, Eskimo, and Aleutians were the lowest at 33 percent (Coelen, 1993). Greene and Forster (2003) reported that black students and Hispanics represented 9 percent and 7 percent of all college freshmen in early 2000. If these students represent such a small proportion of students entering college and college completions rates are as low as those reported by Coelen, then it is clear that the problem that began in high school continues into college. According to the December 2007 Projections in Education (a nonprofit organization formed to administer training, research, and service programs for educational institutions in the Metropolitan Washington D.C., area), in 2005 there were nearly 17.5 million students enrolled in degree-granting institutions. Of those, nearly 12.5 million were white, 2.5 million black, 1.8 million Hispanic, 1.3 million Asian Pacific Islander, and 0.76 million Indian/Alaskan Native. The projections for 2016 indicate a million more white students and a million more Hispanics. Blacks are projected to increase by six hundred thousand, Asians by four hundred thousand, and American Indians by only fifty thousand.

These data indicate that it is very difficult to overcome a history of exclusion and discrimination and challenge society's efforts toward diversity and inclusion. Perhaps more alarming is the impact that education has on economic progress. There is a direct correlation between educational achievement and salary gain.

An examination of earnings in 1975 and 2005 by level of education and race/ethnicity illustrates a clear racial disparity. For example, in 2005 black individuals with a high school degree had a median salary of $23,904 compared to whites with a salary of $30,569. The data are startlingly consistent across thirty years. In fact a look at poverty rates suggests that although white Americans make up the largest percent of individuals living in poverty, racial/ethnic minorities are disproportionately overrepresented in poverty groups. According to the U.S. Census Bureau the rates of poverty in 2003 were 24.4 percent, 11.8 percent, 22.5 percent and 23.2 percent for blacks, Asians, Hispanics and American Indians/Alaska Natives respectively. These rates compare to a rate of 8.2 percent for whites. While there are numerous reasons why these disparities exist, it is clear that some of these groups suffer more than others and that all groups are not fully included in the rewards of society.

The trend of excluding ethnic/racial minorities is also reflected in attitudes toward which jobs groups generally can and do obtain. For example, in the spring of 2007 roughly one hundred individuals who represented varying ethnicities, races (including whites, blacks and Latinos), men and women whose ages ranged from 11 to 80 and incomes from $0 to over $100,000 annually, were asked what the chances were of an individual becoming president of the United States on a scale of 0 to 100 percent. There were 23 categories of people that included individuals from different races and ethnicities to individuals with traits like obesity and beliefs like atheism. Overwhelmingly, the white male was given a 100 percent chance of being elected president, while the others ranged from a 0 to 50 percent chance at best.

In actual data that analyzed presidents of American colleges and universities, we noticed that the trend was not that different from the survey results about the U.S. presidency. In 1986 nearly 92 percent of college and university presidencies belonged to white individuals; blacks were at 5 percent; Hispanics at just over 2 percent and all other ethnic groups were under 1 percent. By 2006 there was slightly more diversity with whites at just over 86 percent; blacks rising to 5.9 percent and Hispanics doubling to 4.5 percent. Asians also doubled their rate to nearly 2 percent and American Indians showed a slight increase to 0.7 percent (Jaschik, 2007). In May 2008 a question was posed to a very active listserv of chief student affairs officers who serve at schools that hold membership in the National Association of State Land Grant Colleges and Universities. The question simply asked how long had the executive management team at their institutions been desegregated. An earlier question was posted on the list in the same week regarding the structure of organizations, and it netted responses from a large number of the nearly two hundred member list; the desegregation question received only about three responses. Those responses indicated that desegregation occurred in the last 6 to 15 years. One could ask why there were so few responses to the question, and there may be many answers, but the results remain the same, and it is known that ethnic/racial issues are difficult to discuss. The lack of discussion could be seen as an indication of a lack of inclusion. But, given that at least 15 of the members are ethnic/racial minorities, other factors could be at play, including the framing of the question.

MICROAGGRESSIONS

In the above example, another reason for the lack of response could be that individuals are hesitant to talk about matters of race and ethnicity on a listserv. My white colleagues have often shared that they are cautious about saying the wrong thing and thus being seen as a racist, while my black colleagues have said they are conscious of the possibility of their remarks being held as overly sensitive to racial matters. It does seem that minority and majority group individuals interpret behaviors both verbal and nonverbal in different ways. John Dovidio and his colleagues (Dovidio & Gaertner, 2004; Dovidio, Gaertner, Hodson, Houlette, & Johnson, 2005) have shown that blacks and whites can walk away from the same interaction and whites will believe that the interaction went well while blacks will believe that they have just been involved in a racist incident. Dovidio and Gaertner (2004) claimed that sometimes that happens because although white individuals espouse egalitarian principles they may exert what is labeled aversive or modern racism. Aversive racism is the unconscious and unintentional racist behavior that white people will sometimes engage in around interactions or attributions regarding race. A series of well-conducted research studies have validated this contention (Gaertner, Dovidio, Anastasio, Bachman, & Rust, 1993). The good news is that the researchers also demonstrated that this behavior can be changed.

A consequence of such behavior could be that white individuals' unintentional racist insult can invalidate people of color. This behavior could influence the retention of some racial and ethnic minorities in educational and employment settings. Derald Wing Sue and others (Brown, 2003; Franklin, 2004; Sue et al., 2007) have described what they call microaggressions. Racial microaggressions have been defined as "brief and commonplace daily verbal, behavioral and environmental indignities, whether intentional or unintentional, that communicate hostile, derogatory or negative racial slights and insults that potentially have harmful or unpleasant psychological impact on the target person or group" (Sue et al., 2007, p. 271). These authors asserted that microaggressions may be more psychologically damaging than hate crimes because the perpetrator is so often unaware that he or she has committed the infraction. And of course since the microaggressions are many times one-on-one private conversations without malevolent intent, there is rarely an institutional process for redress. Numerous individuals have provided examples of microaggressions in studies that were conducted or in the presentation of lived experiences. A. J. Franklin (2004) related the story of a man of color who graduated from Yale University, attained a high ranking management position and took a white client to a business meal. The African American male was overlooked by the restaurant host, the credit card was returned to the white client and, at the end of the meal, the white client easily hailed a taxi for himself while the manager had trouble. I had the same experience trying to get a taxi in Washington D.C., I solved the problem by going to a hotel to get the bellman to hail the taxi.

Other instances of microaggressions include people of color being overlooked when the team is introduced; people of color who are chief executive officers in various areas at educational institutions being overlooked during important discussions in favor of the CEO's assistant. Examples also include comments to capable people of color such as, "You are so articulate," "You are a credit to your race," and "I wish I was Native American." Micro assaults happen in educational settings when all the brochures and academic bulletins show people of color playing sports and all the white students in the science labs. Micro assaults happen when ethnically offensive material is the usual decoration in an officemate's work space. Micro insults occur when ideas of a person of color are attributed to a white colleague. These statements and actions are debilitating because they are cumulative and enduring. "Just like when the disappointed asker asks 'No, where are you REALLY from?' when I say in perfect, unaccented English that I was born and raised in far exotic suburbs of Dayton, OH" (Park, 2007).

We have to wonder about the psychological toll that racial/ethnic minority exclusions and microaggressions take on the mental psyche of people of color. Tony Brown (2003), a critical race theorist, said that "racial stratification can cause mental health problems not systematically described in the existing literature or psychiatric nosology." Brown further claimed a need for mental health researchers to examine more closely what it means to be black or white in the United States in order to understand the correlation between race and mental health. Janet Helms (2007) went on to assert that white people must name and claim their race as whites so that we can move beyond racism in this country because racism also exacts a heavy psychological toll on white people.

THE ECONOMY

Racism, exclusion, and lack of diversity are economically unhealthy for the United States. A look at the high school drop out rate begins to point to the economic drain. Data indicate a significant difference in the salaries of individuals who finish high school versus those who do not. The data further show a difference in high school graduation rates by race and ethnicity. Since many states depend on tax dollars for everything from highways and bridges to schools and scholarships it is easy to see that lower incomes translate into lower taxes. One could frame this scenario through every educational level. There are ethnic and racial salary discrepancies at the bachelor's through doctoral degree levels. More education generally produces higher dollars but not at the same rate for all ethnic groups.

The economic impact from exclusion and discrimination can be felt at the intersection of health and wealth. Depressed salaries or no income burden the health care system. People who make less money will sometimes wait until they are very ill before seeking medical attention. Such delays increase medical costs and cause strains on the family when the ill individual is also the family breadwinner. What's more, lower wages decrease individuals' ability to have adequate medical insurance, further depressing the economy.

Perhaps as troubling as the impact of exclusion and lack of diversity in education and employment is the cost for the United States to participate in the global community. Since 1979 more than 53 million manufacturing jobs have been lost in the United States, most to offshore sites (Johnson & Kasarda, 2008). About half of the job losses occurred between 2000 and 2003 (Press Associates Union News Service, 2003). Such losses mean that the affected individuals must find other ways to earn a living. But what will that be? In a recent National Public Radio interview, commentator Kevin Phillips (2008) claimed that the United States was fast becoming a country that manufactures nothing. What kinds of jobs, then, will replace those well-paying jobs? Some say that people must retool by attending college in order to develop new skills. What happens to people of color who must now make their way to majority race colleges and universities, especially in the face of daily microaggressions? Job loss in and of itself is a psychologically challenging experience, and the challenge is made greater if one is a racial or ethnic minority who must now contend with micro insults and micro invalidations in a majority setting that is quite unfamiliar.

In the early years many of the jobs lost to offshoring and outsourcing were blue collar; however, as U.S. companies sought more access to customers in different countries and sought to deliver services 24/7, more white collar jobs also began to move out of the country (Johnson & Kasarda, 2008). Some of the movement occurred because of the need for more workers in technology fields and later in science, engineering and mathematics. Two problems were immediately obvious. After 9/11 the United States began closing its borders to more foreign students. Graduate schools experienced sharp declines in students in the STEM (science, technology, engineering, mathematics) fields. Therefore fewer of these knowledge workers were available for jobs in the United States. India and China had more of these workers, and the desire to take advantage of the different world time zones made it profitable for some U.S. companies to just move their operations to these countries. Given that there were already large gaps in education between whites and peoples of color in the United States it is easy to see that the problem began to grow exponentially. Exclusionary practices meant that the United States did not have enough people in the pipeline to fill needs in the STEM fields. Clearly, the problem with exclusion, lack of diversity, and discrimination is that they negatively impact the entire society.

Johnson and Kasarda (2008) maintained that for U.S. society to become more robust we must become more innovative and entrepreneurial. They asserted that the United States must move from producing 16 percent of worldwide undergraduates in STEM fields to greater than 50 percent of undergraduate degrees in these areas. We must therefore empower through inclusion all races and ethnicities to participate in the production of this number of undergraduate majors in science, technology, engineering and mathematics. No one can be excluded.

WHAT CAN PSYCHOLOGY DO?

We have an economic and a moral challenge to end the "blood on the floor." We must find ways to more deftly include and diversify education and employment, and we must empower racial and ethnic minorities so that they can become more a part of the U.S. recovery. Psychologists are behavioral experts so we can intervene:

1. Ethnic and racial minorities must support each other. Psychologists know how to help groups deal with inter-group conflicts. During the American Psychological Association annual conventions in 2005 and 2006, workshops were held to tackle head-on such inter-group problems. More such programs are needed.
2. White individuals must end racism. Helms (2007) described from a psychologist's perspective a model about how white people can end racism. The model entails a process for developing a positive white identity, which is essential to ending racism.
3. Because psychologists are experts in behavior, we must use that expertise to increase awareness about microaggressions and intervene to change such behavior.
4. Psychologists must develop research to more intentionally study behavior between culturally, racially, ethnically different groups, not only for resolutions within the United States but also to help end strife between foreign groups. The country, after all, is a part of a global community.
5. Psychologists must become more interdisciplinary in our approaches to understanding human behavior and change. We must help others to see the relationship between the state of the economy in the United States and the state of mental health and the process for change.
6. Psychologists must increase understanding of the power of inclusion in changing oppression and discrimination.

Finally, psychologists must help U.S. society see that change is possible. The very data that demonstrate the problems of exclusion in our society also demonstrate that change is occurring. The number of university and college presidents who are ethnic/racial minorities has increased. While the spring 2007 survey that measured the probability of different groups of individuals becoming president of the United States only showed a fairly small chance for a woman or person of color, the 2008 presidential election demonstrated that a racial minority can be elected president of the United States. The very numbers that revealed that Native Americans have a low high school completion rate also showed that the numbers of Native Americans within the borders of the United States are increasing. Psychologists have been issued numerous calls to help society deal with racism. The American Psychological Association has committed to at least once yearly training for the entire 162 member Council of Representatives. Such behavior demonstrates that we can move from mind to action if we have the will and the knowledge to make the change. Psychology is a favorite undergraduate major; therefore, if academic institutions want to begin to make a change in exclusion in this society, they certainly have enough psychologists to get the job done and move from diversity in mind to diversity in action.

REFERENCES

Brown, H., & Neubig, E. (2006). *Findings from the 2006 CGS international graduate admissions survey phase II: Final applications and offers of admission.* Washington, DC: Council of Graduate Schools.

Brown, T. N. (2003). Critical race theory speaks to sociology of mental health problems linked to racial stratification. *Journal of Health and Social Behavior, 44*(3), 292–301.

Clark, K. B. (1950). *Effect of prejudice and discrimination on personality development.* Paper presented at the Mid-century White House Conference on Children and Youth, Washington, DC.

Clark, K. B., & Clark, M. K. (1940). Skin color as a factor in racial identification of Negro preschool children. *The Journal of Social Psychology, 11,* 159–169.

Coelen, S. P. (1993). *Demographic change, education and the work force: Existing relationships and the prognosis in New England.* Retrieved December 1, 2008, from http://www.nelliemae.com/library/research_1.html.

Dovidio, J. F., & Gaertner, S. L. (2004). Aversive racism. In M. P. Zanna (Ed.), *Advances in experimental social psychology* (pp. 1–52). San Diego, CA: Academic Press.

Dovidio, J. F., Gaertner, S. L., Hodson, G., Houlette, M., & Johnson, K. M. (2005). Social inclusion and exclusion: Recategorization and the perception of intergroup boundaries. In D. Abrams, J. M. Marques, & M. A. Hogg (Eds.), *The social psychology of inclusion and exclusion* (pp. 246–264). Philadelphia: Psychology Press.

Franklin, A. J. (2004). *From brotherhood to manhood: How black men rescue their relationships and dreams from the invisibility syndrome.* New York: John Wiley & Son.

Gaertner, S. L., Dovidio, J. F., Anastasio, P. A., Bachman, B. A., & Rust, M. C. (1993). The common ingroup identity model: Recategorization and the reduction of intergroup bias. *European Review of Social Psychology, 4,* 1–26.

Greene, J. P., & Forster, G. (2003). *Public high school graduation and college readiness rates in the United States* (Education Working Paper No. 3). Manhattan Institute for Policy Research. Retrieved December 1, 2008, from http://www.manhattan-institute.org/cgi-bin/apMI/print.cgi.

Hechman, J. J., & LaFontain, P. A. (2007, December). *The American high school graduation rate: Trends and levels* (Discussion Paper No. 3216). Alexandria, VA: Center for Public Education. Retrieved January 30, 2009, from http://www.centerfor publiceducation.org/site/c.kjJXJ5MPIwE/b.3959021/k.956A/The_American_ High_School_Graduation_Rate_Trends_and_Levels.htm.

Helms, J. E. (2007). *A race is a nice thing to have: A guide to being a white person or understanding the white persons in your life* (2nd ed.). Hanover, MA: Microtraining Associates, Inc.

Hernandez, S. (2007). Where I am from. In S. E. Borrego & K. Manning (Eds.), *Where I am from: Student affairs practice from the whole of students' lives* (pp. 18–19). Waldorf, MD: National Association of Student Personnel Administrators.

Jaschik, S. (2007). *The graying of the presidency.* Retrieved December 1, 2008, from http://www.insidehighered.com/news/2007/02/12/presdata.

Johnson, J. H., & Kasarda, J. D. (2008). Jobs on the move: Implications for U.S. higher education. *Planning for Higher Education, 36*(3), 22–33.

Kayyali, R. (2006). *The people perceived as a threat to security: Arab Americans since September 11.* Retrieved December 1, 2008, from http://www.migrationin-formation.org/Feature/display.cfm?ID=409#top.

Lincoln, A. (1858). *A house divided speech.* Retrieved December 1, 2008, from http://showcase.netins.net/web/creative/lincoln/speeches/house.htm.

NativeAmericans.com. (2008). *American Indians.* Retrieved May 30, 2008, from http://www.nativeamericans.com.

Park, J. J. (2007). Where I am from. In S. E. Borrego & K. Manning (Eds.), *Where I am from: Student affairs practice from the whole of students' lives* (pp. 17–18). Waldorf, MD: National Association of Student Personnel Administrators.

Pavel, D. M., Skinner, R. R., Farris, E., Cahalan, M., Tippeconnic, J., & Stein, W. (1998). *American Indians and Alaska Natives in postsecondary education,* National Center for Education Statistics (NCES). (NCES 98-291.) Washington, DC: U.S. Department of Education, Office of Educational Research and Improvement.

Phillips, K. (2008, April 15). *"Bad money" criticizes Wall Street, U.S. finances.* National Public Radio, Morning Edition.

Press Associates Union News Service. (2003, June 23). *White collar job exodus to increase, panelist warn.* Retrieved December 1, 2008, from http://www.engology.com/ArchPanelistWarns.htm.

Redd, K., Neubig, E., & Mahler, J. D. (2007). *Findings from the 2007 CGS international graduate admissions survey phase I: Applications.* Washington, DC: Council of Graduate Schools.

Rehyner, J. (1993). New directions in United States native education. *Canadian Journal of Native Education, 20*(1), 63–75.

Sue, D. W. (2005, January 28). Town hall meeting at the National Multicultural Conference and Summit, Los Angeles, CA.

Sue, D. W., Bingham, R., Porche-Burke, L., & Vasquez, M. (1999). The diversification of psychology: A multicultural revolution: Report of the National Multicultural Conference and Summit. *American Psychologist, 54,* 1061–1069.

Sue, D. W., Capodilupo, C. M., Torino, G. C., Bucceri, J. M., Holder, A.M.B., Nadal, K. L, et al. (2007). Racial microaggressions in everyday life. *American Psychologist, 62*(4), 271–286.

Wilcox, T. (2007). Where I am from. In S. E. Borrego & K. Manning (Eds.), *Where I am from: Student affairs practice from the whole of students' lives* (pp. 2–3). Waldorf, MD: National Association of Student Personnel Administrators.

CHAPTER 2

Diversity in the Black Community: Implications for Mental Health

Guerda Nicolas, Kimberly A. Prater, and Angela M. DeSilva

The Black population is the largest racial minority group in the United States (with Latinos comprising the largest cultural group), and there exists significant cultural diversity among Black populations. Although native-born Blacks and Black immigrants in the United States share some similarities with respect to phenotypic features and experiences with racism, discrimination, and prejudices, there exists significant differences between the two groups. Specifically, different cultural groups within the Black community vary with respect to sociopolitical history, language, cultural beliefs, family life, and so on. A closer understanding of the diversity among Blacks is paramount in understanding the mental health of individuals who comprise this racial group. In this chapter we provide a summary of the demographic and mental health diversity among native-born Blacks and Black immigrants in the United States. In addition we discuss the importance of understanding and addressing this diversity in mental health work.

BEYOND SKIN TONE: CULTURAL DIVERSITY AMONG NATIVE-BORN AND FOREIGN-BORN BLACKS

According to the 2004 American Community Survey (ACS) report, it is estimated that there are a total of 36.6 million Blacks living in the United States, representing 13 percent of the U.S. population. However, information regarding the specific cultural groups that comprise this number is often not available or included in most population reports. It is often the case that most population data use external characteristics to categorize individuals (as Black or African American [the common politically correct term]) and fail to recognize the cultural diversity that exists within this population.

Eight percent of the total Black population consists of Black immigrants (Schmidley, 2001), with the majority coming from the Caribbean (60%) and Africa (24%). We noted similar trends in our mental health research project among Blacks, from which we found that the majority of the immigrant Black participants reported immigrating to the United States from the Caribbean islands (53.7%) and Africa (40.1%). Because of their physical appearance, these groups are often categorized as "Blacks" or "African Americans" without any consideration of their ethnic and cultural backgrounds. Importantly, however, there are significant cultural differences between the various ethnic groups that comprise the Black population that must be taken into account in understanding this population. Despite such diversity, the literature on Blacks rarely addresses such diversity or takes into account the significant contributions or potential impact of such diversity with respect to research and service delivery.

An Understanding of Terminologies: Native-Born versus Foreign-Born Blacks

Historically, terms such as *Black, Black Americans*, and *African Americans* were used interchangeably to describe "a person having origins in any of the Black racial groups of Africa" (Altman, 1997, p. 30). This definition is then used in most government documents and programs in the country but fails to acknowledge the cultural diversity that exists among Blacks in America. Although the term African Americans implies a description of individuals with African history who are born in America, it is often used to refer to many different cultural Black American groups. Such use of the term fails to recognize the unique cultural differences among the heterogeneous Black community.

Native-born Blacks (African Americans). Native-born Blacks in the United States are individuals who are living in America, are descendants of Africans (specifically Black Africans), and who are born and whose family of origin members (from previous generations) were born in America. These are individuals whose sociopolitical history is grounded in their experiences in American society and not a country outside of the United States. Thus, while there are many Black individuals who are able to trace their ancestry to Africa, the term African American should be designated for individuals who have African heritage, who are born in the United States, and whose parents and grandparents were also born in America. The classification of the term African American is significant because it reflects the social, historical, political, and lifetime experiences and behaviors of Black individuals in America. Thus the term African American is more than a label; it is also an expression of the cultural and historical roots of a group of individuals. When data and reports are produced using the term

African American, a description of the inclusion process used to identify such groups should be clearly delineated. Not doing so can lead to erroneous generalizations of findings to all ethnic and cultural Black groups.

Foreign-born Blacks (Black Immigrants). Although the presence of foreign-born Blacks in the United States is not new, over the last decades the number of foreign-born Blacks has increased from 125,000 in 1980 to 2,815,000 in 2005, with the majority coming from the Caribbean and Latin America (approximately two-thirds) and Africa (approximately one-third), and the remaining from countries such as Europe, Canada, or elsewhere (Campbell & Jung, 2005). When foreign-born Blacks immigrate to the United States, they bring with them their distinctive cultural, social, political, and historical background, which likely differs from those of Blacks born in America. Thus, it is central that individuals become aware of cultural characteristics and backgrounds as they have important implications for research service delivery.

In contrast to the description of African Americans, Black immigrants are individuals of African ancestry who immigrated to the United States from another country. These may be Black individuals who immigrated to America from Africa, the Caribbean islands, Latin America, and so on. This description also includes individuals who are documented, undocumented, as well as those who are naturalized citizens in the United States. While Black immigrants share the status of being immigrants, they often have distinctive migration, immigration, and acculturation patterns that must be taken into account when trying to understand their experiences in the United States. In addition, the distinctive cultural differences between and within these groups of foreign-born Blacks must be recognized and factored into any comparative conclusions that are made about them.

In summary, the cultural diversity in the Black community calls for a greater awareness and integration of cultural issues into understanding and improving the psychological well-being of all Black individuals. Researchers, practitioners, and public officials should cease using terminologies such as "Blacks" and "African Americans" interchangeably as such descriptors do not clearly take into account the cultural uniqueness of individuals from this population. Thus, every attempt should be made to describe the inclusion criteria used to determine such categories for a group of Black individuals.

MENTAL HEALTH AMONG NATIVE- AND FOREIGN-BORN BLACKS

Overwhelmingly the majority of mental health research findings on Blacks are based on racial categorization and not cultural background. This makes it difficult to tease out mental health differences among native-born Blacks and foreign-born Blacks. Recently, research has reported significant health disparities between native-born Blacks and Black immigrants, with

the latter reporting better health (Read & Emerson, 2005). Thus, it is paramount that research focusing on Blacks takes into account the diversity
among Black individuals. The following sections summarize the available
mental health data on Blacks and Black Caribbeans in an effort to highlight the need to further examine the mental health status of specific cultural groups of Blacks.

Mental Health of Blacks

The majority of mental health reports on Blacks are done in comparison
to Whites. These studies have concluded that in comparison to Whites,
Blacks, across all dimensions of health status, report poorer health (Kington & Nickens, 2001). Furthermore, research has demonstrated that the
basic levels of stress for Black men (Myers & King, 1985), women (Anderson, 1996), and children (Myers & King, 1985) are significantly higher compared to the corresponding White groups. For example, Blacks are higher
than Whites with respect to death rates from cardiovascular disease and
strokes (Centers for Disease Control, 2000). It is well known that Blacks in
particular are exposed to numerous specific stressors and many general
stress-producing social conditions that are found to be associated with
major psychiatric disorders. Livingston (1994) reports that over one-third
of Blacks live in poverty, a figure that is three times the number of Whites
who currently live in poverty. In addition, Livingston notes that over half
of the Black population live in urban areas characterized by poor housing
and school standards with a pervasive drug culture. Furthermore, Black
individuals are frequently underemployed and some may be exposed to
an excess of street violence (Livingston, 1994). The combination of these
detrimental factors contributes to high levels of stress among the Black
population.

Black people live with greater stress than do White individuals, but some
have the personal and social resources to maintain a perspective that keeps
the stress external, not permitting it to become internalized or to disrupt
personal integration (Veroff, Kulka, & Douvan, 1981). Jackson (1991) reported that a significant percentage of his sample of Blacks (35%) indicated
no health symptoms or problems, and stated that they were very satisfied
with their health (52%). In fact, Veroff et al. (1981) state that "the experience
of being Black in a society dominated by Whites does not, as is sometimes
incorrectly assumed, lead to deep and corrosive personal demoralization"
(p. 40). Blacks may rely heavily on support systems, such as religion and
the extended family, to help maintain their physical and mental health.

Mental Health of Black Immigrants

In comparison to the research on the mental health of other immigrant
groups such as Latinos and Asians (Alegria et al., 2006), the literature on

the mental health of Black immigrants is scarce. The little mental health research there is was conducted in the 1990s among Black immigrants and is inconsistent, with some reporting a poor mental health status of Black immigrants based on acculturation, acculturative stress, and assimilation. More recent mental health data are showing the opposite, with Black immigrants having better mental health than native-born Blacks in the United States (Malzberg, 1964; Vander Stoep & Link, 1998). Given that Black immigrants account for more than 25 percent of the entire Black population in major cities such as New York, Boston, and Miami, it becomes even more important to understand and investigate their mental health status (Read & Emerson, 2005; Takeuchi et al., 1998). Due to the significant population of Black Caribbeans in the United States and in Europe, the majority of mental health data on Black immigrants focuses on Black Caribbeans and most have been collected in England (Harrison, Owens, Holton, Neilson, & Boot, 1988; Lloyd, 1993). Research by Jackson et al. (2007) is beginning to fill this gap by reporting mental health data for both African Americans and Black immigrants, especially Black Caribbeans. In this section of the chapter, we provide a summary of the international and national research focusing on Black Caribbeans.

International Studies

Mental health researchers in England have found higher rates of schizophrenia diagnoses among Black Caribbeans than Whites (Harrison et al., 1988). Specifically, utilizing several diagnostic classifications, rates for schizophrenia in Afro-Caribbean individuals in England between the ages of 15 and 54 were found to be 12 times higher than in the general population and 18 times higher for second generation British-born Black Caribbeans. It is unclear from these studies whether the cultural backgrounds of the individuals were taken into account. For example, historically, African Americans were often diagnosed with paranoid schizophrenia until researchers began to demonstrate that these individuals were being misdiagnosed due to the lack of understanding of their cultural norms and presentation (Jackson & Jones, 1998; Neighbors, Jackson, Broman, & Thompson, 1996).

With respect to depression, conflicting results have been reported on Black Caribbeans. While Lloyd (1993) found a higher rate of depression among Black Caribbeans than Whites, Shaw, Creed, Tomenson, Riste, and Cruickshank (1999) found that Black Caribbeans were no more likely to have depression symptoms than whites. Interestingly, Shaw et al. did find that Black Caribbean women were more likely to have depressive disorders than White women. Research results indicate that Black Caribbeans were less likely to receive treatment for their mental health needs (Shaw et al., 1999; Williams et al., 2007). Williams et al. (2007) found that although Black Americans are less likely than Whites to have a major depressive disorder (MDD), when they do, it tends to be more chronic and severe. They are also much less likely to undergo treatment. Researchers are urging mental health clinicians and researchers to better understand depression among Black Caribbeans and to develop more culturally appropriate interventions for this population so that effective mental health treatment can be more readily accessible.

National Studies

In reviewing the mental health literature in the United States, one is hard-pressed to find articles pertaining to the mental health of Black Caribbeans. James Jackson's national survey of Blacks' mental health (Jackson et al., 2007) is the first of its kind to include a national sample of Black Caribbeans. The National Survey of American Life (NSAL) is the most comprehensive and detailed study of mental disorders and the mental health of African Americans and Caribbeans. Three recent analyses from the NSAL dataset have yielded interesting comparison results, which ultimately call for further evaluation of mental health disorders among Black adolescents. The first is a study of the prevalence and risk factors of attempted suicide among Black adolescents; the study found that of the respondents 2.5 percent reported one year ideation, 2.3 percent had attempted suicide at least once, and 1.2 percent attempted suicide in the past year. Females accounted for 71 percent of the attempted suicides. There were ethnic differences in suicide attempts, with African Americans and Caribbean adolescents accounting for 81 percent and 19 percent of suicide attempts, respectively. This study underscores the importance of understanding the heterogeneity of the Black population and, by extension, differences in Black ethnic groups.

In another paper, which examined perceived discrimination as a risk factor for mental disorders, the data indicated that an increase in perceived discrimination resulted in significant increases of being diagnosed with MDD, conduct disorder, and oppositional defiant disorder among African American and Caribbean adolescents (Seaton, 2005). Lastly, McCloskey, Berman, Noblett, and Coccaro (2006) recently examined the prevalence rates and psychosocial correlates of intermittent explosive disorder (IED) using the same dataset and found that 9.8 percent of African American and 16.1 percent of Caribbean adolescents met diagnostic criteria for IED. These rates are significantly higher than those suggested by current prevalence estimates. Collectively, these preliminary results indicate that Black Caribbean immigrant adolescents have higher rates of mental health problems than American-born Black adolescents (Joe, 2005), but information with regard to the distribution differences pertaining to the types of mental health disorders is unknown.

Results from the NSAL analyzed by Williams et al. (2007) suggest differences within the Caribbean sample. For instance, within the Caribbean sample, men had higher rates of psychiatric disorders than women, while persons from the Spanish Caribbean had higher rates than those from other ethnic origins. Generational status also emerged as a risk factor for mental illness. Third-generation Caribbean men and women had significantly elevated rates of all disorders, with the exception of anxiety disorders among men, compared with first-generation immigrants. Additionally, second-generation men and women had higher rates of substance abuse disorder, and only men had higher rates of any disorder compared with foreign-born men and women. These results speak to the notion that acculturation and acculturative stress are potentially associated with risk for developing a mental disorder.

In sum, international and national research studies highlight the ethnic and cultural differences between native-born Blacks and foreign-born Blacks and further support the need to look at both between and within ethnic group differences with respect to mental health. In addition, there is also a need to examine intra-group variability within both the native- (i.e., regional differences) and foreign-born Blacks (i.e., within African immigrants) in order to further understand the mental health status of Blacks in the United States.

HELP-SEEKING BEHAVIOR PATTERNS AMONG NATIVE- AND FOREIGN-BORN BLACKS

In addition to examining the mental health status of Blacks in the United States, some scholars have examined the help-seeking behaviors of this population as a means to address the mental health of this population. Mental health research among Blacks and Black immigrants reported differences in help-seeking behavior compared to whites. And while there are some similarities within different cultural groups of Blacks, there are significant differences between native-born Blacks and Black immigrants with respect to seeking help from mental services.

Help-Seeking Behaviors of Blacks

Despite the overwhelming statistics attesting to their poor health and the multiple constraints on their lives, Blacks have been found to report higher psychological well-being than Whites (Miller, 1987) and are thus less likely to utilize professional mental health services. Neighbors (1984) found that less than 10 percent of Blacks who had experienced "serious personal problems" utilized professional services. Regardless of the psychiatric symptoms, Blacks were found to be less likely to voluntarily seek mental health services than Whites (Sabshin, Diesenhaus, & Wilkerson, 1970).

In 1988 over 60 percent of the visits to doctors made by Whites took place in doctors' offices, compared to 49 percent by Blacks (Reed, 1992).

Blacks tend to make more visits to hospital outpatient departments and emergency rooms than Whites, which indicates that Blacks are more likely to go for treatment when they perceive their condition as life-threatening. Furthermore, Blacks tend to use facilities such as the emergency room as their primary care clinic because they often do not have a private physician due to economic disadvantages. In addition, Reed also reports that Blacks are more dissatisfied than Whites with the medical care they receive. Using the National Survey of Black Americans to study mental health, Neighbors (1991) came up with some interesting findings. He found, not surprisingly, that the rich are more likely to seek professional help than the poor, the elderly are more likely to seek medical settings for help with personal problems, and that the severity of a problem is not related to the use of medical organizations.

The lack of utilization of medical services by Blacks may relate to the quality of the services they receive once they actually do seek assistance. Ruiz (1990) reports that Blacks are more likely to receive treatment in public facilities, to be treated with drugs, and to begin treatment with little focus on interpersonal relationships or personality factors. In addition, Adebimpe (1981) found that although Blacks are more likely to be diagnosed with mental disorders, they are also more likely to be treated in group therapy, resulting in a high drop out rate. Black people live with greater stress than Whites, but some have the personal and social resources to maintain a perspective that keeps the stress external, not permitting it to become internalized or to disrupt personal integration (Veroff et al., 1981). While the information on mental health and health service utilization among Blacks is important for the mental health field, it is not clear if these results are consistent among different Black cultural groups in the United States.

Help-Seeking Behaviors of Black Immigrants

Similar to the data on the mental health of Black Caribbeans, the majority of data on the help-seeking behavior patterns within this group has been collected on an international scale. In general research shows that while there is some divergence in the mental health status of native-born and foreign-born Blacks, their patterns of help-seeking behavior are more similar. Research comparing Black immigrants with native-born Blacks has consistently found that both groups tend to underutilize formal mental health services (Jackson et al., 2007). Although both groups are less likely to use formal support systems, there is some variability among the groups. In fact, Jackson et al. (2007) found that Black participants born in the United States were more likely to receive care when it was needed than were first-generation Black immigrants. This suggests that nativity does count in examining the help-seeking behavior patterns among Black individuals.

In a prevalence study comparing the help-seeking behaviors of Black Caribbean and White British women, Shaw et al. (1999) found similar medical help-seeking behaviors among the two groups, but African Caribbeans with mental disorders such as depression and anxiety were likely to seek additional cultural remedies from nonmedical sources. With similar findings in a prenatal study of White and Black British women, Edge, Baker, and Rogers (2004) argue that the lack of help-seeking services among Black British may be associated with cultural conceptualizations of mental illness, mistrust of mental health services, and lack of availability of culturally sensitive services. Gray (2002) argues that due to the stigma associated with seeking assistance from the mental health system, mental health practitioners need to integrate traditional healers into mental health interventions.

In conclusion, factors such as gender, cultural beliefs, and previous history with mental health systems are likely to have an impact on the help-seeking behavior patterns for many individuals, and this is especially true for Black immigrants in the United States. In addition, a closer examination of the many barriers (i.e., perceived helpfulness, satisfaction, trust of the system, cultural sensitivity of the service, generational status) to help-seeking behaviors for both native and Black immigrant groups is necessary in order to understand the unique needs and help-seeking patterns of these groups.

THE IMPLICATIONS OF CULTURAL DIVERSITY AMONG BLACKS AND MENTAL HEALTH

Given the increase in Black immigrants from Africa and the Caribbean, it is becoming increasingly more urgent for mental health professionals to distinguish between African Americans and Black immigrants. Failure to recognize and consider one's country of origin can lead to inappropriate and ineffective mental health assessments and treatment programs. As a result, the cultural diversity in the Black community has significant implications for how we assess mental health status and design and implement mental health interventions for this racial group.

In response to increasing cultural diversity in the United States, the American Psychological Association (APA) put forth guidelines for providing appropriate mental health care to multicultural populations and for conducting culturally sensitive research. The guidelines call for the need to consider the ethnic and cultural background of clients and research participants in order to provide ethical mental health services and conduct ethical research. The guidelines also provide a foundation from which service providers and researchers can effectively account for the ethnic background of clients and research participants.

The following are APA's six multicultural guidelines (APA, 2002): (1) Psychologists are encouraged to recognize that, as cultural beings, they may hold attitudes and beliefs that can detrimentally influence their perceptions of and interactions with individuals who are ethnically and racially different from themselves; (2) Psychologists are encouraged to recognize the importance of multicultural sensitivity/responsiveness, knowledge, and understanding about ethnically and racially different individuals; (3) As educators, psychologists are encouraged to employ the constructs of multiculturalism and diversity in psychological education; (4) Culturally sensitive psychological researchers are encouraged to recognize the importance of conducting culture-centered and ethical psychological research among persons from ethnic, linguistic, and racial minority backgrounds; (5) Psychologists strive to apply culturally appropriate skills in clinical and other applied psychological practices; (6) Psychologists are encouraged to use organizational change processes to support culturally informed organizational (policy) development and practices.

When thinking about mental health services or research with the Black community in the United States, it is important to follow these guidelines, particularly the second and fourth guidelines. Unfortunately, however, much of the research and clinical reports available on the mental health of Black individuals fails to adhere to these guidelines, since they group all Black individuals into one group irrespective of their specific ethnic or cultural background. Moving forward it will be important for clinicians and researchers to integrate the APA guidelines into their mental health work (i.e., research design, assessment procedures, and treatment plans) with the Black community in the United States.

As alluded to previously, the second and fourth guidelines put forth by the APA are the most pertinent to this chapter. Therefore, the following section will focus specifically on the application of these guidelines to mental health work with Black populations. In accordance with the second guideline, which emphasizes the importance of multicultural sensitivity and responsiveness, knowledge, and understanding about ethnically and racially different individuals, clinicians must have an awareness and understanding of a client's birth country from the onset of therapeutic work, in order to gain potentially invaluable information regarding the beliefs, values, and norms held by that client. The knowledge necessary to provide culturally sensitive mental health services can be obtained beginning with the initial intake assessment. Intake interviews should be structured to include a comprehensive assessment of the client's cultural background. Simply documenting the race of the client will not provide information sufficient enough to develop a culturally sensitive and responsive conceptualization of the client's present problems. Research has documented strong connections between culture and mental health. Therefore, intake assessments with Black individuals need to gather information about the cultural background of Black clients and take into account their unique sociopolitical history.

Treatment plans, modalities, and styles utilized in clinical work also need to be sensitive to the country of origin of Black clients. As discussed above, many Black immigrants tend to rely on religious leaders as well as close family members for support and care during times of distress. Therefore, treatment for Black immigrants may need to include religious practices and/or leaders, as well as family members. The therapist's therapeutic style may also need to be adapted based on the cultural background of Black clients. Clinical interventions cannot be selected or adapted based on the client's racial status. Rather, any selections or adaptations that need to be made must be based more pointedly on the specific cultural background of the client. Failure to distinguish between native-born and foreign-born Blacks may result in treatment plans that are inappropriate and ineffective for Black clients.

A similar level of rigor must be used in research work with Black populations. The fourth guideline put forth by the APA highlights the importance of conducting culture centered psychological research. Therefore, according to this guideline, psychological research with Black individuals must account for participants' country of origin. This can be done through demographic questionnaires that ask for specific information regarding the birth country of the participants, birth countries of their parents and grandparents, age of immigration, languages spoken, and so on. When research projects involve Black individuals from different birth countries, it is imperative that researchers assess the potential differences between the groups instead of reporting general information about the mental health of "Blacks" or "African Americans." In a similar vein, it is important to try to gain an understanding of the norms and values of the participants' specific ethnic backgrounds as this may impact the ways in which individuals respond to the general research process, as well as to specific questions or areas of examination in the research. Additionally, it is important to factor cultural values and norms alongside the sociopolitical histories of different Black populations into research findings and interpretations. Results should be interpreted within the context of the participants' birth countries and not simply their racial categorization.

Central to ensuring that psychologists are able to provide culturally responsive mental health services and to conduct culturally sensitive research are training programs that address the importance of examining the specific cultural background of Black clients. As mentioned earlier, Black individuals—both native-born and foreign-born—are often grouped together as "Blacks" or "African Americans" regardless of their specific cultural background or country of origin. If psychologists can learn from the onset of their training the importance of looking more scrupulously at the cultural backgrounds of Black clients, it is likely that they will carry such a practice into their professional work. Therefore, given the increasing diversity among the Black community in the United States, training programs must begin to educate their students about the importance of distinguishing between African Americans and Black immigrants when working within the Black community in the United States.

CONCLUSIONS

While often viewed as one homogenous group by previous research, the Black population is exceedingly diverse and heterogeneous. Significant differences exist within the different ethnic groups of Blacks. For instance, Jackson et al. (2007) show that Black Caribbean immigrant men were more likely than African American men to have experienced mood and anxiety disorders in the last year. Black Caribbean immigrant women, however, were less likely than African American women to have experienced anxiety or substance abuse disorders in the last year and over their lifetimes. Additionally, results from the NSAL study analyzed by Williams et al. (2007) suggest ethnic differences in regards to mental health within a Caribbean sample. For instance, men had higher rates of psychiatric disorders compared with women, and persons from the Spanish Caribbean had higher rates compared with those from other ethnic origins. Furthermore, those individuals born in the United States had elevated rates compared with immigrants, and third-generation immigrants had markedly higher rates of mental illness compared with other Caribbean immigrants. Nativity differences as well as age of immigration were also associated with lifetime risk for psychiatric disorders. For example, immigration as a young adult (aged 18–34) was associated with a significantly reduced risk for all disorders among women and for all but mood disorders among men (Williams et al., 2007). Collectively, the results of these studies support the general notion that the cultural background of individuals is essential to promoting their psychological well-being.

Help-seeking behavior patterns also differ by ethnic and cultural backgrounds. Jackson et al. (2007) found that African Americans are more likely to receive care than first-generation Black immigrants. But immigrants who had lived in the United States for more than 21 years reported the highest use of services. "The longer Black Caribbeans live in the U.S. and the younger they are when they immigrated, the more likely they are to use mental health services," Jackson reported. "This suggests that socialization and access may play an important role in seeking and receiving treatment for mental health problems" (p. 2).

In sum, this chapter stresses the need to understand the cultural context and experiences of all Blacks in order to decrease the disparities that exist. It is hoped that the present chapter contributes to the building of a model for understanding within and between cultural differences that likely exist within the Black community. In fact grouping native-born and foreign-born Blacks is likely to disguise important mental health differences for these groups. Thus we must move beyond looking at Blacks as a whole and beyond native versus foreign Blacks so as to be able to understand the experiences, behaviors, and attitudes of specific cultural groups within the Black population. Such examination holds promise in understanding the mental health disparities among different racial groups in the United States. Aldarondo (2007, p. 15) states that "culture and diversity influence the way that mental illness manifests itself, how individuals and communities perceive and cope with this illness, and how health care providers diagnose, treat, and care for persons with mental illness." Thus, all services, including mental health, must be culturally sensitive and take into account the country of origin as well as the cultural background of the individual.

REFERENCES

American Psychological Association. (2002). *Guidelines on multicultural education, training, research, practice, and organizational change for psychologists.* Retrieved February 22, 2005, from http://www.apa.org/pi/multicultural guidelines.pdf.

Adebimpe, V. R. (1981). Overview: White norms in psychiatric diagnosis of Black patients. *American Journal of Psychiatry, 138,* 279–285.

Aldarondo, E. (2007). *Advancing social justice through clinical practice.* New York: Routledge.

Alegria, M., Cao, Z., McGuire, T. G., Ojeda, V. D., Sribney, B., Woo, M., et al. (2006). Health insurance coverage for vulnerable populations: Contrasting Asian Americans and Latinos in the United States. *Inquiry, 43,* 231–254.

Altman, S. (1997). *The encyclopedia of African-American heritage.* New York: Facts-on-File.

Anderson, L. P. (1996). Perceived stress and social support among single and married black mothers. In J. Stewart & L. Burton (Eds.), *The black family: Contemporary issues.* University Park, PA: Penn State University Press.

Campbell, G., & Jung, K. (2005). *Historical census statistics on the foreign-born population of the United States: 1850 to 2000* (Population Division Working Paper No. 29). Washington, DC: U.S. Bureau of the Census.

Centers for Disease Control. (2000). *Racial and ethnic approaches to community health (REACH 2010): Addressing disparities in health.* Atlanta, GA: U.S. Department of Health and Human Services, Centers for Disease Control, Division of Data Services.

Edge, R., Baker, D., & Rogers, A. (2004). Perinatal depression among black Caribbean women. *Health & Social Care in the Community, 12,* 430–438.

Gray, J. A. (2002). Stigma in psychiatry. *Journal of the Royal Society of Medicine, 95,* 72–76.

Harrison, G. D., Owens, A., Holton, D., Neilson, D., & Boot, D. (1988). A prospective study of severe mental illness among Afro-Caribbean patients. *Psychological Medicine, 18,* 643–657.

Jackson, J. J. (1991). Ordinary husbands: The truly hidden men. In R. Staples (Ed.), *The black family: Essays and studies* (4th ed.). Belmont, CA: Wordsworth.

Jackson, J. S., & Jones, N. A. (1998). New directions in thinking about race in America: African Americans in a diversifying nation. *Looking Ahead, 20*(3), 3–19.

Jackson, J. S., Neighbors, H. W., Torres, M., Martin, L. A., Williams, D. R., & Baser, R. (2007). Use of mental health services and subjective satisfaction with treatment among black Caribbean immigrants: Results from the National Survey of American Life. *American Journal of Public Health, 97,* 60–67.

Joe, S. (2005). *Prevalence and correlates of black adolescent suicidal behavior in the United States.* Paper presented at the Annual APA Convention, Washington, DC.

Kington, R., & Nickens, H. W. (2001). Racial and ethnic differences in health: Recent trends, current patterns, and future directions. In N. Smelser, W. Wilson, & F. Mitchell (Eds.), *America becoming: Racial trends and their consequences* (pp. 253–310). Washington, DC: National Academy Press.

Livingston, I. L. (1994). *Handbook of black Americans health: The mosaic of conditions, issues, policies, and prospects.* Westport, CT: Greenwood Press.

Lloyd, K. (1993). Depression and anxiety among Afro-Caribbean general practice attenders in Britain. *International Journal of Social Psychiatry, 39,* 1–9.

Malzberg, B. (1964). Mental disease among native and foreign born whites in New York State. *Mental Hygiene, 48,* 478–99.

McCloskey, M. S., Berman, M. E., Noblett, K. L., & Coccaro, E. F. (2006). Intermittent explosive disorder-integrated research diagnostic criteria: Convergent and discriminant validity. *Journal of Psychiatric Research, 40*(3), 231–242.

Miller, S. M. (1987). Race in the health of America. *Milbank Quarterly, 65,* 500–531.

Myers, H. F., & King, L. M. (1985). Mental health issues in the development of the black American child. In G. J. Powell (Ed.), *The psychosocial development of minority group children* (pp. 275–306). New York: Brunner/Mazel.

Neighbors, H. W. (1984). The use of informal and formal help: Four patterns of illness behavior in the black community. *American Journal of Community Psychology, 12,* 629–644.

Neighbors, H. W. (1991). Improving the mental health of black Americans: Lessons from the community mental health movement. In D. P. Willis (Ed.), *Health policies and black Americans* (pp. 348–380). New Brunswick, NJ: Transaction Publishers.

Neighbors, H. W., Jackson, J. S., Broman, C., & Thompson, E. (1996). Racism and the mental health of African Americans: The role of self and system blame. *Ethnicity & Disease, 6,* 167–175.

Read, J. G., & Emerson, M. O. (2005). Racial context, black immigration and the U.S. black/white health disparity. *Social Forces, 84,* 181–199.

Reed, W. L. (1992). *The health and medical care of African Americans* (Vol. 5). Boston: William Monroe Trotter Institute.

Ruiz, D. S. (1990). *Handbook of mental health and mental disorders among black Americans.* New York: Greenwood Press.

Sabshin, M., Diesenhaus, H., & Wilkerson, R. (1970). Dimensions of institutional elements in a black church service. *Hospital Community Psychiatry, 35,* 464–469.

Schmidley, A. D. (2001). *Profile of the foreign-born population in the United States: 2000* (U.S. Current Population Reports, Series P23–206). Washington, DC: U.S. Government Printing Office.

Seaton, E. K. (2005). Perceived discrimination and racial identity profiles among African American adolescents. Unpublished manuscript.

Shaw, C. M., Creed, F., Tomenson, B., Riste, L., & Cruickshank, J. K. (1999). Prevalence of anxiety and depressive illness and help seeking behavior in African Caribbeans and white Europeans: Two phase general population survey. *British Medical Journal, 318,* 302–306.

Takeuchi, D., Chung, R. C., Lin, K. M., Haikang, S., Kurasaki, K., Chun, C., et al. (1998). Lifetime and twelve-month prevalence rates of major depressive episodes and dysthymia among Chinese Americans in Los Angeles. *American Journal of Psychiatry, 155,* 1407–1414.

Vander Stoep, A., & Link, B. (1998). Social class, ethnicity and mental illness: The importance of being more than earnest. *American Journal of Public Health, 88,* 1396–1403.

Veroff, J., Kulka, R., & Douvan, E. (1981). *Mental health in America: Patterns of help-seeking from 1957 to 1976.* New York: Basic Books.

Williams, D. R., Gonzalez, H. M., Neighbors, H., Nesse, R., Abelson, J. M., Sweetman, J., et al. (2007). Prevalence and distribution of major depressive disorder in African Americans, Caribbean blacks, and non-Hispanic whites: Results from the National Survey of American Life. *Archives of General Psychiatry, 64,* 305–315.

CHAPTER 3

Beyond Access: Culturally Competent Training and Workforce Development

D. J. Ida

GOING BEYOND ACCESS

Increasing access to services is frequently cited as key to improving care for communities of color. While this is clearly an important factor, it is imperative to look beyond access alone as a means of eliminating disparities in quality care for African Americans, Asian Americans, Native Hawaiians, Pacific Islanders, Latinos/Hispanics and Native Americans. The sad reality is the fact that many who are from underserved populations have few options for them *to* access.

At the heart of the matter is the need to overhaul the current workforce that has failed to meet the mental health needs of diverse populations (Hoge, Huey, & O'Connel, 2004; Hoge & Morris, 2007; Institute of Medicine, 2002; President's New Freedom Commission on Mental Health, 2003; Vega, Kolody, & Aguilar-Gaxiola, 2001). This chapter will explore issues related to access, which include the cost of unmet mental health needs, barriers to access, and an assessment of the current workforce. It will also look at why it is critical to diversify the workforce, not only in terms of increasing the number of providers from each of the four major ethnic groups, but to also recruit and retain consumers, family members and paraprofessionals as providers, as well as train interpreters to work specifically in the mental health arena.

Efforts to diversify the workforce must also be partnered with improved training of providers. Without changes in training and without modifying how services are provided, little progress will be made towards improving the quality of care for vulnerable populations. Often we talk about being "culturally competent" but do not clearly define what that means.

This chapter will therefore identify five core competencies that also look at how an effective workforce must develop training models that focus on a consumer-centered, strengths-based recovery model that coordinates primary health, mental health and substance abuse. It looks at the role and impact of culture in making an appropriate assessment, diagnosis, and treatment plan. Last but not least, policies must be developed that ensure the successful implementation of changes made for a culturally and linguistically competent workforce.

COSTS OF UNMET MENTAL HEALTH NEEDS

Approximately 217 million days of work are lost annually due to lost productivity related to mental illness and substance abuse disorders (U.S. Department of Health and Human Services, 1999). Costs for mental disorders are the leading cause of disability in the United States and Canada for people ages 15 to 44 (World Health Organization, 2004). It is estimated that the indirect cost for untreated mental health problems is $94 billion (Substance Abuse and Mental Health Services Administration [SAMHSA], 2008).

Untreated conditions exist because of either the actual absence of services or because of poor treatment that in essence results in the person not having received any services. In some instances, the latter can be more damaging if there is a misdiagnosis that results in improper treatment. A poorly trained workforce adds to mounting costs by failing to provide competent services. The result is prolonged treatment, the prescribing of unnecessary medications, and increased severity of symptoms that may result in costly hospitalization stays, stays that could have been avoided had the person received proper care. Untreated mental illness can also result in a person becoming homeless and/or getting involved with the criminal justice system.

The greatest cost of all, however, is the loss of life. More than 90 percent of people who commit suicide have a diagnosable mental disorder. Nearly 20 percent of persons diagnosed with bipolar disorder and 15 percent of persons diagnosed with schizophrenia die by suicide (Center for Mental Health Services, 2000). Individuals with serious mental health problems have a life expectancy that is twenty-five years less than the average individual (Lutterman et al., 2003; Parks, Radke, & Mazade, 2008).

Untreated depression can lead to other serious physical health problems, including diabetes, cardiovascular disease and stress disorders that incur additional health-related costs. The burden of mental illness has become such a critical issue that the World Health Organization (WHO) has become increasingly concerned with it on a worldwide basis. The WHO, in collaboration with the World Bank and Harvard University, found that mental disorders are so disabling in countries like the United States that they are considered equal to cardiovascular disease and cancer in their impact on disability (Murray & Lopez, 1996). Five of the top ten health disabilities are mental health related: depression, bi-polar disorders, alcoholism, schizophrenia, and obsessive compulsive disorders (Harnoid & Gabriel, 2000; Wijnant, 2000). Individuals with untreated mental health conditions utilize health care services more frequently than the general population (Greenberg, Stiglin, Finkelstein, & Berndt, 1993; National Mental Health Association, Mental Health America, 2006) and in a crisis will most likely end up in the emergency room.

The Medical Expenditure Panel Survey (Machlin, 2006) reported that expenses for emergency room visits in 2003 were generally higher than for other ambulatory visits to hospital, outpatient department or office-based settings. In 2003 the average expenditure for an emergency room visit was $560, while the median expenditure was $299. In Washington State, 9 out of 10 aged and disabled clients who visited the emergency room 31 or more times in FY 2002 had a substance abuse disorder, a mental illness, or both.

Not all costs can be accounted for in financial terms. There are also emotional costs that can be devastating for the consumer as well as for family members and that are impossible to calculate. If one takes into consideration the additional financial burden placed on family members, the costs are even higher. Assuming primary responsibility of raising children may prevent a spouse of an individual with serious mental health problems from seeking employment of their own, or, if employed, may affect their productivity on the job because they have to cope with the dual responsibilities of taking care of their children and having to cope with the emotional problems of their spouse. The outcome could also have a long-term negative effect since children growing up in an emotionally unhealthy environment are at greater risk for experiencing mental health problems themselves. The financial costs of untreated or improperly treated mental health conditions can therefore carry over from one generation to another.

Those with untreated psychiatric illnesses comprise one-third of the six hundred thousand individuals who are homeless. Belying the myth that individuals with mental health problems are violent, they are actually far more likely to be the victim rather than the perpetrators of violent crime (Appleby, Mortensen, Dunn, & Hiroeh, 2001; Hiday et al., 1999).

There are social and fiscal costs associated with individuals becoming involved with the criminal justice system. The cost to imprison a person is $22,650 per year (U.S. Department of Justice, Office of Justice Programs Bureau of Justice Statistics, 2004) compared to the average cost for outpatient care of $1,800 and $6,800 for long-term residential care (Physician Leadership on National Drug Policy [PLNDP] National Project Office, 1998).

According to a special report by the Bureau of Justice Statistics, more than half of all prison and jail inmates in 2005 had a mental health problem (James & Glaze, 2006). About 23 percent of state prisoners and 30 percent of jail inmates reported symptoms of major depression. An estimated 15 percent of state prisoners and 24 percent of jail inmates reported symptoms that met the criteria for a psychotic disorder. While African Americans and Latinos make up only 12 and 13 percent of the total adult population respectively, approximately 40 percent of all jail inmates were African American and another 15 percent were Latino (U.S. Department of Justice, Office of Justice Programs Bureau of Justice Statistics, 2004). A similar picture emerges when looking at the adolescent population. Latino and African American males constitute approximately 32 percent of the youth population but make up 68 percent of those in secure confinement and detention (Office of Juvenile Justice and Delinquency Prevention, 1997). The odds of them receiving quality care while incarcerated is virtually nonexistent, increasing the likelihood of there being additional costs down the road due to untreated mental health needs.

Barriers to Access

Barriers to receiving competent care exist in many forms. There may be a lack of providers who reflect the cultural and language background of the intended population, negative perceptions about mental health conditions that keep a person from seeking help, a fragmented system that makes it difficult for an individual to receive care, the lack of resources to pay for services, lack of information about where to receive help, or the time and location of services that are not conducive to the individual accessing services.

The lack of a properly trained workforce, however, is one of the biggest barriers to receiving care. The President's New Freedom Commission on Mental Health (2003) clearly outlined the workforce challenges when it stated, "The current mental health system has neglected to incorporate, respect or understand the histories, traditions, beliefs, languages and value systems of culturally diverse groups. Misunderstanding and misinterpreting behaviors have led to tragic consequences, including inappropriately placing individuals in the criminal and juvenile justice systems. There is a need to improve access to quality care that is culturally competent" (p. 49).

Another major barrier to accessing care is the discrimination against mental health that results in the lack of fair, equitable and affordable insurance coverage for mental health services (Thomas & Snowden, 2001). Mental health parity legislation that would provide equal coverage for mental health and physical health in insurance plans was first introduced in the United States Congress in 1992. In 2003 it became the Paul Wellstone Mental Health and Addiction Equity Act, so named after the untimely death of Senator Paul Wellstone from Minnesota who was a champion for mental health issues. Congress finally passed the Paul Wellstone and Pete Domenici Mental Health Parity and Addiction Equity Act of 2008 in October 2008. While passing parity legislation is a major victory for the provision of mental health services, it is just the beginning. There are millions who do not have insurance coverage of any kind, thereby making parity legislation moot. Parity legislation also does not guarantee that services that are available are culturally and linguistically competent.

Congress also passed the State Children's Health Insurance Program (SCHIP) on January 29, 2009, which was signed into law by President Obama on February 4, 2009. The legislation expands the coverage to an estimated four million children who would otherwise be uninsured and will benefit at least 11 million SCHIP recipients overall. It is historic in that it is the first time that mental health parity has been implemented in the SCHIP plan. Like the Wellstone Parity Act, however, insurance coverage alone does not guarantee quality of services. A properly trained workforce is key to addressing this issue.

Those who argue that it will increase costs ignore the fact that early intervention and appropriate treatment can actually save costs in the long run. Shifting the workforce to address mental health, substance abuse and primary health can ease the perceived additional financial burden. Implementing a collaborative model may initially be resource-intensive but in the long run can provide an effective model to serve a needy population in light of increased cuts to Medicaid (Grazier, Hegedus, & Carli, 2003).

The current health care system is fragmented with different funding streams, training programs, service delivery systems, and policies for reimbursement. The lack of coordination makes it extremely difficult for the consumer to navigate through multiple systems and discourages them from seeking help. This is particularly true for individuals for whom English is a second language. Having to go from one site to another, tell their story over and over, fill out multiple forms, and have multiple treatment plans only results in frustration and delivery of poorer quality of services (Davis, 2003; Hoge, 2002; Lee, 1997). The lack of coordination between education, juvenile justice and child welfare systems further complicates the process of securing services for children with co-occurring disorder (President's New Freedom Commission on Mental Health, 2003).

Implementing services that are not designed for a particular population can also be a major barrier to receiving quality care. There is a growing trend toward requiring the implementation only of strategies that are considered "evidence based practices." The use of "evidence based practices" is in and of itself an appropriate strategy to follow and is designed to implement services that have been shown to be effective. The challenge comes with determining "whose evidence" gets used (Bernal & Scharro-del-Rio, 2001; Davis et al., 2002; Fortier & Bishop, 2003). Unfortunately, communities of color have been all but ignored in the research. The implications for this failure of current research practices can be very detrimental to communities of color. The book *The Spirit Catches You and You Fall Down* (Fadiman, 1997) is an excellent example of what happens when good people provide bad services and the dire consequences that can occur.

It forces community-based organizations to seek funding for and implement practices that have not been evaluated for effectiveness with the intended population and may be inappropriate, ineffective, and potentially
damaging to their consumers. There are also practices that are known to
be effective within the community but lack the "scientific rigor" required
to be deemed evidence based. Without proper resources and support,
these practices cannot be evaluated adequately enough to get the evidence
proving their efficacy.

The U.S. Department of Health and Human Services (2001) provides a
comprehensive overview of research on different mental health conditions.
Of the 7,670 individuals included in clinical trials for major depression,
bi-polar disorders and schizophrenia, only 1 percent of the participants
were identified as either African American, Latino, Asian American or
nonwhite. A similar picture emerged when looking at research on attention deficit hyperactivity disorder (ADHD) in children. Of the 1,675
children included in the study, only 182 or 1 percent were identified as
African American, Latino or Asian American. No Native American adults
or children were identified in the studies. Further review of the literature revealed that not one of these studies looked at the impact of race,
language or ethnicity in the outcomes for any of these populations (U.S.
Department of Health and Human Services, Appendix A).

Another major barrier to seeking and receiving care includes the negative perceptions about mental health within the community itself. Because
of the stigma and shame, individuals are afraid of seeking help for fear of
being labeled and shunned. A public awareness campaign that normalizes
mental health problems, raises awareness about what mental health is and
is not, and provides hope for those with serious issues can help establish a
healthy atmosphere that makes it "safe" to talk about mental health.

Diversifying the Current Workforce

Diversifying the current workforce falls into four broad categories of
change. The first is to increase the number of providers from each of the
major ethnic groups. The second is training interpreters to work specifically in the mental health field. The third is to broaden the current workforce to encompass other disciplines including primary health, substance
abuse and educators. The fourth area is the inclusion of consumers and
peer specialists as providers.

*Increase the Number of Providers from Each of the
Major Ethnic Groups*

In spite of their growing numbers, communities of color are greatly underrepresented in the number of available mental health service providers
that reflect their ethnic/racial background. According to the 2000 census,

African Americans, Latino/Hispanics, Asian American, Native Hawaiians, Pacific Islanders, and Native Americans comprised 30 percent of the total population in the United States, and by the year 2025 the numbers will grow to 40 percent. Unfortunately, only 6.6 percent of psychologists, 12 percent of social workers, 9.8 percent of psychiatric nurses, 17.4 percent of counselors, 7.5 percent of marriage and family counselors, 4.9 percent of school psychologists, and 17 percent of pastoral counselors represent professionals from any of the four major ethnic groups (Center for Mental Health Services, 2004). There are even fewer providers who have the bilingual capability of communicating effectively with individuals with limited English proficiency, leaving this vulnerable population without appropriate services.

Studies have indicated that matching ethnicity between providers and consumers, particularly among Asian Americans and Hispanic/Latinos increased positive outcomes (Snowden, 1999). Providers who are unfamiliar with a particular population may not recognize the relevance of culture, may misinterpret unfamiliar beliefs or fail to understand the significance of historical trauma. There may also be major differences in how the provider and consumer define the problem and determine what constitutes success.

Clinicians, like consumers, bring their own cultural values and beliefs into the therapeutic session (Comas-Diaz & Jacobsen, 1991; Davis, 2003; Hays, 2001; Hunt, 1995). When the provider and consumer are from different cultural backgrounds and/or speak different languages, the likelihood of miscommunication increases greatly. It is important, however, to remember that ethnic match alone does not guarantee cultural competence. In fact, making the assumption that any clinician of a particular background will automatically be competent to work with another person of similar background can be very dangerous. They may bring certain strengths and insights into the situation, but they must also have their own biases, which can negatively influence the therapeutic relationship, dismissing certain cultural beliefs as being old-fashioned or assuming that everything is attributed to race or culture. Assuming that culture accounts for everything can be as dangerous as saying that it plays no role at all. It is important to keep a balanced perspective in providing culturally and linguistically competent care.

Training only providers of color is insufficient because the entire workforce must be culturally sensitive and competent. This is also a practical matter since the number of providers from the different ethnic minority populations will never catch up with the needs of their respective communities. Being culturally competent should therefore be the responsibility of all providers, regardless of ethnic, cultural or language background. A review of the literature in *Setting the Agenda for Research on Cultural Competence in Health Care* (Fortier & Bishop, 2003) found that cross-cultural training did improve the quality of care and that it also led to significant

increase in the use of services and reduction of drop out rates by consumers of color (p. 69). The evaluation of the "Growing Our Own" curriculum designed by the National Asian American Pacific Island Mental
Health Association indicated that training increased the ability of interns
to do a comprehensive, culturally appropriate assessment, regardless of
ethnicity.

Training Interpreters to Work Specifically in the Mental Health Field

Properly trained bilingual, bicultural service providers represent the
gold standard for providing culturally and linguistically competent mental
health services for individuals with limited English proficiency. Unfortunately, it is unrealistic to think that their numbers will increase sufficiently
in the near future, leaving a major gap in the system's ability to provide
quality services to this vulnerable population. Use of a properly trained
interpreter, however, can go a long way in reducing disparities and improving communication between the consumer and provider.

The rapid increase in those who are foreign-born presents a special
challenge for the mental health workforce. According to the 2000 census,
88 percent of Asian Americans are either foreign-born or have at least
one foreign-born parent. The Hispanic population has also seen a major
increase in their numbers. Some 35.2 million Hispanics now live in the
United States, of which 40 percent are foreign-born, with the majority living in California, Texas, and Florida.

There is also a small but growing number of African Americans who
are foreign-born. According to the U.S. census, there are approximately
one million foreign-born African Americans residing in the United States,
and they make up three percent of the total foreign-born population. A
large percentage of immigrants come from Nigeria and Ethiopia, while a
large percentage of refugees come from Sudan and Somalia. There are also
some Native Americans who speak their native language and may not be
fluent in English.

Frequently, bilingual staff are used to providing interpreting services,
even if they have never been trained to be an interpreter or have any mental health training. They are asked to do this in addition to their regular
job responsibilities and may or may not get compensated at a higher rate
because of their language skills. Not only is it unfair to place this burden
on the bilingual staff, but it is also unethical, as it compromises the quality
of care for the consumer.

Interpreters must be trained to work specifically in the mental health
arena. There are unique challenges to helping a clinician understand
whether a person is hearing voices because of a belief in spirits, or the
voices are symptoms of psychosis. One role of an interpreter is that of
a cultural broker. They provide the clinician with cultural information

that will help the clinician make a culturally appropriate assessment and diagnosis. While the interpreter is a key member of the clinical team, it is the responsibility of the provider to be both clinically and culturally competent. Few providers know how to properly use interpreters so that they're more than a human dictionary to them. At the same time, an interpreter should not be viewed as a clinician who can provide a clinical diagnosis. An untrained interpreter could seriously alter the assessment and diagnosis, thereby compromising the quality of care of a consumer.

A Spanish-speaking consumer may receive a written notice instructing them to take the pills *once* daily. The doctor may think he/she is asking the person to take one pill per day, but the consumer may think the instructions are to take 11 pills since *once* is "11" in Spanish. An interpreter could help minimize such miscommunication. It is imperative to use only trained interpreters and *never* use a child as this is fraught with many problems.

Federal laws, under Title VI of the Civil Rights Act of 1964, requires that "no person in the United states, shall, on grounds of race, color, or national origin, be denied the benefits of, or be subjected to discrimination under any program or activity receiving federal financial assistance." This includes individuals with limited English proficiency.

Training both interpreters and providers is necessary because:

- Most interpreters are not trained to work in mental health settings
- Most providers are neither culturally competent nor skilled in using interpreters properly
- Most non-English-speaking clients are ill-informed as to their right to receive service in their own native language.

Broaden the Workforce to Encompass Other Disciplines Including Primary Health, Substance Abuse, and Education

Integrating mental health and primary health: Collaborative model. There is no health without mental health. An effective workforce recognizes this and works across disciplines to include those in the primary health and substance abuse fields. There is practical value to this as many consumers enter the service delivery system through the healthcare door. Unfortunately, most healthcare providers are not trained to address mental health concerns nor are they trained to work with diverse populations, leaving many consumers unhappy with the quality of their care.

Addressing both physical and mental health is also important because of the direct correlation between the two (Hamid, Abanilla, Bauta, & Huang, 2008; Oxman, Dietrich, & Schulberg, 2005; Rollman, Weinreb, Korsen, & Schulberg, 2006; Unützer et al., 2002). According to the National Institutes for Health, the chances of becoming depressed increase as diabetes complications worsen and vice versa. People with depression are at greater risk for developing heart disease (Anderson et al., 2000; Musselman, Evans, & Nemeroff, 1998) and may have difficulty taking medications and following through with their treatment plans (Ciechanowski, Katon, Russo, & Hirsch, 2003).

The Commonwealth Fund 2001 Health Care Quality Survey found that 33 percent of Latinos, 27 percent of Asian Americans and 23 percent of African Americans reported that their doctor did not listen to everything they said, that they did not fully understand their doctor, or that they had questions during the visit but did not ask them. This compares with only 16 percent of the white population, which indicated they had difficulty with their provider. In addition, 45 percent of Hispanic and 44 percent of Asian American patients were the least likely to report that it was very easy to understand their doctors' information, including instructions for prescription medicines and materials from the doctor's office, compared to other racial/ethnic groups. Nearly half of the Asians (46%) said their doctor's advice was too difficult to follow and almost one-third (32%) said they did not follow the doctor's advice because it went against their personal beliefs.

There are several models of integrated care. Each has different levels of effectiveness. The most common models focus on either referrals or co-location. In the referral model, the physical health care provider makes a referral when they feel their patient is in need of mental health services. The patient is usually limited to no follow-up once the referral is made. In the colocation model, the mental health and primary care providers are located in the same physical location, making it easier for the individual to access both mental health and primary health care services. There is no guarantee, however, that service providers from different disciplines will discuss the case with each other nor develop a comprehensive treatment plan. Because of this, neither model alone guarantees that there will be long-lasting, positive outcomes.

The Hogg Foundation (2005) reports that after 20 years of research, the most effective model of integrated health care is the collaborative model. It goes on to define collaborative care as an integrated model in which providers from both the physical and mental health arena develop a partnership to manage the treatment of mild to moderate psychiatric disorders and stable to severe psychiatric disorders, usually in the primary care setting. The Hogg Foundation identifies effective collaborative models as those having the following four elements:

1. A mental health assessment tool used to evaluate the presence of psychiatric disorders;
2. A clinical care manager who is a professional or paraprofessional responsible for following patients with identified mental health needs in the primary care setting. They serve a vital role in helping the individual maintain their treatment adherence and may provide education about the psychiatric disorder and address the stigma associated with it. The clinical care

manager may also do outreach to the family as well as educate them on related issues;

3. A patient registry used by the clinical care manager to track the mental health needs of the individual. The registry includes scores on the mental health assessment tools as well as records of all contacts with the primary care physician and care manager; and

4. A psychiatric consultation that provides supervision for the clinical care manager to review patient progress and make recommendations for any adjustments that may be needed in the treatment plan.

One word of caution in developing integrated programs: There is a tendency to want to place mental health service in medical settings. While this is an appropriate strategy, it may draw valuable resources away from ethnic-specific, community-based organizations that have effectively served diverse populations for many years. In times of economic hardships, it is important to not take resources from one entity to support another.

Educators as Partners: Suicide is the third leading cause of death in youth aged 10 to 24. More youth and young adults die from suicide than from cancer, heart disease, AIDS, birth defects, stroke, pneumonia, influenza, and chronic lung disease combined (SAMHSA, 2001). At least 1 in 5 children and adolescents have a mental health disorder. At least 1 in 10, or about 6 million people, have a serious emotional disturbance (Center for Mental Health Services, 2000).

In the documentary *I Have Tourette's, but Tourette's Doesn't Have Me* (Kent et al., 2007), young children talk about the challenges of having a disorder that causes them great emotional pain. Some are teased by classmates. One student said the most difficult thing for him was having to deal with an insensitive teacher. In an effort to limit such incidences, an initiative was started in Minnesota and several other states to require mental health training as one of the topics for continuing education credits when teachers seek recertification.

Mental health problems that are undetected or untreated can result in serious emotional and behavioral problems that can rob children and adolescents of critical developmental years that cannot be reclaimed. Untreated mental health disorders can lead to school failure, family conflicts, drug abuse, violence, and suicide and can be very costly to families, and the communities at large. Columbine has become synonymous with school violence, and unfortunately this is not an isolated incident; it reflects a greater problem in our schools.

Teachers and school personnel are in a unique position to help with early identification of mental health problems in students before it reaches a crisis. They would not be expected to serve as a clinician but as part of a team that can improve the emotional well-being of children and adolescents. They can establish an atmosphere that reduces stigma and helps at risk youth feel like they belong.

Consumers and Peer Specialists as Providers

The mantra for the consumer movement is "nothing about us without us." They can be a powerful change agent in the mental health workforce and provide a unique perspective that is invaluable to service providers. Consumers in Georgia took the lead nationally and developed the Certified Peer Specialist program that increases the involvement of individuals with mental disorders and their families in mutual support services, consumer-run services, and advocacy.

The Certified Peer Specialist (CPS) serves as a role model to other consumers and provides peer support services; serves as a consumer advocate; provides consumer information and peer support for consumers in emergency, outpatient or inpatient settings. The CPS helps consumers clarify their personal goals for recovery as well as determine appropriate means to reach their goals. They help the consumer develop and track individualized treatment plans that meet the consumer's specific needs. Other job-related activities include helping the consumer build social skills that will improve their chances of finding and maintaining jobs, obtain decent and affordable housing, help nonconsumer staff identify environments that are conducive to recovery and help providers gain insight into mental illness and what makes recovery possible. They attend treatment team meetings and promote the consumer's use of self-directed recovery tools. The CPS will also continue their training and stay on top of current trends in the field to assist in the recovery process.

Consumers in the role of provider can be tremendous help to other consumers. There is also another benefit to using the peer specialist model. The act of helping others can also be therapeutic for the peer specialist as it continues to help build their competency skills.

DEVELOPING A STRENGTH-BASED, RECOVERY-FOCUSED WORKFORCE

In December 2004 the Substance Abuse and Mental Health Services Administration within the U.S. Department of Health and Human Services and the Interagency Committee on Disability Research (alongside six other federal agencies) convened the National Consensus Conference on Mental Health Recovery and Mental Health Systems Transformation. Experts representing different areas of focus developed a consensus statement on recovery that said: "Mental health recovery is a journey of healing and transformation enabling a person with a mental health problem to live a meaningful life in a community of his or her choice while striving to achieve his or her full potential" (SAMHSA, 2004).

Participants at the summit identified "10 Fundamental Components of Recovery," which were: (1) self-direction, (2) individualized and person-centered, (3) empowerment, (4) holistic, (5) non-linear, (6) strengths-based, (7) peer support, (8) respect, (9) responsibility, and (10) hope.

The recognition that recovery is possible is one of the most important paradigm shifts in the mental health field and a far cry from the times when those with serious mental health problems were literally chained to the walls of asylums. Recovery is more than symptom reduction. It looks different for each person. It increases a person's skills, allowing them to engage effectively with the world around them. Knowing recovery is possible gives hope to individuals and can help reduce much of the stigma around mental health. The shift toward a strength-based, consumer-driven recovery model is critical to helping consumers become productive members of society.

Being seen as someone who is competent is critical to restoring self–esteem, which in and of itself is an essential part of the recovery process (Deegan, 2003; Fisher & Ahern, 1999; Provencher, Gregg, Mead, & Mueser, 2002). Having an opportunity to engage effectively can be of particular importance for those who are isolated and disenfranchised because of cultural and language barriers, stereotypes, biases and prejudices.

Recovery occurs at multiple levels and involves the person in recovery, the service provider, the larger community and the system that establishes policies that often work against those who do not fit the mold of what mainstream society considers "the norm." In this context, the definition of the mental health workforce can be broadened yet again to encompass anyone involved in the larger service delivery system.

Recovery must also address the issue of trauma, which can occur for many reasons, including personal and physical trauma, natural disasters, the trauma associated with coming to a new country and, for refugees, the trauma brought on by war (Ida, 2007). Persons of color may also experience historical trauma brought on by discrimination due to ethnicity, race, place, or immigration status. This type of historical trauma goes deep and can leave invisible scars that lasts for generations (Davis & Bent-Goodley, 2004; Hunter, Shannon, Knox, & Martin, 1998). For Native Hawaiians, the term *Kaumaha Syndrome* literally means "heavy." Figuratively, it signifies the sadness, depression and dreariness brought on by oppression, discrimination, poverty, homelessness, and the cultural and spiritual disintegration of the Native Hawaiian people (Rezentes, 1996).

For Southeast Asian refugees, trauma may be associated with the horrors of war (Kinzie, 1993; Kinzie, Leung, & Boehnlein, 1997; Mollica, 2000, 2007). Regardless of the source, it is important to address trauma if the recovery process is to be successful (President's New Freedom Commission on Mental Health, 2003). In the case of discrimination, the intervention strategy must include changing a toxic environment that caused much of the trauma to begin with. A workforce that does not understand the impact of trauma cannot effectively serve those who have experienced it in any of its forms.

IMPROVE TRAINING—OPERATIONALIZING CULTURAL COMPETENCE

It is easy to ask providers to be culturally competent, but describing *how* to do it has always been a challenge. In an attempt to clarify what this might look like, the National Asian American Pacific Islander Mental Health Association (NAAPIMHA) developed the first national multidisciplinary curriculum to train master's and doctoral level interns and residents to provide culturally and linguistically competent services for Asian Americans, Native Hawaiians, and Pacific Islanders.

Called Growing Our Own, this curriculum was developed with funds from the U.S. Department of Health and Human Services, Substance Abuse Mental Health Services Administration, Center for Mental Health, Workforce Development grant, and it was recognized by the Annapolis Coalition for Workforce Development as a best practices model. The project brought together experts on Asian American, Native Hawaiian, and Pacific Islander (AANHPI) mental health from the Asian Counseling and Referral Services in Seattle, Washington; the Asian Pacific Development Center in Denver, Colorado; Hale Na'au Pono, Wai'anae Coast Community Mental Health Center, Wai'anae, Hawaii; the Hamilton Madison House, New York, New York; RAMS, Inc., San Francisco, California; and San Francisco General Hospital, San Francisco, California. These sites were chosen because of their history of providing culturally and linguistically competent services to AANHPI communities, their experience with training, and their ability to provide supervision. In order to assess different systems issues, the sites were also chosen to represent different geographical locations.

The focus of the training is to help the clinician learn how to think, how to analyze the situation by considering the role of culture and language at each step of the assessment, and how to respect the consumer's perspective and see things through a strength-based recovery lens. It was developed with input from consumers when asked what they thought was helpful on their road to recovery. It also recognizes that having clarity on one's own personal biases, strengths, and challenges are essential to being an effective clinician.

While the curriculum was designed to provide services for AANHPI consumers, it can be easily modified to work with other populations because it steers clear of simplistic approaches that say, for instance, "When you see a Chinese person, you do this. When you see a Latina, you do that." The following is an outline of the five modules with the corresponding core competency for each.

Module I: Self-Assessment

Core Competency: The Ability to Critically Self-assess. This requires the individual to look at his/her own beliefs about mental health, culture and language, how they view their role as a provider, and the impact this has on the therapeutic relationship. It challenges the belief that if I am from the community I do not need training or if I am not from the community I cannot be effective. It also challenges the traditional belief that the only expert in the room is the person with the degree.

Module II: Connecting with the Consumer

Core Competency: The Ability to Effectively Engage with the Consumer. This assesses their ability to develop a healthy rapport with the consumer and requires that the clinician be familiar with different communication styles, is sensitive to nonverbal cues, and understands the impact of culture and language in the therapeutic process. Providers learn how to change engagement strategies depending on age, gender, nationality, language, and other critical factors. It also assesses their ability to appropriately use an interpreter if necessary.

Module III: Culturally Responsive Assessment and Diagnosis

Core Competency: The Ability to Do a Culturally and Linguistically Appropriate Assessment and Diagnosis. The clinician learns how to use the *Diagnostic and Statistical Manual of Mental Disorders' (DSM–IV)* "Outline for a Cultural Formulation" to accurately assess and diagnose the current situation. A cultural formulation takes into consideration different world views of health and pathology and the potential impact of culture and language. It is important for the clinician to maintain a balanced perspective and not assume that culture and language alone always account for everything or, conversely, that it has no impact at all. The clinician must also be respectful of the consumer's perspective on what is considered a problem or what the solution might be.

Module IV: Culturally Responsive Intervention

Core Competency: The Ability to Develop a Culturally and Linguistically Appropriate Intervention Strategy Based on the Cultural Assessment. Developing a culturally responsive intervention uses a public health approach that looks at the individual within the context of his or her environment. It may involve the use of medications, individual/group/family therapy, use of traditional healers and herbal medicine, employment and training, housing, medical services, substance abuse counseling, learning English, and educating others about cultural beliefs and behaviors. It is important to note that teaching English should not be seen as implying that English is better than the person's native language. It is just another skill that will enhance their ability to communicate effectively.

Interventions may involve the use of traditional healers to help with problems that are viewed as psychological in nature (Chung, 2002; Jilek,

1994). Traditional tribal healing practices for Native Americans are tied to their tribal language, values, and beliefs (Nebelkopf & Phillips, 2004). African Americans, Asian Americans, Hispanics, Latinos, Native Americans, and Native Hawaiians and other Pacific Islanders all have different practices that may involve the use of traditional healers, curanderas, shamans, medicine men, midwives, acupuncture, ayurvedic medicine, herbal medicine, meditation, *ho'oponopono*, *morita*, *naikan*, t'ai chi ch'uan, and yoga (Kendziora, Bruns, Osher, Pacchiano, & Mejia, 2001; Lee, 1997; Rezentes, 1996).

Module V: System Cultural Competence

Core Competency: The Ability to Effectively Negotiate Systems. This means recognizing how different systems impact the individual and being able to effectively move from one system to another and develop a comprehensive intervention strategy. Examples of systems issues include the ability to get reimbursed for interpreting services or use of traditional healers or providing services to "ineligible" immigrants who may or may not have legal status. It involves the availability of quality supervision that respects the role of culture and language in the therapeutic process and involves outside issues such as anti-immigrant legislation that may keep a person from seeking help for fear of being turned in to Immigration and Naturalization Services.

SPECIAL WORKFORCE ISSUES: RECRUITMENT, RETENTION, AVOIDING BURN OUT AND SUPERVISION

Building the pipeline must go deep and wide, deep in the sense of starting early in the recruitment process and wide to capture a broader range of providers, a range that cuts across disciplines and includes paraprofessionals, consumers, interpreters and professionals from other fields (i.e., health and education).

Recognizing the stigma associated with the mental health field poses a barrier to people entering the field. To ameliorate this, a clear, proactive, recovery-oriented public campaign could be established to educate the general population about mental health. Messages could be tailored to address unique cultural and language needs in the different communities.

A common dilemma faced by community-based organizations is the ability to retain bilingual and bicultural interns, particularly those with graduate degrees. It is frustrating for agencies to provide quality training and supervision only to lose the intern or clinician to social services, a hospital or a large HMO that can pay a higher salary. Agencies' difficulty in finding resources to increase their capacity to hire and retain new clinicians continues to place a heavy burden on the remaining staff. They are at risk for burn out because they are almost always from the community and are willing to work at a lower rate on account of personal commitment. Their lack of a degree makes it difficult for them to move up the career ladder, and few advance to senior clinical or managerial positions.

The newly trained interns are also caught in a bind. Those with bilingual capabilities are very marketable with their much-coveted graduate degree. Being in high demand, they can get paid a higher salary than their counterparts who lack a formal education. Many feel caught between working for a community-based organization that gives them easier access to consumers from their own community (a desirable situation) and working for a larger agency that helps them pay their bills but has them work with a different population.

Supervision is a critical workforce issue that does not get much attention. This is unfortunate since much rests on their ability to provide ongoing training to improve the clinical skills of the clinician. As the field shifts its focus to being more culturally competent, the issue becomes: who supervisors the supervisor? Most are trained in graduate programs that fail to provide adequate training in cultural and linguistic competence. Some may be unfamiliar with the consumer movement or a strengths-based recovery model. An intern may receive the best clinical training but will have an uphill battle if his/her supervisor feels that issues of culture and language are unimportant, unnecessary, or, worse yet, something to overcome. The same goes for supervisors who focus solely on the individual, failing to understand the impact of historical trauma, the distinction between being a refugee and an immigrant, and the ongoing influences of the social/political/economic environment.

The supervisor must also be aware of the dynamics that arise when the consumer, clinician and supervisor are of the same or of a different cultural/racial/ethnic/sexual orientation background (Comas-Diaz & Jacobsen, 1991). Each combination has its own set of dynamics that the supervisor must be able to provide guidance on. The supervisor must understand how a particular combination might impact communication and, by extension, the therapeutic process. The supervisor must also be able to look at different intervention strategies that may be contrary to the way they were trained. This may include home visits, use of traditional healers, use of interpreters, doing case management, and integrating health and substance abuse.

Supervisors also need support, supervision or some means of getting a consult when needed. Many inherited their roles by virtue of the fact that they had seniority at an agency and may not have had any previous training on how to do supervision. Just because a supervisor is from a particular ethnic group does not mean they know how to do a cultural formulation; nor is it fair to expect them to be an expert on all issues. Developing a format for them to seek consultation and address issues of supervision could greatly enhance the quality of supervision.

Developing regional training clusters could draw on the expertise of the clinicians and supervisors across multiple agencies in a cost-saving effort that pools resources. Training could be attached to a local institution of higher education when available, but efforts should always be coordinated with the local community-based organization that provides access to the focus population.

Regional cultural competency centers that work with institutions of higher education can also: (1) provide training and support to faculty, administration and staff on cultural competence, (2) provide technical assistance in creating culturally competent training programs, (3) provide a venue for faculty, administrators and staff of different programs to discuss theories, teaching methods, and address students' need to work with culturally diverse populations, (4) provide evaluation and feedback to students and faculty on cultural competency skills, (5) develop programs of credentialing for paraprofessionals, interpreters, consumer- and/or family-assisted mental health providers, (6) develop training programs that address health, mental health and substance abuse, and (7) conduct research that includes diverse populations that will add to the body of knowledge on what constitutes a culturally competent workforce.

POLICY RECOMMENDATIONS

Training, recruitment efforts, and ongoing supervision are critical elements to improving the mental health workforce. Developing clear policies is how to bring the plan to fruition. This will be accomplished by gathering accurate data, assessing the current workforce, determining needs, and recognizing what steps are required to improve quality of services for diverse populations.

Recommendation 1: Improve data collection to include communities of color. Data must be disaggregated to reflect cultural and language differences within each of the four major ethnic groups, as this has direct bearing on our ability to gain a clear picture of the depth and breadth of the issues for each community. This provides the necessary information to modify and improve the current workforce. Data-collecting methods must also be appropriate and responsive to the needs of the community (i.e., do not send out evaluation forms in English to individuals who may not be literate in any language and/or who may not understand English).

Recommendation 2: Improve research and evaluation to include outcome measures that are culturally and linguistically appropriate. Include communities of color in clinical trials and research that assess the effectiveness of different intervention strategies. This will inform training efforts designed to improve the workforce competence.

Recommendation 3: Diversify the current workforce by recruiting individuals who reflect the makeup of different communities of color. This includes those seeking graduate training, consumers, and paraprofessionals and interpreters. Recruitment efforts should start early to bring people into the pipeline.

Recommendation 4: Diversify the workforce by including those from the mental health, primary health, substance abuse and education arenas, regardless of ethnicity.

Recommendation 5: Train interpreters to work specifically in the mental health arena and develop policies that clearly define roles and provide salary increases for language skills.

Recommendation 6: Train teachers how to address mental health issues in the classroom. This would include early identification and referral to appropriate sources.

Recommendation 7: Identify, implement and evaluate training programs that address cultural and linguistic competence and focus on a strengths-based, consumer-driven recovery model.

Recommendation 8: Increase supervision efforts and develop strategies to support supervisors, share resources and provide ongoing training for clinicians.

Recommendation 9: Establish appropriate rates of reimbursement and develop resources to cover additional costs. Without added resources, the financial burden falls back onto community-based organizations that cannot afford the increased costs.

Recommendation 10: Enforce Executive Order no. 13166, Improving Access to Services for Persons with Limited English Proficiency, which was signed by President Bill Clinton in 2000. The Executive Order requires Federal agencies to examine the services they provide, identify any need for services to those with limited English proficiency (LEP), and develop and implement a system to provide those services so LEP persons can have meaningful access to them.

ACKNOWLEDGMENTS

A special thank you to Janet Soohoo, Ree Ah Bloedow, and Jocelyn Lui who did a superb job taking material from NAAPIMHA's Workforce Development Executive Committee to organize and edit the *Growing Our Own* curriculum. The executive committee included Kinike Bermudez, Eddie Chiu, Davis Ja, Frank Kim, Poka Laenui, Evelyn Lee, Francis Lu, Joanne Sakaguchi, Steven Shon, Ann Yabusaki, and Paul Yew. Their expertise was invaluable in conceptualizing the curriculum. Thank you also to Meekyung Han and Yu-Wen Ying, who assisted with the evaluation process, and Kana Enomoto, project officer for the Center for Mental Health Services, which funded the project.

REFERENCES

Anderson, R., Freedland, K., Clouse, R., & Lustman, P. (2001). The prevalence of co-morbid depression in adults with diabetes: A meta-analysis. *Diabetes Care* 24: 1069–1078. Retrieved March 22, 2009, from http://care.diabetesjournals.org/cgi/content/abstract/24/6/1069.

Appleby, L., Mortensen, P. B., Dunn, G., & Hiroeh, U. (2001). Death by homicide, suicide, and other unnatural causes in people with mental illness: A population-based study. *The Lancet, 358,* 2110–2112.

Bernal, G., & Scharro-del-Rio, M. (2001). Are empirically supported treatments valid for ethnic minorities? Toward an alternative approach for treatment research. *Cultural Diversity and Ethnic Minority Psychology, 7*(4), 328–342.

Center for Mental Health Services. (2000). *Cultural competence standards in managed mental health care services: Four underserved/underrepresented racial/ethnic groups.* Rockville, MD: Substance Abuse & Mental Health Services Administration, USDHHS.

Center for Mental Health Services, Mental Health, United States. (2002). Manderscheid, R. W., and Henderson, M. J. (Eds.). DHHS Pub No. (SMA) 3938. Rockville, MD: Substance Abuse and Mental Health Services Administration, 2004.

Chung, H. (2002). The challenges of providing behavioral treatment to Asian Americans: Identifying the challenges is the first step in overcoming them. *Western Journal of Medicine, 176,* 222–223.

Ciechanowski, P. S., Katon, W. J., Russo, J., & Hirsch, I. B. (2003). The relationship of depressive symptoms to symptom reporting, self-care and glucose control in diabetes. *General Hospital Psychiatry, 25,* 246–252.

Comas-Diaz, L., & Jacobsen, F. (1991). Ethnocultural transference and countertransference in the therapeutic dyad. *American Journal of Orthopsychiatry, 61*(3), 392–402.

Davis, J., Erickson, J., Johnson, S., Marshall, C., Running, W., & Santiago, R. (2002). *Lifespan issues related to American Indians/Alaska Natives with disabilities.* Paper by the Work Group on American Indian Research and Program Evaluation Methodology (AIRPEM), presented at the Symposium on Research and Evaluation Methodology, Flagstaff, AZ.

Davis, K. (2003, March 13). *The disparity hypothesis: An overview of current research findings on mental health of people of color in the United States.* Paper presented at the American College of Mental Health Administration Summit, Santa Fe, NM.

Davis, K., & Bent-Goodley, T. (2004). *The color of social policy.* Alexandria, VA: Council on Social Work Education.

Deegan, G. (2003). Discovering recovery. *Psychiatric Rehabilitation Journal, 26*(4), 368–376.

Fadiman, A. (1997). *The spirit catches you and you fall down: A Hmong child, her American doctors, and the collision of two cultures.* New York: Farrar, Straus and Giroux.

Fisher, D., & Ahern, L. (1999). *People can recover from mental illness.* National Empowerment Center, Inc. Retrieved August 15, 2006, from http://www.power2u.org/articles/recovery/people_can.html.

Fortier, J., & Bishop, D. (2003). *Setting the agenda for research on cultural competence in healthcare: Final report* (C. Brach, Ed.). Rockville, MD: U.S. Department of Health and Human Services, Office of Minority Health, and Agency for Healthcare Research and Quality.

Grazier, K. L., Hegedus, A. M., & Carli, T. (2003). Integration of behavioral and physical health care for a Medicaid population through a public-public partnership. *Psychiatric Services, 54*(11), 1508–1512.

Greenberg, P. E., Stiglin, L. E., Finkelstein, S. N., & Berndt, E. R. (1993). The economic burden of depression in 1990. *Journal of Clinical Psychiatry, 54,* 405–418.

Hamid, H., Abanilla, K., Bauta, B., & Huang, K-Y. (2008). Evaluating the WHO assessment instrument for mental health systems by comparing mental health policies in four countries. *Bulletin of the World Health Organization, 86*(6), 417–496.

Harnoid, G., & Gabriel, P. (2000). *Mental health and work: Impact, issues and good practices.* Geneva: World Health Organization.

Hays, P. A. (Ed.). (2001). *Addressing cultural complexities in practice: A framework for clinicians and counselors.* Washington, DC: American Psychological Association.

Hiday, V. A., Swartz, M. S., Swanson, J. W., Borum, R. I., & Wagner, H. R. (1999). Criminal victimization of persons with severe mental illness. *Psychiatric Services, 50,* 62–68.

Hoge, M. (2002). The training gap: An acute crisis in behavioral health education. *Administration and Policy in Mental Health, 29*(4–5), 305–317.

Hoge, M., Huey, L., & O'Connel, M. (2004, November). Best practices in behavioral health workforce education and training. *Administration and Policy in Mental Health, 32*(2), 91–106.

Hoge, M., & Morris, J. (2007). *An action plan for behavioral health workforce development: A framework for discussion.* (Prepared by the Annapolis Coalition on Workforce Development under Contract Number 280-02-0302 with SAMHSA, U.S. Department of Health and Human Services.)

Hogg Foundation. (2005). *Integrated health care.* Retrieved April 5, 2008, from http://www.hogg.utexas.edu/programs_ihc.html.

Hunt, G. J. (1995). Social and cultural aspects of health, illness, and treatment. In H. H. Goldman (Ed.), *Review of general psychiatry* (pp. 362–368). Norwalk, CT: Appleton and Lange.

Hunter, S., Shannon, C., Knox, J., & Martin, J. (1998). *Lesbian, gay, and bisexual youths and adults.* Thousand Oaks, CA: Sage Publications.

Ida, D. J. (2007, Summer). Cultural competency and recovery within diverse populations. *Psychiatric Rehabilitation Journal,* 49–53.

Institute of Medicine. (2002). *Unequal treatment: Confronting racial and ethnic disparities in health care.* Washington, DC: National Academy Press.

James, D., & Glaze, L. (2006, September). *Mental health problems of prison and jail inmates.* U.S. Department of Justice, Office of Justice Programs, Bureau of Justice Statistics Special Report, NCJ 213600.

Jilek, W. G. (1994). Traditional healing in the prevention and treatment of alcohol and drug abuse. *Transcultural Psychiatric Review, 31,* 219–258.

Kendziora, K., Bruns, E., Osher, D., Pacchiano, D., & Mejia, B. (2001). *Systems of care: Promising practices in children's mental health, 2001 Series* (Vol. 1). Washington, DC: Center for Effective Collaboration and Practice, American Institutes for Research.

Kent, E. G., Aala, B., Benaroya, S., Bernstein, S., Morris, D., & Nevins, S. (Producers). (2007). *I have Tourette's but Tourette's doesn't have me* [Television broadcast]. Tourette Syndrome Association, Bayside, New York, and HBO Productions, New York.

Kinzie, J. (1993). Posttraumatic effects and their treatment among Southeast Asian refugees. In J. Wilson & B. Raphael (Eds.), *International handbook of traumatic stress syndromes* (pp. 311–320). New York: Plenum Press.

Kinzie, J., Leung, P., & Boehnlein, J. (1997). Treatment of depressive disorders in refugees. In E. Lee (Ed.), *Working with Asian Americans: A guide for clinicians.* New York: Guilford Press.

Lee, E. (1997). The assessment and treatment of Asian American families. In E. Lee (Ed.), *Working with Asian Americans: A guide for clinicians.* New York: Guilford Press.

Lutterman, T., Ganju, V., Schacht, L., Shaw, R., Monihan, K., et al. (2003). Sixteen State Study on Mental HealthPerformance Measures. (DHHS Publication No. [SMA] 03-3835.) Rockville, MD: Center for Mental Health Services, Substance Abuse and Mental Health Services Administration.

Machlin, S. R. (2006, January). *Expenses for a hospital emergency room visit, 2003* (Medical Expenditure Panel Survey: Statistical Brief #111). Retrieved April 2008, from http://www.meps.ahrq.gov/mepsweb/data_files/publications/st111/stat111.pdf.

Mollica, R. (2000). Invisible wounds: Waging a new kind of war. *Scientific American, 282*(6), 54–57.

Mollica, R. (2007). *Healing invisible wounds: Paths to hope and recovery in a violent world.* New York: Harcourt Press.

Murray, C. J. L., & Lopez, A. D. (1996). *The global burden of disease.* Cambridge, MA: Harvard University Press.

Musselman, D. L., Evans, D. L., & Nemeroff, C. B. (1998). The relationship of depression to cardiovascular disease epidemiology, biology, and treatment. *Archives of General Psychiatry, 55,* 580–592.

National Mental Health Association, Mental Health America. (2006). Mental health: Pay for services or pay a greater price. Retrieved April 5, 2008, from http://www1.nmha.org/shcr/community_based/costoffset.pdf.

Nebelkopf, E., & Phillips, M. (2004). *Healing and mental health for Native Americans speaking in red.* Walnut Creek, CA: Atlamira Press.

Office of Juvenile Justice and Delinquency Prevention. (1997). *Juvenile offenders and victims: 1997 Update on Violence* (Report number NCJ 165703). Washington, D.C.

Oxman, T. E., Dietrich, A. J., & Schulberg, H. C. (2005). Evidence-based models of integrated management of depression in primary care. *Psychiatric Clinics of North America, 28,* 1061–1077.

Parks, J., Radke, A. Q., & Mazade, N. (2008). *Measurement of health status for people with serious mental illnesses.* (Technical Report No. 16.) National Association of State Mental Health Program Directors Medical Directors Council.

Physician Leadership on National Drug Policy (PLNDP) National Project Office. (1998, March). Brown University Center for Alcohol and Addiction Studies. Retrieved July 12, 2008, from http://www.drugpolicy.org/docUploads/New MexicoTreatmentVIncarcerationFactsheet.

President's New Freedom Commission on Mental Health. (2003). *Achieving the promise: Transforming mental health care in America. Final report* (DHHS Pub. No. SMA–03–3832). Rockville, MD.

Provencher, H., Gregg, R., Mead, S., & Mueser, K. (2002). The role of work in the recovery of persons with psychiatric disabilities. *Psychiatric Rehabilitation Journal, 26*(2), 132–144.

Rezentes, W. C. (1996). *Ka lama kukui hawaiian psychology: An introduction.* Honolulu, HI: A'ali'li Books.

Rollman, B. L., Weinreb, L., Korsen, N., & Schulberg, H. C. (2006). Implementation of guideline-based care for depression in primary care. *Administration and Policy in Mental Health and Mental Health Services Research, 33*(1), 43–53.

Snowden, L. R. (1999). African American service use for mental health problems. *Journal of Community Psychology, 27,* 303–313.

Substance Abuse and Mental Health Services Administration (SAMHSA). (2001). National Strategy for Suicide Prevention (Inventory Number SMA01-3518). Rockville, MD.

Substance Abuse and Mental Health Services Administration (SAMHSA). (2004). National Consensus Statement on Mental Health Recovery. Retrieved October 2007, from http://mentalhealth.samhsa.gov/publications/allpubs/sma05-4129/

Substance Abuse and Mental Health Services Administration (SAMHSA). (2008). What you need to know about mental and substance use disorders (Issue Brief #4 for Employees, SMA 08-4350.) Retrieved January 25, 2009, from http://www.csat.samhsa.gov/IDBSE/employee/Mentaland SubstanceUseDisorders.

Thomas, K., & Snowden, L. R. (2001). Minority response to health insurance coverage for mental health problems. *The Journal of Mental Health Policy and Economics, 4*, 35–41.

Unützer, J., Katin, W., Callahan, C., Williams, J., Hunkeler, E., Harpole, L., et al. (2002). The IMPACT investigators: Collaborative care management of late-life depression in primary care: A randomized controlled trial. *Journal of American Medical Association, 288*(2), 2836–2845.

U.S. Department of Health and Human Services. (1999). *Mental health: A report of the Surgeon General—Executive summary.* Rockville, MD: U.S. Department of Health and Human Services, Substance Abuse and Mental Health Services Administration, Center for Mental Health Services, National Institutes of Health, National Institute of Mental Health.

U.S. Department of Health and Human Services. (2001). *Mental health: Culture, race, and ethnicity–A supplement to mental health: A report of the Surgeon General.* Rockville, MD: Author.

U.S. Department of Justice, Office of Justice Programs Bureau of Justice Statistics. (2004, June). Special Report State Prison Expenditures 2001 (Report number NCJ 202949). Washington, D.C.: Stephan, J. J.

Vega, W., Kolody, B., & Aguilar-Gaxiola, S. (2001). Help-seeking for mental health problems among Mexican-Americans. *Journal of Immigrant Health, 3*(3), 133–140.

Wijnant, I. H. (2000). *The challenges and opportunities for mental health in the third millennium:* Perspectives in health (Vol. 5). World Health Organization. Retrieved July 12, 2008, from http://www.paho.org/English/DPI/Number9_article3.htm.

World Health Organization. (2004). *The World Health Report 2004: Changing history, annex table 3: Burden of disease in DALYs by cause, sex, and mortality stratum in WHO regions, estimates for 2002.* Geneva, Switzerland: WHO.

CHAPTER 4

The Impact of Health Beliefs on Health and Health Care

Jean Lau Chin

Culture provides the context in which we live. There can be little doubt that it provides the context for the provision of culturally competent health care services, including diagnosis, managing medical compliance, and improving patient outcomes. Yet, some still wonder: What does culture have to do with health care? They will argue that disease and good health care delivery are color-blind and culturally neutral. As the Surgeon General's Report (U.S. Public Health Service, Office of the Surgeon General, 1999) demonstrated, culture counts in the delivery of health care services and in the prevalence of disease.

DIFFERENTIAL INCIDENCE OF DISEASE

Heckler's report (1985), the Institute of Medicine's report (Smedley, Stith, & Nelson, 2002), and other policy reports documented significant disparities in the burden of illness and mortality experienced by blacks and other minority groups in the U.S. population. They also set an ambitious national agenda for the elimination of health disparities among racial and ethnic minority groups in the United States, yet differential incidence of disease and response to treatment among these groups still remain.

DIFFERENTIAL ACCESS TO CARE

While biological and genetic differences exist among communities of color, the predominant cause of these disparities are environmental, social, and cultural barriers that result in differential access to and utilization of care. With regard to access to care, high rates of people uninsured and a low utilization of regular sources of care are some factors. They are compounded by provider-patient miscommunication, lack of culturally competent providers knowledgeable about the patient's culture, and linguistic barriers in which providers cannot communicate with patients in their language.

Yet, we have a health care system that views culture as relevant only for newly arrived immigrants who do not speak English. Racial and ethnic differences in cultural attitudes and health behaviors are often unaccounted for in our health care delivery system and its providers. Consequently, racial disparities in health status will exist, and the competence of providers and a health care delivery system dealing with diverse racial and ethnic populations is inadequate and will continue to be until we view and address the cultural attitudes and health beliefs that patients bring to the provider-patient encounter. Disparities will exist when a system of care has not been culturally competent in serving diverse groups and communities.

HOW CULTURE INFLUENCES HEALTH AND HEALTH CARE UTILIZATION

People have views of themselves and of their environment that will influence their behaviors. This is also true of health—health views and health behaviors. Many times, these views and behaviors operate outside consciousness and will not appear overtly in the patient encounter, unless they are elicited. Moreover, providers are unlikely to elicit them if they view them as irrelevant to patient care or if they assume that they and their patients share similar views.

With growing diversity in our communities, these views and behaviors may differ across diverse groups because of cultural values and beliefs. The values and beliefs of the dominant culture will influence the cultures that are developed within our health care delivery system and in the views and behaviors of its providers. Unless we have a framework for examining and identifying these differences, providers are likely to interpret patient behaviors as noncompliant or resistant when they do not behave as providers might expect.

Views of Health

First, how do patients view health? Does the patient define himself or herself as sick or in ill health when they seek health care? Patients may deny their illnesses, view the illness as caused by personal carelessness or weakness, or have feelings of inadequacy or powerlessness about being ill. They may self-blame, feel punished, or view the illness as caused by external forces over which they have no control and for which they cannot be responsible.

Practitioners may view the same illness as related to diet, genetics, or occupational hazards, such as a disease. In the mental health arena patients may need to define themselves as sick or "crazy" to seek mental health treatment. They may need to have specific somatic symptoms to define themselves as ill. One way to characterize these differences in views of health between patient and practitioners is that a disease is what practitioners objectively discover, while an illness is what patients subjectively experience. Illness is the psychological experience of disease as defined by individual and community views of health. Patients who fail to see themselves as ill will fail to go for care and refuse to be compliant when they do.

Sometimes the definition of ill health is determined by the ability to carry on daily functions. Without overt symptoms, patients are prone to denial because they may not appear sick. Sometimes this denial is associated with economic factors: the person needs to keep working. It may be sociocultural: the person has difficulty asking for help because social conditioning within his or her culture demands stoicism. The decision to seek help is often related to sociocultural factors rather than the severity of the illness. Thus, success or failure of treatment is often related to how the patient perceives the problem or their health.

It is not uncommon for patients from racial and ethnic minority communities to hold holistic views of health. In contrast to Western views of health, which deal with everyone separately and focus on the individual as patient, many in the Latino, Asian, and Native American communities hold the belief that body, mind, and soul are interconnected. Moreover, views of family and community may result in a greater inclusion of family members in their health care; different definitions of kinship may result in practitioners denying access to information for family members against the patient's wishes. Worldviews may cause them to blame their illness as something beyond their control in spite of views that press them to fight and conquer.

Different Health Care Sectors

Where do people seek care? We might make a distinction between the different health care sectors in which people seek care; these have been called the popular, folk, and professional sectors (De La Cancela, Chin, & Jenkins, 1998). With advances in technology and medicine, the emphasis on health care delivery in the professional sector is an antiseptic environment with a highly stratified hierarchy. While physicians may view the professional sector of clinics, hospitals, and doctors' offices as the places in which health care is provided, patients often view places to seek care in a broader cultural context.

Ill health is often first recognized and defined by relatives, friends, neighbors, or workmates who collectively comprise the popular sector.

Credentials are often based on one's own experience with a specific illness. Over the counter remedies or home remedies may be used on account of one another's personal experience.

Patients may view hospitals as places to go when one is dying, or seek care in the professional sector only for severe illness. Patients often use health care in the professional as well as the folk sector simultaneously. The folk sector has also been termed alternative medicine, traditional healing, or herbal medicine. Patients may seek care from healers who are either sacred or secular, such as herbalists, spiritual healers, Buddhist monks, clairvoyants, fortune tellers, naturopaths, shamans, and acupuncturists. Physicians are now beginning to recognize the need to inquire into these practices because they often do not come up in the medical encounter unless elicited. Patients either find that physicians do not care to know, or they may be reluctant to disclose these practices as superstitious, folklore, or home remedies. Moreover, the U.S. health care system is often segmented—mental health services are separate from medical services; specialty care focuses only on the body part in question. Consequently, patients and physicians may fail to attribute importance to how the different health sectors interact.

The culture of hospitals and health care settings in the United States is important to identify; perceptions of the context in which health care is delivered may differ between provider and patient. It is not uncommon for patients to view the professional sector as trade-driven and to view the provision of health care as antiseptic and disease-oriented. Patients in hospitals often experience loss of control over their bodies, personal space, privacy, behavior, diet, and use of time; they often feel they are given limited knowledge of their conditions. They may experience the formality to be depersonalizing, to reflect a lack of respect for the human body, or as dispassionate reactions to medical conditions. They may experience the routines in health care settings to be ritualistic and highly scripted; they may react to the many ways in which these settings denote status and confer power rather than competence—for example, restricted areas for physicians only, white-coat-costumed uniforms for high status providers; objects, space and people all classified as sterile or nonsterile; heavy use of technical jargon.

Culturally Competent Health Care

These views of health and health care are influenced by cultural values and beliefs, as well as different perspectives and experiences. Differences between practitioner and patient with these views will also influence access, utilization, and quality of care; if not addressed, they will result in higher rates of poor compliance and resistance to care. A culturally competent approach is essential to avoid miscommunication and poor care and to eliminate racial and ethnic disparities in health. Practitioners must not only understand the importance of culture in disease management and medical compliance, but they also must ensure that the system is responsive to diversity throughout the organization if quality services are to be provided (i.e., its policies, governance, providers, and environment).

Health disparities are the result of a system failing to provide culturally competent care to all segments of the population. Culturally competent health care is responsive to population-specific needs and indicators and incorporates cultural beliefs into disease management and health care delivery (Chin, 1999).

CULTURAL BELIEFS INFLUENCE LIFESTYLE BEHAVIORS

In recognizing the different health care sectors, practitioners are increasingly recognizing the importance of and attending to health behaviors outside the clinical encounter. Illness and disease are increasingly viewed along a continuum to health and wellness; this means placing increased emphasis on prevention and lifestyle behaviors as important to disease management. Lifestyle behaviors include exercise, diet, and stress, which can greatly influence the progression of disease and the management of health outside the health care setting; these are, in turn, influenced by cultural attitudes and health beliefs.

Exercise

In our modern, technological society, lifestyles tend to be more sedentary. Whereas exercise was part of our daily work, we now need to plan our exercise by joining health clubs and use machines to mechanically assist our movements, all in order to maintain a regimen of physical fitness and health. It is planned and artificial as we fight the progression toward a more obese society.

Diet

The same is true with diet. Unlike the places from which our ancestors came, where starvation was or is widespread, we now show no want for food in our more affluent society. Our food choices are not limited by geography, but are imported fresh from all parts of the globe. Not only is it abundant, it is often wasted. We now face the challenge of moderation with the proliferation of low sodium, low carbohydrate, low cholesterol, low fat, low sugar, and low protein diets. We fight these excesses on a daily basis, and are preoccupied with high calories and carbohydrates. We worry about having too much compared with previous eras of having enough as we fight high cholesterol, high blood pressure, and high blood sugars.

Stress

Stressors in our environment are many and more complex in today's diverse, global society. For racial/ethnic minority groups, these are compounded by several things, namely discrimination associated with racism, classism, losses related to immigration trauma, wartime experiences, family separation, glass-ceiling effects and underemployment when it comes to jobs, and adjustments associated with living in a bicultural environment. A constant vigilance of the effects of racism can be stressful. Effects of immigration and posttrauma can be lifelong. Coping with differences between immigrant cultures of origin and the American culture can be challenging and increase stress levels. The race to get ahead and the need to balance work and family can also increase stress, especially if different cultural beliefs and practices come into play.

How people manage their stress has major consequences on health. The difference between type A and type B personalities, for example, has been found to correlate with heart attacks and stroke. There is also the stress "let down" response, and the absence of psychosocial supports that contribute to healthy fitness or fitful stress. Often, people experiencing stress tend to eat more, which only compounds existing health problems.

Recognition of lifestyle behaviors is important to disease management because it has been shown in Asian, Latino, African and Native American communities that mind, body, and soul are not disconnected. While lifestyle behaviors often involve the interaction of these components, our health care system has historically kept them separate. Our health and mental health systems of care are separate on many levels. Religion and spirituality are often kept separate until the exercise of last rites. Cultural views of health and health care are seen as superstition, folklore, or emanating from the ignorant; they are tolerated at best. Thus, promoting a holistic approach to life and health care is good prevention.

ASIAN HEALTH BELIEFS

Asian health beliefs are presented here as an example because they contrast with Western health beliefs. It is important to appreciate the diversity within Asian American communities caused by factors such as country of origin, period of immigration, generation in the United States, and age. Moreover, traditional Asian health beliefs are often held by many Asian Americans, transmitted as they are through the generations. At the same time, vestiges of these beliefs often operate outside of consciousness to the point that individuals deny the influence of culture on their behaviors. These beliefs are often unspoken and will not emerge in routine clinical practice unless they are actively elicited.

Therefore, it is incumbent on practitioners to actively invite patients to think about the things that were said to them growing up and the practices with which they lived. Oftentimes, even those who claimed to have lived a completely Western lifestyle will recall the influence of Asian values and beliefs from their parents' behaviors. There may have been herbal tonics that they were asked to drink. There may have been admonitions about not going to sleep with wet hair. They may have been told to sweat out a fever rather than taking a cool bath. Sometimes these beliefs and behaviors can appear confusing and contradictory when living in a bicultural world. Sometimes practitioners or patients or both will actively seek to eradicate them.

In disease management we need to weigh the importance of these belief systems and how they influence utilization patterns, provider choice, and medical compliance. They pervade our service delivery system since provider and patient sometimes interact with differing beliefs; providers may view patient behavior as poor compliance, while patients may view providers as lacking in knowledge or insensitive to their values and beliefs. Providers, for example, may recommend a high fruit and vegetable diet, while Asian patients may refuse to eat certain fruits, peaches because of their yang quality or salads because they're uncooked and have too much of a yin quality. Asian patients may also refuse to follow a certain regimen because it is viewed as disruptive to their Qi energy. Ice cold drinks and overexertion, for instance, are believed to deplete Qi energy and lead to blood deficiencies. Practitioners need to be aware of how strong and how subtle these influences may be when making treatment recommendations. Otherwise, they could run the risk of losing credibility or encountering poor medical compliance.

ASIAN HEALTH BELIEFS ABOUT
WELLNESS AND DISEASE

Asian views of health embrace a more holistic view of well-being. In embracing this notion, health can be described as a dynamic relationship in which the physical, social, psychological, and spiritual well-being of the individual interacts with the physical and social environment. As such, we should not talk of disease management in terms of health, but of health promotion.

Asian cultures tend to embrace a holistic approach to health that includes the body, mind, and soul. It is not uncommon for Asians to use herbal medicine and traditional Asian methods of health care in combination with Western health care methods. Health beliefs underlie these practices. Asian cultures hold views that all things, including people and foods, have yin and yang properties (commonly known as "hot" and "cold"), and they associate these with medicinal value and healing powers.

In order to understand Chinese medicine and Asian health beliefs, one also needs to understand some differences between Eastern and Western ways of thinking. How people think about direction is one way to characterize these differences. Western culture is characterized by striving toward movement and exploration. Common images are the herding of cattle, the pioneers in caravans going West across deserts and plains, ships sailing in search of new lands, and voyages through space, perhaps guided by the North Star as a point of orientation. The West is yang. By contrast, in Eastern cultures, the orientation towards life and health is based on cultivating "what is." This is based on farming, voyages that bring you home (the sojourner), and Confucian principles of striving toward scholarship and self-actualization. They orient to the East and South. This difference is aptly illustrated by the use of the compass, which orients to the North for Westerners and to the South for Chinese (Kim, 1996; Lu, 1986).

In health and science, meditation and the flow of Qi energy in the body were the keys to restoring health. Asians look at everything in context compared to the Western way of isolating, dissecting, and analyzing (Kim, 1996). The cure in Western culture is to tear apart and destroy (i.e., germs, pain, parasites), while the cure in Asian cultures is to restore the body to its natural condition in its environment (i.e., balance of yin and yang and Qi energy).

ASIAN HEALTH BELIEFS ABOUT THE BODY

According to Asian culture, the basic essences of the body include: Qi (wind), blood, and yin/yang qualities. This is the basis for Asian health beliefs and the practice of Chinese medicine. The balance of yin/yang qualities in one's body is considered critical to good health and one's well-being. Deficiencies of yin will give rise to symptoms of dryness (e.g., cough), and heat (e.g., inflammation, fever), while deficiencies of yang give rise to symptoms of poor vitality and strength (e.g., fatigue, impotence) and lack of adequate warmth (e.g., chills). Deficiencies are caused by the failure of one to regulate the other to achieve a yin/yang balance. Tonics are frequently used to restore the balance of yin/yang qualities.

Pathologic factors of wind (Qi), moisture, and toxins cause illness. The primary means to maintain and restore health are to open Qi stagnation in the body and to revitalize body functions. This requires an understanding of how body systems are interconnected. Qi Gong breathing and Tai Chi exercise are methods to promote health by feeling centered and calm.

As Kim (1996) writes, "Disease can be caused by: 1) six exogenous factors, seven emotions, diet and nutrition, physical activity, scars and trauma, improper medical treatment, improper Qi Gong practice, astronomical influences, technological influences, infection, spirit possession, genetics, and stress" (p. 12). The six exogenous factors are wind, cold, summer heat, dampness, dryness, and heat, all of which account for many practices within Asian cultures.

Wind usually attacks the upper part of the body (i.e., respiratory); people will avoid sitting near the air conditioner or catching the wind. Exposure to cold temperatures for long periods is viewed as losing body warmth and thus their yang or Qi. The belief is that cold causes the arteries to constrict in order to conserve heat, disturbing Qi flow and resulting in "wind pain," chronic muscle spasms, and headaches. Summer heat occurs as a result of exposure to extreme heat; this can injure yin and deplete the body fluids, and is associated with symptoms of fever and heavy sweating. Dampness includes activities such as getting caught in the rain, having wet hair or clothes for too long, or drinking too many cold liquids or food too rapidly, and is associated with symptoms of lethargy, indigestion, nausea, and vomiting. Admonitions not to go to bed with wet hair and to avoid drinks with ice are common examples. The belief is that this can cause arthritis. Dryness during the fall is associated with dry cough and skin.

ASIAN BELIEFS ABOUT FOOD

Asian cultures hold views that all foods have yin and yang, that is, "hot" and "cold" properties, and they associate these with medicinal value and healing powers. In a Chinese diet, it is considered bad for someone with constipation to drink tea; it is good for someone with a cough to eat apple with honey. When sick, Asians want to know which foods to avoid in order to prevent the problem from becoming worse. This contrasts with the Western emphasis on diet primarily for weight loss; Asians tend to view diet as a way to maintain and restore health.

Secondly, in Western diets foods are considered for their protein, calorie, carbohydrate, vitamin, and other nutrient content. In Chinese diets foods are considered for their flavors, energies, movements, and organic actions. For example, if I feel cold in my body and limbs, naturally I should eat something that will warm me. Ginger will warm me because it has a warm energy; sugar can make my stomach stronger because it tastes sweet and acts on the stomach (Lu, 1986).

Health care providers need to realize that these cultural beliefs and behaviors are explanatory models for health and illness and will often occur in tandem with Western practices and beliefs. They influence medical compliance and disease management. Failure of practitioners to incorporate them will pose barriers to care and result in inappropriate care.

Socioeconomic factors also influence food habits and nutrition. Food preservation methods, related to the absence of refrigeration, resulted in high salt intake among Cantonese and Toisanese Chinese immigrants. Foods high in salt and fat content alongside organ meats were more readily available to the poor, resulting in nutrition habits that are now considered unhealthy. Obesity is associated not only with stress-related eating, but also with the value placed on obesity as a sign of prosperity in China. Higher rates of nasopharyngeal, esophageal, stomach, and liver cancer among Chinese, Japanese, and Filipinos has been correlated with dietary and food preservation methods common to certain locales (Rosenblatt, Weiss, & Schwartz, 1996), while migrant studies have shown that Asian immigrants will show alteration in cancer rates more similar to patterns found in the country to which they have immigrated (Li & Pawlish, 1998).

Stress and psychological distress have been linked to daily exposure to societal disorders of racism, sexism, and classism; hypertension has been associated with the internalization of these emotional states. We see these phenomena within the African American and Latino American communities as well. Losses due to immigration will also compound such stress.

IMPLICATIONS FOR PATIENT CARE

If culture is important to all aspects of health care, then quality health care means that physicians must:

1. Be aware of culture in defining health and health care.
2. Understand racial/ethnic differences in incidence and prevalence of disease.
3. Conduct culturally competent clinical assessments to arrive at accurate diagnoses.
4. Manage compliance by addressing cultural attitudes and beliefs in the patient-doctor relationship.
5. Treat disease and prescribe care relevant to the patient's culture and relative to the patient's individual history and beliefs.

The patient-doctor relationship is a relationship; patient care is provided within a cultural context that includes several cultures, that of the patient, practitioner, and health care system, at the very least. Practitioners must demonstrate an awareness of cultural biases, values and beliefs, develop a cultural knowledge of the beliefs and history of the patient they treat, recognize the importance of differences between patients and between cultures, and apply this information to optimize and provide quality health care. Those who fail to incorporate culture into their practice will run the risk of miscommunication, resulting in poor patient care, inaccurate patient histories, faulty diagnoses, suboptimal screening and follow-up, and poor patient compliance.

Assessing Efficacy of a System of Care

All cultures and individuals have explanatory models for health and illness. The efficacy of a system of care and the competence of its practitioners can be measured by its responsiveness to cultural factors, beliefs and health practices, which in turn influence access, utilization, quality, and outcomes. Some basic questions to evaluate the efficacy of a system are:

1. How easy is it to get in the door? (Access)
2. Once there, do they get the care they need? (Access)

3. Are they using services when they should? (Utilization)
4. Does it do any good? (Quality)

Eliciting Explanatory Models of Health and Illness

Practitioners should realize that their own explanatory models of health and illness, whether personal or professional, may differ from that of patients; self-reflection is important to determine if these differences will interfere with appropriate care. Questions (adapted from Kleinman, 1980, p. 79) to elicit a patient's explanatory model and beliefs about health and illness could include:

1. Is there a specific time of day the problem is more severe?
2. What do you think it does to you?
3. How do family and other around you respond to the problem?
4. What activities lead to an increase or decrease in the problem?
5. What can you no longer do because of the problem?
6. What are the results you hope to receive from the treatment?
7. What are the problems your sickness has caused you?

IMPROVING MEDICAL COMPLIANCE

Medical compliance is enhanced when practitioners support the beliefs, values, and behaviors articulated by the patient. Practitioners need to ask themselves what it is that prevents patients from complying with "doctors' orders" to stop smoking, start exercising, and so on. Attention to how cultural beliefs and practices contradict a recommended regimen is essential if we are to help patients manage their illnesses and promote healthy lifestyle behaviors in ways that are culturally syntonic. To improve medical compliance, physicians need to "treat the illness and the disease!" (De La Cancela et al., 1998). Specifically, this might mean:

1. A more informal or personal approach during history-taking to engage the patient
2. Increased emphasis on explaining the problem and validating a patient's health beliefs
3. Responding to the personal, family, and community context surrounding illness
4. Identifying and acknowledging the importance of social roles and social distance in treating the patient
5. Being respectful of cultural differences even if they appear strange from your perspective

CONCLUSION

In conclusion, culture counts! Cultural views and beliefs of health and health care strongly influence health outcomes, disease management, lifestyle behaviors, and medical compliance. Patients typically do not bring these views and practices into the clinical encounter because our health care system is not designed to elicit them. Practitioners need to elicit these beliefs with respect for the patient and value for the answer. Practitioners need to help patients to achieve a healthy balance via a holistic and culturally competent approach. This is needed to transform our health care delivery toward a more integrated system of care.

REFERENCES

Chin, J. L. (1999). *Cultural competence and healthcare in Massachusetts.* Waltham, MA: Massachusetts Health Policy Forum, Brandeis University.

De La Cancela, V., Chin, J. L., & Jenkins, Y. M. (1998). *Community health psychology: Empowerment for diverse communities.* New York: Routledge.

Heckler, M. M. (Ed.). (1985). *Report of the secretary's task force on black and minority health, Vol. 2: Crosscutting issues in minority health.* Washington, DC: U.S. Department of Health and Human Services.

Kim, M. C. (1996). *Oriental medicine and cancer.* Belmont, MA: Seven Galaxy Publication.

Kleinman, A. (1980). *Patients and healers in the context of culture: An exploration of the borderland between anthropology, medicine, and psychiatry.* Berkeley, CA: University of California Press.

Li, F. P., & Pawlish, K. (1998). Cancers in Asian Americans and Pacific Islands: Migrant studies. *Asian American and Pacific Islander Journal of Health, 6,* 123–129.

Lu, H. C. (1986). *Chinese system of food cures: Prevention and remedies.* New York: Sterling Publishing Co, Inc.

Rosenblatt, K. A., Weiss, N. S., & Schwartz, S. M. (1996). Liver cancer in Asian migrants to the United States and their descendents. *Cancer Causes Control, 7,* 345–350.

Smedley, B., Stith, A., & Nelson, A. (2002). *Unequal treatment: Confronting racial and ethnic disparities in health care.* Washington, DC: Institute of Medicine.

U.S. Public Health Service, Office of the Surgeon General. (2001). *Mental health: Culture, race, and ethnicity—A supplement to mental health: A report of the Surgeon General.* Washington, DC: Author.

CHAPTER 5

Reform or Revolution?: Curricular Change in Higher Education

Melanie E. L. Bush

During the last decades of the twentieth century a movement developed to incorporate greater diversity in the academy. To reflect upon its impact, it is important to consider the historical development of public higher education, the struggles for societal transformation in the 1960s from which it emerged, and the broader social landscape in which it developed. The mission of higher education has always embodied a tension between creating a more educated populous with greater engagement in the social process and functioning as a vehicle for "generating little more than obedient citizens who are prepared to work within society" (Glisczinski, 2007, p. 317) thus reinforcing the existing positioning of groups in the social structure. Issues of diversity and power in education are implicitly linked to this tension. A more engaged and educated society would theoretically be more equal; one structured to maintain the status quo and replicate the existing social structure would more likely have higher levels of inequality. In this context, student and faculty demography, as well as the orientation and content of curricular and co-curricular life, affect how educated populations understand social realities such as inequality. This, in turn, influences normative thinking for the public at large.

This chapter analyzes the impact of the trend toward greater diversity in curricula and considers the extent to which it challenged traditional

The discussion related to the City University of New York is based on research conducted in 2004–2005 and partially funded by the CUNY Diversity Projects Development Fund of the University Affirmative Action Committee, Office of the Vice Chancellor for Faculty and Staff Relations.

patterns in the structure of U.S. society. To what degree has consideration been given to addressing group positioning in addition to issues of inclusion? How have differences been approached and inequalities explained? Are they presumed "natural" and "immutable" or social and historical realities that demand redress?

From the late 1960s onward, U.S. society experienced demographic shifts due to increased immigration, a dramatic polarization of wealth with corresponding downward pressures on the poor, middle, and working classes, alongside a dismantling of the social safety net that had been erected in the 1960s, and a vast expansion of the military and prison industries (Pew Center on the States, 2008). These transformations were paralleled in universities with an era of expanded privatization and institutionalization of neoliberal policies evidenced by increases in the proportion of part-time to full-time faculty, rising tuition rates, and moves to reshape universities in the business model. Despite the rhetoric of unlimited possibilities for upward mobility articulated in the construct of the "American Dream," the life chances for many became increasingly constricted (Lardner & Smith, 2005). Did these social, political and economic trends have an impact on efforts made to incorporate greater diversity in university curricula during this period? Does the academy have a responsibility to educate about social realities? How much agreement is there that "The university is also a 'critic'—a forum for debate about the 'status quo.' In this way, the university is at the margins of society, just as in its roles as creator and curator it is at the center. As critic, it raises ethical questions—questions of fairness and justice. It is in these ways that universities are unique" (Scott, 2008).

This chapter examines the movement to diversify curriculum that occurred in the second half of the twentieth century. We first explore the history of public higher education and the multicultural education movement and then discuss research findings about the process inside one of the largest urban public institutions of higher education in the United States. We conclude with questions that can frame this inquiry into: *How should diversity be represented within academic curricula* and *what principles should guide our decisions?*

TRENDS IN THE HISTORY OF PUBLIC HIGHER EDUCATION

The universalistic discourse of the Founding Fathers of the United States conveyed that all men were created equal. However, until the mid-nineteenth century, education was considered appropriate solely for the sons of propertied men of European descent. All others were believed either not to need education for their station in life or unfit for the rigors of scholarly engagement. In fact, legislation in 1829 established as a criminal offense the teaching of African-descended peoples to read or write, regardless of their status as free or enslaved (Du Bois, 1936/1979, p. 644).

After the presidency of Andrew Jackson and the celebration of the "Common Man," the Free Academy (now known as the City University of New York) opened in 1847, establishing the first public institution of higher education (Gorelick, 1981, p. 194). From inception, this university provided thousands of poor and working people an opportunity to obtain a college education. Despite this, as Crain (2003) points out, "African Americans were largely absent from a college that was emblematic of democratic opportunity" (p. 46) until after the Civil War.

During Reconstruction (1860s and 1870s) the idea emerged that education, including college, should be made available to all people at the public's expense, not just to elites or those of European descent (Du Bois, 1936/1979, pp. 637–669). The move to expand educational access as a social good emanated from black leaders (particularly in the South), who associated knowledge with power as a means to achieve status and respect, and as a benefit to society as a whole (Du Bois, 1936/1979, p. 641). With the opening of the first public schools, whites and blacks more frequently interacted and some progress was made in eliminating prejudice and educational inequalities. Along with the movement toward inclusion, "American colleges explicitly taught civics and morality and expected their students to incur moral obligations" (Carnegie Foundation for the Advancement of Teaching & CIRCLE, 2006, p. 1). Education, was viewed not just a means of developing a skilled workforce but also as an important vehicle for cultivating social responsibility.

When Confederates returned to power in the late 1870s, many public schools were closed since they represented the possibility that racial equality could be achieved (Du Bois, 1936/1979, pp. 644–645). Additionally, education was believed to encourage insolence; the idea of teaching all children to read and write was considered "revolutionary" and "poisonous" (Franklin, 2003, p. 10). Higher education was again deemed for those with "leisure time," not poor and working people (Franklin, 2003). This rationale was later articulated in relationship to the idea of educating women, viewed as interfering with the "appropriate" duties of wives and mothers. Those with power best positioned to facilitate inclusion were generally those least likely to be inclined to do so. An educated workforce and population are generally more difficult to control. A diverse educational system with equal access for all had the potential to reshape the social order.

From the late nineteenth century to World War II, after a period of massive immigration and heightened U.S. nationalism, the Americanization movement shifted the public focus from a pursuit of communal progress to an individualist orientation emphasizing the idea that individuals determine their own success. Civic engagement was to a large extent localized and privatized (e.g., voting) and schools moved away from teaching morality (Carnegie Foundation for the Advancement of Teaching & CIRCLE, 2006, p. 1). Numerous symbols of national loyalty, such as the pledge of allegiance, emerged at this time, fostering patriotic declarations and displays (O'Leary, 1999).

This period extended until the mid-twentieth century when along with anticolonial struggles around the globe and demands for the expansion of human and civil rights to all populations in the United States, a movement emerged in the late 1960s to diversify the academy. This had far-ranging consequences, in particular "open admissions" policies within institutions like the City University of New York and efforts addressing campus climate, intergroup relations, hiring, and curricular transformation.

In line with the spirit of the 1960s, public demands were made that "rather than defining human need in corporate terms, colleges must serve the needs of working-class minority communities, including their need for fundamental social change" (Gorelick, 1981, p. 194). The doors of the university were opened to previously excluded communities. The open admissions policy generated heated opposition: "In 1971 vice president Spiro Agnew said that CUNY would give away '100,000 devalued diplomas'" (Crain, 2003, p. 47), further claiming that equal access could not be achieved while maintaining excellence. Indeed, in later years some have asserted that excellence cannot be achieved without equal access. Similar language resonated when a key educational advisor to Nixon proclaimed that U.S. society was in "danger of producing an educated proletariat. That's dynamite!" (Franklin, 2003, p. 10)

By the late 1970s, when a majority of CUNY students were people of color, both the state and city university systems imposed tuition (Crain, 2003, p. 5). Some people assert this move was an attempt to erect another barrier to the expansion of educational opportunity to all by eroding the funding base of public higher education. A conservative political and economic agenda was on the rise, including a national trend that expanded what is known as the "prison industrial complex." Corrections' share of all state and local spending grew 104 percent from 1980 to 2000, while higher education's share dropped by 21 percent ("Incarcerate or Educate?" 2008, p. 14).

Another development further provided a counterpoint to the opening of the academy. Media images depicting "urban youth as dangerous, pathological and violent," and the expansion of "get-tough policies" contributed to the "growth of a highly visible criminal justice system that disproportionately targeted on poor black and brown youth" (Giroux, 1999). This contradictory reality entailed, on the one hand, expanded opportunities for previously excluded populations and, on the other, increasingly higher tuitions and the criminalization of young men of color. The contradiction provides a context for our discussion of the curricular change movement. An analysis of what took place is not entirely separate from who is included in the discussion.

MULTICULTURALISM IN HIGHER EDUCATION

The multicultural education movement (sometimes described as a "project") took root as a result of the convergence of numerous historic

realities in the late 1960s. Post–World War II economic expansion provided an environment that allowed for the reconstitution of the national
image along the lines of the "Great Society." The Hart Cellar Act of 1965
abolished national origin quotas and led to dramatically expanded immigration. Anticolonial struggles were being waged globally, while within
the United States poor and working people, communities of color, women,
gays and lesbians demanded justice, equality, and inclusion in the American Dream. Education was deemed the primary route toward upward mobility for previously disenfranchised and marginalized groups; academic
institutions thus became prime targets for transformation. The percentage of female college students grew from 40 percent in 1966 to 58 percent
in 2005; the percentage of white college students decreased from 90.7 to
74.4 percent in 2006. The percentage of people (aged 25 or older) who
completed 4 or more years of college increased from 9.8 to 27.6 percent in
this same period ("By the Numbers," 2006).

Institutional change was set in motion around the country. Organizations such as the Association of American Colleges and Universities, American Council on Education, Carnegie Foundation for the Advancement of
Teaching, Ford Foundation, National Endowment for the Humanities, William and Flora Hewlett Foundation, James Irvine Foundation, and Richard
Parsons Family Foundation were involved in a multitude of projects to
enhance this process.

The orientation of curricular change primarily emphasized either an
additive process (including information about previously underrepresented groups) or sought transformations in orientation, perspective, and
pedagogical style. Some believe that "as multicultural content has become
infused into the curriculum of required courses and standardized in college and high school texts, its political and economic tendencies have been
gutted . . . Celebrating differences is a far cry from dismantling inequalities" (Platt, 2002). This distinction is generally described as those seeking
curricular infusion versus curricular transformation (Banks, 2008, p. 39).
Unlike other aspects of the diversity education movement, relatively little
has been written documenting and analyzing the curriculum retrospec-
tively and nationally (Antonio & Muniz, 2007, p. 279).

Increased numbers of women and faculty of color within the academy
also had impact on the development of knowledge. However, though
increased faculty hiring of women and persons of color has occurred,
changes have not been as widespread as many had hoped. Moreover, recent claims that liberals, democrats and radicals are overrepresented in the
academy reveal that what was accomplished was not universally accepted
(Bush, 2005). Some maintain the view that diversity is not relevant to intellectual pursuit and that curricular transformation is an expression of
special interests. This was explicitly articulated in an article that appeared
in the *Chronicle of Higher Education:* "The opposite of being pro-diversity
is not being anti-diversity. It's being diversity-indifferent, and that's me.

My T-shirt would not say 'Diversity Sucks.' It would say, 'Diversity—Who Cares?'" (Clegg, 2000, p. B8).

While many studies document the widespread perception of an educational system that embraces diversity and engages students in learning about the social world, public knowledge about society is often filled with misperceptions. About 80 percent of the U.S. population believes that the average person has more than $40,000 income, despite the fact that only 44 percent actually do ("How Class Works," 2005). A study by the *Washington Post*, Harvard University, and the Kaiser Foundation found that 40 to 60 percent of all whites believe that the average black is faring as well or better than the average white (Morin, 2001, p. A1), yet black households earn on average two-thirds of what is earned by white households (U.S. Census Bureau, 2000, p. 12-2). For those who believe we have achieved gender equity, data shows the gender wage gap to be approximately 73 percent (Eitzen & Zinn, 2004, p. 348).

Many scholars view the educational system as a locus where racialized images, beliefs, and ideologies are produced and reproduced despite denial by many that this occurs (Delpit, 1995; Delpit & Perry, 1998; Giroux, 1997; McIntyre, 1997). While misperceptions are certainly not solely the consequence of miseducation and a balanced curriculum will not automatically lead to a systematic overhaul of the dynamics of power in society or the elimination of white supremacy and of gender and class structures, the relationship between knowledge, exposure, perception and action is clearly documented in scholarship about diversity (Chang, 2005; Humphreys, 1998, 1997; Morin, 2001; Williams, Berger, & McClendon, 2005).

Beverly Daniel Tatum (1997), renowned psychologist, speaks of this: "Stereotypes, omissions, and distortions all contribute to the development of prejudice" (pp. 5–6). Tatum discusses the significant consequences of Eurocentric curricula reflected in the remark of one of her white students: "It's not my fault that Blacks don't write books" (p. 5). She wonders whether any of his teachers had actually told him that there were no black writers, or whether, given the omission, he had drawn his own conclusion (p. 5). Young people also learn about society from the media, especially when there is little challenge to the messages conveyed about the social world in school curricula.

A lack of curricular coverage of the experiences, accomplishments, and struggles of communities of color contributes to a distorted view of history and perpetuates notions of the inferiority of marginalized groups. This void also conveys that race, class and gender are matters of "identity" only, and that patterns such as hierarchies and group positioning are a result of individual actions and interpersonal relations rather than systemic and institutional social problems of concern to all. These ways of thinking impact the decisions that people make at the polls, in their jobs, policies they support and the opinions they form about society. How diversity is approached in curricula matters.

CHANGES IN ACADEMIC CURRICULA

> The curriculum is the battlefield at the heart of the institution. (Hefferlin
> quoted in Yamane, 2001, p. 127)

Debra Humphreys (1998) of the Association of American Colleges and
Universities (AAC&U) and the Ford Foundation Campus Diversity Initiative reported that "more and more colleges and universities across the
nation are transforming their curricula because college leaders increasingly recognize that knowledge about the diversity of American history
and culture and knowledge about international diversity are essential
for today's students." This is particularly important given demographic
shifts in the U.S. population and the way that the political, economic,
business and social environments in which we live have become increasingly globalized. Humphreys (1997) found that of 65 institutions
involved in an AAC&U curriculum transformation project, almost
60 percent required students to take at least one course addressing diversity. A survey of 196 colleges and universities revealed that 34 percent
had a multicultural general education requirement, 33 percent offered
course work in ethnic and women's studies, and 54 percent had introduced multicultural material into departmental course offerings (Light
& Cureton, 1992). In the process academic leaders have discussed what
constitutes an appropriate knowledge base for the twenty-first century
(Association of American Colleges and Universities [AAC&U], 1997a,
1997b, 2000, 2001, 2005). Women's studies, Africana, Asian and Latino
studies programs and courses challenged the narratives and parameters
of intellectual work within and without the academy, along with explora-
tions of sexuality, gender, ability, labor and other subjects. These follow a
longtime engagement of scholars of color and women who have taken the
lead in critiquing patriarchy, white supremacy and capitalism. This most
recent "curricular transformation" movement occurred within a longer
historic tradition.

For example, African American and Africana studies emerged from the
civil rights and Black Power movements, occurring in the larger context of
the black freedom struggle. Du Bois' pronouncement that the problem of
the twentieth century would be the problem of the color line was a clarion
call for what followed. After blacks migrated north, concentrating themselves in urban centers, a political moment emerged that facilitated intellectual and material alliances with anticolonial forces around the globe.
Demands were made for widespread social change within specific institutions and for an anti-hegemonic and systemic transformation of U.S. and
global society. By 1969, black students had staged takeovers on 50 campuses, with demands for black studies, faculty hiring, inclusion and other
students' rights (Alkalimat, 2007; Bush, in press).

The objectives of this movement were viewed by different actors
in divergent ways. Many foundations saw the development of black

studies as a means to foster the integration of people of African descent into white Euro-dominated society with little change to the social structure (Rooks, 2006, p. B9). This had significant consequences
as establishment and funding sources sought means to contain the parameters of change. Forces of conservatism also emerged to replace the
New Deal Left's notion of a "century of the common man" and the
trend toward democratization in the 1960s. These organizations and
individuals sought to contain the possibility of radical change and nar-
row the scope of theorizing about race and racial discrimination to the
attitudes and practices of individuals, rather than an examination of
social patterns and responsibilities (Bush, 2005). In previous eras belief
in the biological superiority of Europeans was dominant; this shifted
toward discourse about the "culture of poverty" and a belief in the
social survival of the fittest that rationalized inequality as the outcome
of deficient cultural habits of particular groups (Bush, 2004; Steinberg,
2001).

The tension between democratization and conservatism—most clearly
marked by Ronald Reagan's presidency—gradually undermined the possibilities of radical social change envisioned by the social forces that they
represented. This was no longer the multiculturalism of the Third World
Liberation Front of 1969, which struck the University of California at
Berkeley with demands for an autonomous Third World College (Bush,
in press). An opening existed to reshape U.S. and global society with mass
mobilizations of large sections of the population for an increase in the
democratic and egalitarian character of U.S. society. That possibility became increasingly unlikely by the 1990s. Curricula would most certainly
incorporate greater content related to diversity, but it would not call into
question broader issues of structural inequalities that could transform
power relations overall.

Those fields that fell under a broad banner of "ethnic studies" experienced contested histories, with periods of expansion and support inter-
spersed with times of contraction and consolidation (Darder & Torres,
2003; Flores, 1999). Women's studies had its roots in earlier struggles
for women's rights and gender equality and made significant progress
in the movement toward greater diversity in the curriculum. "Whereas
in 1969 there had been only 16 women's studies course syllabi, by 1982
there were some 20,000 courses and 450 certificate- or degree-granting
programs in the United States" (Stimpson, 1983, p. 1). By the turn of the
twenty-first century, however, feminists were asking, "Is women's studies dead?" (Zalewski, 2003). They were posing questions about whether
women's studies is a discipline in and of itself or actually an interdisciplinary pursuit, changing social conditions, relationship to projects
addressing other forms of oppression (Wiegman quoted in Luhmann,
2004, p. 150).

CASE STUDY: THE CITY UNIVERSITY
OF NEW YORK (CUNY)

Few publications comprehensively document and analyze institutional history related to diversity in the curriculum around the nation. Publications by the National Center for Curricular Transformation Resources on Women (1997) and by the Association of American Colleges and Universities are exceptions, as is David Yamane's (2001) writing on the University of California at Berkeley and the University of Wisconsin at Madison.

In the City University of New York, women's studies, Africana, and Puerto Rican studies programs were developed in several colleges (and a few departments); curriculum was reviewed and revised. From 1975 to 1980 a budget crisis resulted in significant faculty retrenchment; curricular change was not the priority. Efforts picked up again in the 1980s. A Task Force for Balancing the Curriculum for Pluralism and Diversity recommended setting up a structure for accountability in upholding pluralism and diversity on campuses and having diversity-related core curriculum and distribution requirements at each college. In 1988 the CUNY Board of Trustees adopted a resolution concerning cultural pluralism and diversity, following a recommendation from the Council of Presidents in support of a multifaceted approach—curricular, co-curricular—to hiring and admission. A policy statement was issued mandating that students in every school within CUNY take at least one course in a diversity-related subject.

Between 1987 and 1999 the Balancing the Curriculum Project (under the leadership of Dorothy O. Helly, Barbara Omolade, Marie Buncombe, Joan Tronto, Altagracia Ortiz, and Marina Heung) held seminars around the university, infusing great energy into the process. In December 1991 a conference called One University for Many Cultures drew over 250 participants from within the CUNY system. Fourteen workshops identified strategies and asserted recommendations for diversity and pluralism in the university, particularly related to the curriculum. In the 1990s scholars from around the United States participated in an event called the Seminar on Scholarship and the Curriculum, which was hosted by the CUNY Academy for the Humanities and Sciences. Participants examined the impact of new scholarship in areas of race, class, gender and ethnicity on the shaping of the disciplines. The result was a series of seven booklets entitled *CUNY Panels: Rethinking the Disciplines* (Helly, 1993).

Between 1988 and 2000 these seminars and conferences provided an opportunity for a focused review of the curriculum, established networks of faculty interested in issues of diversity, and offered significant opportunities for faculty development. However, the late 1990s were characterized by retrenchment and challenges to remediation programs in the senior colleges. The last Balancing the Curriculum Seminar was held during the 1998–1999 academic year. From that point on, questions were increasingly raised about diversity-oriented courses, portraying them as "special interest" and the locus of "left-wing indoctrination" and further questioning why these seminars should be funded over others that might, for instance, increase the use of technology. Internal and external pressures sought to discredit the value of the changes that were made to balance the curriculum and open admissions, claiming academic standards had dropped as a result. Remediation programs were targeted, though according to the Federal Department of Education, remedial courses are offered at three-quarters of four-year colleges and taken by one-third of all freshmen in the United States (Harden, 1998). This reflected a belief that not everyone is "college material," and someone who takes more than four years to graduate lacks intelligence or commitment rather than funds, time or prior training. At issue was whether access (by way of diversity) and excellence are deemed inextricably linked or whether the achievement of one virtue could only occur to the detriment of the other (Romer, 1999, p. 47). As mentioned earlier in this chapter, the question of who is in the classroom (faculty and student) is inherently related to what is taught and learned.

After a period of diminished hiring in the 1980s and 1990s, CUNY schools began to bring in new faculty, the drawback being that there was no generative process to integrate them into the project of balancing the curriculum. Additionally, with the exception of the Balancing the Curriculum Project, curricular changes took place in individual departments or colleges with little coordination or discussion about what was occurring across the university. This led to a somewhat ad hoc nature to the way that curriculum was revised, especially when individual interests drove the changes taking place. That said, diversity-related courses were mostly clustered into programs, minors or scattered across the disciplines. This provided a disincentive for students to enroll in the courses, as they were often not integrated into disciplinary requirements. This was also problematic from a political point of view, as resources for diversity-related courses proved vulnerable to political tides, especially during periods of fiscal constraint. Though earlier there was support for diversity-oriented requirements in general education, it appeared to dissipate. The courses exposed more students to thinking about diversity, however, they also provide opportunities for interpretations of "diversity" that may be quite different from those who fought for the changes (Goodstein, 1994, p. 83). There are also diverging narratives and inconsistencies about what changes actually took place in the curriculum, as well as what their impact has been (Williams, Berger, & McClendon, 2005, p. 28). This makes assessment and planning more difficult.

Over the last several years there has been an increase in opposition to diversity requirements in curriculum courses, alleging they are not academically sound, too interdisciplinary and/or represent special and ideologically vested interests. As a result of the stigma and de-legitimization of these courses and programs, students sometimes express preference for courses in "traditional" disciplines with less diversity-oriented titles. This impacts enrollment, which in turn affects the support provided. As political and economic pressures have been brought to bear on students who are concerned about finding jobs after college, students look more to business and technical careers and majors. Business as a major has witnessed a significant increase, up 59 percent between 1969–1970 and 1993–1994 (Yamane, 2001, p. 137). Most of the recent decade's attention to civic engagement has taken the form of expanded opportunities for community service and volunteerism. While these are of value in their own right, they are not directed to changing the underlying structural causes of the problems being addressed through "service." This has resulted in students being politicized in a different way, with less knowledge of or involvement in the act of addressing institutional issues of equity, opportunity and justice.

As public institutions receive fewer state and federal funds, they become increasingly vulnerable to the private interests of donors, be they successful alumni or corporate entities. This has an impact on the possibility of change, since administrations are concerned about external pressures and thus vulnerable to the interests of the economically powerful. Another trend has been to hire in traditional departments with joint appointments to departments such as women's studies, Africana or Asian studies. This means that the directors of those programs have little if any say in the hiring and promotion of faculty. This provides a disincentive for new faculty to develop the programs rather than develop work that supports the traditional departments where they were hired.

All times are political times, and curriculum is particularly susceptible to questions of power. In the subsequent decade some of these programs and departments have experienced vulnerability. Many people believe we have dealt with multiculturalism and diversity and need to move on to other concerns regardless of the indicators of racial and gender inequality evident throughout academia and society at large. While hundreds of new diversity-related courses were developed and revised throughout the City University of New York, they often remain marginalized rather than viewed as central to the core curriculum. Departments and majors with a primary focus on previously ignored areas (e.g., Africana studies at Brooklyn College or women's studies at Hunter College) are rare; programs and minors are more common; select courses with a diversity-related component are most common. Diversity appears to have become just another requirement to be fulfilled rather than a value intrinsically linked to the mission of education.

DIVERSITY IN THE CURRICULUM TODAY

"One of the most striking shifts in university education during the last two decades has been the increased commitment to teaching diversity and multiculturalism. . . . There is much disagreement, however, about the contents of the multicultural canon, which range from 'teaching tolerance' to postmodernist construction of race, gender and sexuality" (Platt, 2002). Academic curricula now include significantly more content about "the 'no-name' people" (Kingston, 1975), and critiques of monoculturalism and ethnocentrism. However, "complexity is often sacrificed for morality lessons" such that the history and interlocking nature of social hierarchies are only superficially engaged and cultural celebration is often substituted for political, economic and social analysis; after all, "old-style modernist critiques of racism are out of fashion in academia" (Platt, 2002). Contemporary multiculturalism is typically framed as appreciating differences and cultivating interpersonal communication in contrast to the early developments of ethnic and women's studies that had been rooted in political praxis both on and off campus (Platt, 2002).

Other evidence of the struggle over the political nature of diversity includes the following recent developments: Since 2004, an "academic bill of rights" has been proposed (though not passed) in 17 state legislatures seeking to institute legislative rather than scholarly oversight of academic curricula. Similar language was included in the Higher Education Act Amendments of 2005. In 2006 the National Council for Accreditation of Teacher Education received endorsement from the U.S. Department of Education's National Advisory Committee on Institutional Quality and Integrity only after it agreed to eliminate "social justice" as a possible standard that schools of education could include in their conceptual frameworks. Further evidence of the struggle is found in debates over whether intelligent design and evolution are two equally valid perspectives about the origin of humankind; over whether economics as a discipline is almost uniformly considered part of business school curricula rather than the social sciences; and over attacks on programs such as women's studies at North Carolina State University and peace studies at Ball State University (Indiana). It is truly time for reflection about the state of the movement for diversity and multiculturalism in higher education curricula.

Initiatives such as the AAC&U's American Commitments Initiative (2001), three recent studies linking "Diversity, Equity, and Educational Excellence" ("Greater Expectations: A New Vision for Learning as a Nation Goes to College," "Making Diversity Work on Campus: A Research-Based Perspective," and "Achieving Equitable Educational Outcomes with All Students: The Institution's Roles and Responsibilities" [AAC&U, 2005]), and projects at institutions such as the University of Maryland at College Park, University of Michigan, and University of California provide examples of what can be done when attention is paid to diversity in the curriculum. To a large extent, however, attention has turned elsewhere as political and budgetary pressures mediate against diversity-related curricular transformations to focus on other priorities.

Education in support of diversity involves curricula that include not only the history, struggles, concerns, and accomplishments of all people, but also training in understanding the social, political, and economic forces of history. In this way an academic curriculum can engage public discourse about the dynamics of global capitalism, corresponding racialized structures of power and subordination, and the impact that these systems have on ordinary people's lives. Education can foster awareness about the dynamics of power, but this requires "hard intellectual and pedagogical work necessary to connect the categories (of race, class and gender) analytically and politically" (Platt, 2002, para. 11).

Inclusion of multiculturalism in the curriculum is often viewed as an issue of self-esteem and individualistic empowerment for those people who have been historically left out. It is also viewed as enriching everyone's knowledge of history through a more complete picture of what occurred. While these are important functions, multiculturalism and diversity training can also shed light on historical social patterns that undergird current systemic and institutional realities. Drawing this connection between the past and present provides the greatest possibilities for changes in the future because it provides a context for understanding history by examining its structural patterns.

Diversity and multicultural education pose their greatest challenge to existing social hierarchies when they include a broad-based examination of the politics and economics of social inequality nationally and globally. It is in this context that a multicultural curriculum can have its most powerful impact. If education included information about how Wall Street functions, the cyclical nature of capitalism, profit on a global scale and the concrete implications of these processes on real people's lives, then poverty, wealth and group positioning can be contextualized within social patterns rather than explained as a result of one group's superiority and the other's inferiority on account of biological or cultural prejudices.

This call for deepening the curricular emphasis on diversity and race within an economic framework differs from most recent multicultural scholarship, which often focuses on culture, identity, intentions and intergroup relations. Group experiences are frequently analyzed as if groups are just collections of individuals rather than functioning within a society and positioned within structural realities. "If multiculturalism is not going to take seriously the link between culture and power, progressive educators will have to rethink collectively what it means to link the struggle for change within the university to struggles for change in the broader society" (Giroux, 1999).

The pedagogy suggested here promotes a social vocabulary of cultural difference that links strategies of understanding to strategies of engagement, recognizes the limits of the university as a site for social engagement, and refuses to reduce politics to matters of language and meaning that erase broader issues of systemic political power, institutional control,

economic ownership and the distribution of cultural and intellectual resources in a wide variety of public spaces (Giroux, 1999).

To quote Carol Geary Schneider (1999), president of the Association of
American Colleges and Universities, "Very few courses in the contemporary undergraduate curriculum directly address democratic principles
and/or aspirations" (p. 9). She asks where in the curriculum are students
engaged in concepts of justice, democracy, equality, opportunity, and liberty, and suggested that these challenging topics belong in general education because they are integral dimensions of American pluralism and
must be understood in the context of their historical connections (p. 9).
This engagement is central to the development of civic responsibility and
social awareness as a core tenet of higher education. This returns us to
the first discussion of this chapter related to tensions within the mission
of public higher education as an institution that has simultaneous capacity to serve democracy (through a more highly educated populous and
as a locus for inquiry and critique of the status quo) and also to reinforce
the structural allocation of groups to different sectors of the political, economic and social spheres of society. Public education in the United States
has always had to struggle with being an institution of possibility within a
society that inconsistently demonstrates a commitment to a popular democratic tradition, and those times primarily as a result of struggles on the
part of ordinary people.

The principles that should guide our decisions on how diversity should
be framed within academic curricula need to begin with conscious explo-
rations about what function higher education is to serve within society.
These questions assist us in that reflection:

- What is the relationship between access and excellence—can we have one
  without the other?
- How is democracy served by diversity—how is it challenged?
- How concerned are we as a society about inequality? Is addressing it in our
  control?
- Can diversity be reconciled with power? Are social hierarchies worth
  preserving?
- What is the relationship between knowledge and power, and what does that
  imply for our educational system?
- What role should public higher education play in addressing social problems?

Principles of inclusion, balance, justice, equality, intellectual integrity,
and caring for the common good are central to the ability of educational
systems to function most effectively in society. We must take seriously
the notion that "change is political, keeping things the same is not" (Graff
quoted in Yamane, 2001, p. 129). Perhaps our first task is to ask whether
this is in fact true, for the implications either way are tremendously
consequential.

REFERENCES

Alkalimat, A. (2007, March). *Africana studies in New York State*. Retrieved July 1, 2008, from http://eblackstudies.org/su/complete.pdf.

Antonio, A. L., & Muniz. M. (2007). The sociology of diversity. In P. Gumport (Ed.), *Sociology of higher education: Contributions and their contexts* (pp. 266–294). Baltimore: Johns Hopkins University Press.

Association of American Colleges and Universities (AAC&U). (1997a, Winter). *Advice on effective curriculum transformation*. AAC&U's American Commitments Project. Retrieved July 1, 2008, from http://www.diversityweb.org/digest/W97/advice.html.

Association of American Colleges and Universities (AAC&U). (1997b, Winter). *Curricular recommendations from American commitments*. AAC&U's American Commitments Project. Retrieved July 1, 2008, from http://www.diversityweb.org/Digest/W97/currrec.html.

Association of American Colleges and Universities (AAC&U). (2000, August). *Survey on diversity requirements overview*. Retrieved July 1, 2008, from http://www.aacu.org/divsurvey/irvineoverview.cfm.

Association of American Colleges and Universities (AAC&U). (2001). *American commitments: Diversity, democracy, and liberal learning*. Retrieved July 1, 2008, from http://www.aacu.org/american_commitments/index.cfm.

Association of American Colleges and Universities (AAC&U). (2005, September 12). *New reports provide campus roadmap for making excellence inclusive*. Press release. Washington, DC. Retrieved July 1, 2008, from http://www.aacu.org/press_room/press_releases/2005/IE_Papers.cfm.

Banks, J. A. (2008). *An introduction to multicultural education* (4th ed.). New York: Allyn & Bacon/Pearson.

Bush, M. E. L. (2004). *Breaking the code of good intentions: Everyday forms of whiteness*. Lanham, MD: Rowman and Littlefield Publishers, Inc.

Bush, M. E. L. (2005, April). The movement for an "academic bill of rights": A new assault on academic freedom. *North American Dialogue: The Newsletter of the Society for the Anthropology of North America Section of the American Anthropological Association, 8*(1), 16–19.

Bush, R. D. (in press). *The end of white world supremacy: Black internationalism and the problem of the color line*. Philadelphia: Temple University Press.

By the numbers: How higher education has changed in 40 years. (2006, November 24). *The Chronicle of Higher Education*, p. A17.

Carnegie Foundation for the Advancement of Teaching & Center for Information and Research on Civic Learning and Engagement (CIRCLE). (2006, February). *Higher education: Civic mission and civic effects*. Stanford, CA: The Carnegie Foundation.

Chang, M. J. (2005, Winter). Reconsidering the diversity rationale, *Liberal Education, 91*(1), 6–13.

Clegg, R. (2000, July 14). Why I'm sick of the praise for diversity on campuses. *The Chronicle of Higher Education*, p. B8.

Crain, W. (2003, July–August). Open admissions at the City University of New York. *Academe: Bulletin of the American Association of University Professors, 89*(4), 46.

Darder, A., & Torres, R. D. (2003, July). Mapping Latino studies. In S. Oboler (Ed.), *Latino studies* (Vol. 1, No. 2, pp. 303–324). New York: Palgrave Macmillan.

Delpit, L. (1995). *Other people's children: Cultural conflict in the classroom.* New York: New Press.

Delpit, L., & Perry, T. (Eds.). (1998). *The real Ebonics debate: Power, language, and the education of African-American children.* Boston, MA: Beacon Press.

Du Bois, W. E. B. (1936/1979). *Black reconstruction in America: 1860–1880.* West Hanover, MA: Atheneum Publishers.

Eitzen, E. S., & Zinn, M. B. (2004). *Conflict and order: Understanding society.* New York: Allyn and Bacon.

Flores, J. (1999). Latino studies: New contexts, new concepts. In J. A. Segarra & R. Dobles (Eds.), *Learning as a political act* (pp. 341–352, Reprint Series No. 33). Cambridge, MA: Harvard Educational Review.

Franklin, H. B. (2003, Summer). Under attack for 150 years. *Clarion: Newspaper of the Professional Staff Congress/City University of New York,* p. 10.

Giroux, H. (1997, Summer). Rewriting the discourse of racial identity: Towards a pedagogy and politics of whiteness. *Harvard Educational Review, 67*(2), 285.

Giroux, H. (1999, April). Substituting prisons for schools. *Z Magazine: A Political Monthly.* Retrieved December 16, 2002, from http://www.zmag.org/zmag/viewArticle/12708.

Glisczinski, D. J. (2007, October). Transformative higher education: A meaningful degree of understanding. *Journal of Transformative Education, 5*(4), 317–328.

Goodstein, L. (1994, Spring). The failure of curriculum transformation at a major public university: When 'diversity' equals 'variety.' *National Women's Studies Association Journal, 6*(1), 82–102.

Gorelick, S. (1981). *City College and the Jewish poor: Education in New York, 1880–1924.* New York: Schocken Books.

Harden, B. (1998, June 2). Reading, writing and ruckus; City University of New York's tougher standards anger many. *Washington Post,* p. A3.

Helly, D. O. (Ed.). (1993). *CUNY panels: Rethinking the disciplines series.* Towson, MD: National Center for Curriculum Transformation Resources on Women (NCCTRW).

How class works. Class matters: A special section. (2005). [Interactive graphic]. *The New York Times.* Retrieved July 1, 2008, from http://www.nytimes.com/packages/html/national/20050515_CLASS_GRAPHIC/index_04.html?adxnnl=1&adxnnlx=1134601581-jydhmvQpCXlJlSz8NyzEmA.

Humphreys, D. (Ed.). (1997). *General education and American commitments: A national report on diversity courses and requirements.* Washington, DC: Association of American Colleges and Universities.

Humphreys, D. (Ed.). (1998). *Diversity and the college curriculum: How colleges and universities are preparing students for a changing world.* Retrieved August 24, 2004, from http://www.diversityweb.org/diversity_innovations/curriculum_change/principles_and_practices/curriculum_briefing.cfm.

Incarcerate or educate? (2008, May/June). *AFT on Campus,* p. 14.

Kingston, M. H. (1975). *The woman warrior: Memoirs of a girlhood among ghosts.* New York: Vintage Books.

Lardner, J., & Smith, D. (2005). *Inequality matters.* New York: The New Press.

Light, R., & Cureton, J. (1992, January/February). The quiet revolution: Eleven facts about multiculturalism and the curriculum. *Change, 24*(1), 24.

Luhmann, S. (2004). Trying times for women's studies: Lost pasts, ambivalent presents and predetermined futures. In A. Braithwaite, S. Held, S. Luhrmann, &

S. Rosenberg (Eds.), *Troubling women's studies: Pasts, presents and possibilities* (pp. 147–194). Toronto: Sumach Press.

McIntyre, A. (1997). *Making meaning of whiteness: Exploring racial identity with white teachers.* Albany: State University of New York Press.

Morin, R. (2001, July 11). Misperceptions cloud whites' view of blacks. *Washington Post*, final edition, p. A1.

National Center for Curriculum Transformation Resources on Women (NCCTRW). (1997). *Directory of curriculum transformation projects and activities in the United States.* Baltimore: Uptown Press.

O'Leary, C. E. (1999). *To die for: The paradox of American patriotism.* Princeton, NJ: Princeton University Press.

Pew Center on the States. (2008). *One in 100: Behind bars in America 2008.* Washington, DC: The Pew Charitable Trusts.

Platt, T. (2002). Desegregating multiculturalism: Problems in the theory and pedagogy of diversity education. *Social Justice, 29*(4). Retrieved July 1, 2008, from http://www.socialjusticejournal.org/Pedagogy/Syl-platt1.html.

Romer, N. (1999, Winter). The CUNY struggle: Class and race in public higher education. *New Politics, 7*(2), 47–56.

Rooks, N. M. (2006, February 10). The beginnings of black studies. *The Chronicle of Higher Education,* pp. B8–B9.

Schneider, C. G. (1999, Fall). Democratic principles and the undergraduate curriculum. *Peer Review,* 7–9.

Scott, R. (2008, February 28). *The challenges facing higher education in America today.* Invited Keynote Address by the President of Adelphi University. Luncheon Roundtable, Naples, Florida.

Steinberg, S. (2001). *The ethnic myth: Race, ethnicity and class in America.* Boston: Beacon Press.

Stimpson, C. R. (1983, May). Our search and research: The study of women since 1969. *Comment,* 14.

Tatum, B. D. (1997). *Why are all the black kids sitting together in the cafeteria? And other conversations about race.* New York: Basic Books.

U.S. Census Bureau. (2000). Money matters: Money income, 2000. In *Population profile of the United States: 2000* (p. 12-2, fig. 12-2). Internet release. Retrieved July 1, 2008, from http://www.census.gov/population/pop-profile/2000/chap12.pdf.

Williams, D. A., Berger, J. B., & McClendon, S. A. (2005). *Toward a model of inclusive excellence and change in postsecondary institutions.* Association of American Colleges and Universities. Retrieved July 1, 2008, from http://www.aacu.org/inclusive_excellence/pdfs/Williams_Final.pdf.

Yamane, D. (2001). *Student movements for multiculturalism: Challenging the curricular color line in higher education.* Baltimore: Johns Hopkins University Press.

Zalewski, M. (2003). Is women's studies dead? *Journal of International Women's Studies, 4*(2), 117–133.

CHAPTER 6

Cultural Competence in High Schools: Present Status and Future Directions

Gargi Roysircar, Dana L. Caruso, and John C. Carey

High schools are fundamental in forming the knowledge, beliefs, attitudes, and vocational skills students need to live in a diverse society; they also provide the academic contexts in which students can develop their intellectual pursuits. High schools, both public and private, mirror the changing demographics of the United States and offer important opportunities to expand students' multicultural awareness, comfort, and competence. Through multicultural education, schools strive to prepare students to become healthy, productive adult members of a diverse society. Multicultural education helps the entire academic community, both minorities and nonminorities. For instance, a multicultural framework benefits white, middle-class students by (a) expanding their knowledge of diversity, (b) expanding their cultural awareness through a multicultural school environment, and (c) preparing them to live and work in a diverse nation, the United States of the twenty-first century. Furthermore, schools that emphasize diversity provide access to minority and marginalized students (Roysricar, 2006; Sciarra, 2001). Thus, multicultural education is an important part of a well-rounded education from which all high school students can benefit.

This chapter compares and contrasts private and public high schools in terms of their current major diversity issues and the implications of these issues for counselors and psychologists, and discusses diversity-based approaches to increase the quality of education for all students. There are two parts to this chapter. The first part addresses the organizational structures of nondenominational private high schools in the New England area with regard to their challenges in incorporating multiculturalism into their leadership, faculty, students, social climate, and curriculum. The second part addresses the achievement gap between students of color and white students in public high schools and the needed organizational roles and functions of school counselors and psychologists to change this gap and improve learning outcomes for all students. Developing an understanding of the structural and systemic changes in both independent and public high schools that undergird a transition to more culturally competent practices will enable school-based counselors and psychologists to reconstruct their roles and effectively participate in the change process.

CHANGING DEMOGRAPHICS IN SCHOOLS IN THE UNITED STATES

School-aged children are the most diverse age group in the United States, with 37 percent of this group being nonwhite, as opposed to 28 percent nonwhite people in the general population (Roysircar-Sodowsky & Frey, 2003). Some researchers estimate that under these trends, by the year 2025, the typical public school classroom will be 50 percent nonwhite.

This increasing diversity is typically viewed as a phenomenon in the public school classrooms of the United States, alongside the stereotype that all private schools are elitist, white, upper-class institutions. However, according to 2005 data from The Association of Boarding Schools Web site (http://www.schools.com), today's boarding schools are also rich in diversity. An individual student's identity is represented across multiple group-specific identifications, including, race, ethnicity, international student status, gender, language dominance, ability status, social class, educational background, religion, sexual identity, and hobbies/recreational interests. Additionally, according to 2005–2006 data collected from the National Association of Independent Schools' affiliates (http://www.NAIS.org), the overall percentage of American-born students of color enrolled in independent schools rose significantly over the last decade, a trend that shows no signs of slowing down. Furthermore, by offering incentive grants, organizations like the E. E. Ford Foundation (http://www.eeford.org) have enabled independent schools to employ faculty of color. The Association of Boarding Schools asserts that boarding schools' diverse student and faculty body enriches both academic learning and social climate.

Sociopolitical Context

Arguably, the landmark 1954 court case, *Brown v. Board of Education*, resulted in a larger, collective, systemic consciousness about the inextricable relationship between diversity and education. However, recent studies, cited by Smith (2004) from Harvard University's 2003 Civil Rights Project, reveal that segregation currently permeates all schools, regardless of geographic location or demographic composition (see also Tatum, 1999).

Kozol (2005) has posited that while no one wants to call it *segregation* within American public schools, segregation in the millennium is actually worse than during the civil rights movement. Kozol (2005) also identified three factors that contribute to segregation in public schools: (1) inequitable distribution of resources, (2) mandated academic testing that is culturally biased, such as the Massachusetts Comprehensive Assessment System Examination, which students must pass successfully in order to be promoted to the next grade level, and (3) the nationwide devaluing of public school teachers.

Jay (2003) asserted that traditional curricula tend to be "organized around concepts, events, and paradigms that reflect the experiences of Anglo Saxon Protestant men" (p. 3). Educational materials written by those who are part of the white culture about the white culture fail to include the students outside of that group, thereby implying that the cultural experience of anyone outside the dominant group is not worth learning. Ironically, this results in cultural marginalization and segregation, which is the opposite of the spirit of the civil rights movement. Therefore, a diversity-affirmative school expands the ways in which it addresses multiculturalism by including biraciality and multiraciality, as well as by educating on the negative effects of heterosexism, classism, religious prejudice, and discrimination against people with disabilities (Anderson, MacPhee, & Govan, 2000). Many educators agree that learning about other cultures in school is an important part of the whole education experience. In a world characterized by increasingly interconnected economies, the emergence of new economic powers like China and India with accompanying shifts in the international power structure, and increased competition for basic energy and food resources, having all students graduate from high school aware of other cultures, comfortable with other cultures, and capable of interacting effectively across cultures is critical for our nation's stability, prosperity, and perhaps even survival.

One caveat, however, to this multicultural approach is that students can be required to learn about diversity in an environment that is hostile to students and faculty who are culturally different from white Americans, which further marginalizes these minority constituents. Marginalization is defined by what minority students experience, such as being outliers, with school personnel, other student groups (Kuriloff & Reichert, 2003), as well as with a school's evaluation methods and its observation of due process.

On the other hand, ideally, multicultural education emphasizes learning from the voices of groups that are not from the dominant culture in order to broaden students' perspectives and help them shift from a "deficiency-based" to a "difference-based" mode of understanding human diversity. Once limited to addressing racism, multicultural education in today's schools is much broader; it includes population groups such as gender, socioeconomic class, disability, religion, and sexual identity (Roysircar, Arredondo, Fuertes, Ponterotto, & Toporek, 2003) as well as issues like power, access, and oppression (Toporek, Gerstein, Fouad, Roysricar, & Israel, 2006); and values, such as social justice and equitable distribution. In essence, multicultural education honors and gives a voice to people from underrepresented groups as a part of the overall educational experience (Green, 1989; Nichols, 2003; Sleeter & Grant, 1996).

Curriculum

Frequently, when multicultural education is provided, it is included more as an add-on to the core curriculum. For example, when a teacher designates a time that is separate from the typical school lesson or day for a multicultural topic, it can marginalize and isolate a culture about whom the students are expected to learn (Boatright & Little, 2003). Banks and Banks (1997) refers to this way of teaching as the "additive" approach, which is often combined with the "contribution" approach. The contribution approach involves learning about difference primarily through focusing on the superficial features or "eccentricities" of that culture, which also often results in stereotyping and marginalization (Banks & Banks, 1997). An example of the contribution approach occurs when students are taught about various cultures' holidays or celebrations, and the focus is mostly on what is odd or different from the dominant culture's benchmark holidays. This results in the students from those minority cultures feeling over-observed and socially alienated. There are more effective ways than the well-intended additive or contribution approach to teach about human diversity.

Hayes's (1996) research of educators' understanding of multiculturalism, as measured by looking at their knowledge of diversity, perceptions of differences, and professional attitudes, revealed a great need for teacher training in multicultural education. Parallel to the ways in which multicultural education is taught to high school students, teacher-trainees are often taught about diversity through the additive or contribution approach, or at most, through one course on multiculturalism (Hayes, 1996). Therefore, when an educator is faced with teaching about diversity in high school, it is likely that he or she will, in turn, teach in the same way he or she was taught as a teacher-trainee. Thus, when a high school emphasizes a multicultural curriculum, teachers benefit by filling gaps in their teacher training and making themselves well-rounded educators.

School Climate

In addition to course material, schools educate about difference by creating a climate that fosters a sense of belonging, respect, recognition, and access for all students. Students' sense of affiliation and equity can impact their interpersonal as well as academic functioning. For example, in examining the high school experiences of African American and Latino American adolescents, Van Buren (2005) found that negative interracial experiences and perceptions resulted in reduced overall functioning for Latino American youth. He also learned that when African American male youth internalized discrimination, their academic functioning became impaired. Van Buren concluded that students who perceived school-wide fairness and equity had a reduced perception of educational, institutional, and peer discrimination. Similarly, Gonzalez (2003) showed that in addition to responding positively to an implemented multicultural curriculum, Latino American students credited positive race relations as contributing to their placing value on their education. When Latino American students perceived their school to value their ethnicity, they were more actively involved in their education.

INDEPENDENT SCHOOLS

Both public schools and independent schools, faced with the challenges of managing multiculturalism, approach this challenge in different ways. While public schools have a mandate to serve all students, independent schools need to define their own mission and have the flexibility to be creative (or not) in terms of how multiculturalism is reflected in that mission.

In 1996 the NAIS Board of Directors completed their two-year task of designing a Strategic Diversity Plan, which emphasized widespread development in diversity and multiculturalism for private schools (see summary in http://www.NAIS.org). The approval of this plan dovetailed the organization's 2002 "Principles of Good Practice for Equity and Justice" (see summary in http://www.NAIS.org). In these principles, NAIS directors made known their commitment to establishing a "bias-free environment, and develop[ing] a sense of responsibility for equity and justice in the broader community" (Braverman & Looney, 1999, p. 32). The board's approval of the 1996 Strategic Diversity Plan, later updated in 2000, demonstrated its dedication to diversity at both organizational and constituent levels.

There are many ways that independent schools are different from their public school counterparts in regards to managing issues of diversity. Independent schools are not accountable to state- and federally-mandated curricula and test scores. At many independent schools, valuable forces that influence the schools' policies and practices are the voices of the school's many constituents. Many public schools are faced with budgetary constraints that can result in eliminating programs and positions seen as "nonessential." Contrarily, many independent schools are able to establish and support a position of director of diversity, who oversees the issues surrounding the school's diversity initiatives, while also acting as a liaison between the school's stakeholders and diverse constituents of the school and community (Kaufman, 2003). In summary, independent schools are well positioned to become multiculturally competent institutions if they embrace the change that is required to achieve this end.

However, simply because a private school has more flexibility in what it teaches and how it teaches does not mean that a private school will automatically create a learning environment for its actively recruited diverse student body. In fact, racial and ethnic minority students who have the resources to access private education or have been awarded high financial aid and scholarships may find themselves in a predominantly white environment that does not support multicultural education. Therefore, if independent schools are not willing to implement diversity-enhancing strategies, their many systemic and financial advantages are of no help. Similarly, because an organization has the resources to manage an issue of diversity does not mean that the organization has the wherewithal to be successful at it. Creating an organization that is culturally competent is a complex, multidimensional task that needs to be applied across multiple levels of its community, policy, and roles (American Psychological Association, 2003).

Independent School Diversity: An Organizational Perspective

For youth who board at independent schools, the school community takes on a greater family role, with faculty members, staff, administration, and other students becoming critical influences in the child's educational life. Because an adolescent's interpersonal attachments have effects on his or her psychological health, it is important that he or she feel supported by and connected to the adults and peers who surround him or her (Willkinson, 2004). While a boarding school can provide an opportune environment for nurturing and educating students and adult constituents about diversity, it is an organization and, therefore, is confronted with many of the same challenges around diversity that affect all organizations in the United States.

In his 1992 article, "Organizational Vices: A Cautionary Tale," James Buckheit (1992) illustrated those areas in which independent schools hinder their own growth as culturally competent organizations. First, Buckheit stated that independent schools, like many organizations, tend to conceptualize diversity as a problem that must be solved. Second, he noted that private educational institutions often isolate themselves, without understanding the larger context of diversity in the nation. Eschewing isolation requires an honest review and admission of how it is that a school may perpetuate the status quo. Otherwise, the school does not successfully address deeper and often uncomfortable issues around diversity. Third, independent school bureaucracies promote inequity and limit access through rigid roles, rules, and boundaries. Finally, Buckheit countered that independent schools are not immune to the larger U.S. issues of lowering standards for the core principles of a well-rounded education. Thus, Buckheit suggested that independent schools have lost quality education in the midst of larger systemic reinforcements of meaningless measures, such as graduation rates and norm-referenced tests.

Diversity and the Independent School Leadership

Contrary to the local, state, and federal influences and mandates faced by public schools, independent school systems are accountable to heads of school (the headmaster or headmistress), boards of directors, and, to some degree, parents and alumnae. In the independent school community, these systems both affect and are affected by multiculturalism and diversity; everyone is a stakeholder affected by the ways these issues are or are not managed. Clashes between different stakeholders regarding the importance of or regarding institutional approaches to achieving multicultural competence can disable the school. Ideally, organizations that utilize systems approaches value shared vision and alignment of thoughts and action and encourage leadership and decision-making across all levels of the system. However, to implement action and sustain long-term community change, buy-in regarding the importance of multiculturalism among those who hold power (the headmaster or headmistress, boards of directors, parents and alumnae) is vital.

In an article addressing issues of leadership in the independent schools, Donna Orem (2002) cited Ben Bradlee, former executive editor of the *Washington Post*, who was interviewed by the *Harvard Business Review* about his World War II experiences. Specifically, Bradlee was asked about the qualities of a good leader. In addition to citing the ability to make quick, intelligent decisions, Bradlee emphasized the importance of a leader surrounding himself or herself with "good people" to help make those decisions: "If you're smart, you'll hire and inspire people who are smarter than you—or at least know more than you do about a lot of things" (Orem, 2002, p. 40). Here, the implication is that important and difficult decisions affecting the larger group and the school climate should not be made in isolation. The question arises, who are the power brokers in an organization that must be involved in a school's transition towards a more fully multiculturally competent institution?

Board of Trustees

In the independent school environment, particularly for multiculturalism, the three-fold power structure consists of the board of trustees, the head of the school, and the director of diversity. An independent school's board of trustees is often comprised of elected alumnae, parents of current students, and other individuals who have a connection to the school. Boards are primarily responsible for overseeing important institutional issues, such as hiring the head of school and dictating a school's long-term master plan. Because the board's primary goal is to always have the best interest of the school in mind, "strategic" is a theme that underscores every decision they make (Bassett, 2001). Bassett (2001) noted that while a director of diversity (the diversity point person) is fundamental to sustaining campus-wide climate change, the board still plays an important role in creating a multicultural community. Examples of the board's tasks include: approving or initiating a plan that promotes community diversity, supporting a diversity task force, and remaining actively involved in community-wide diversity training (Bassett, 2001). Bassett stated that including the board in a variety of hands-on diversity initiatives that are not strictly administrative, per se, can facilitate opportunities for multicultural interactions similar to those experienced daily by students, teachers, and the head of school.

Head of School

Internally, the head of the school is the face of leadership. Citing NAIS research that was conducted in the early 2000s, Orem (2002) presented the data of a survey that summarized characteristics of current heads of independent schools. The survey was mailed to 502 randomly selected NAIS-member school heads, and 351 heads responded, yielding a 70 percent response rate. Of those who responded to the survey, 71 percent were male and 29 percent were female. Cultural demographics revealed that of the respondents, 91 percent were European American; 2 percent were Asian or Pacific Islander, and 1 percent was identified as African American, Latino or Hispanic, and bi- or multiracial. According to the NAIS survey, many heads of school had an average of 24 years of experience working in independent schools. Orem reported that while most had been teachers, some had been department chairs, deans, or other administrators, prior to their roles as heads of school. None of the survey's respondents had ever held the position of director of diversity. This may be due to the fact that director of diversity is a relatively new position, and many of the current Directors of Diversity have not yet "come of age" to hold the position of head of school. At the same time, undoubtedly there were many pioneers, particularly women and people of color, who addressed issues of equity in the independent school environment long before there was the formal position of director of diversity. Most likely, at least some of the respondents had experience dealing with issues of multicultural climate change in their school community, though they may not have identified these activities in their response to the NAIS survey, thus suggesting the perceived low worth of their diversity efforts.

Because of the lack of diversity in the position of heads of school (Orem, 2002), respondents were questioned about their perceptions of a "glass ceiling effect" for multicultural individuals striving to attain leadership roles in independent schools. The data yielded mixed results to this question: few respondents thought a glass ceiling effect was true "all of the time" for people of color and women; 16 percent of respondents thought this was true "most of the time" for people of color, and 8 percent thought it was "true" for women. Orem notes that a "significantly higher percent" thought the glass ceiling was true "some of the time" for people of color and women—40 percent and 37 percent, respectively. When school heads were questioned about the factors that may be contributing to the lack of diversity in the head of school position, the following reasons were cited, with percentages given of how many respondents gave a particular reason:

- 79 percent believed that there were too few people of color in other positions at independent schools.
- 51 percent believed that trustees and search committees were often reluctant to hire nontraditional heads of school.
- 36 percent believed that there were too few students of color to attract professionals of color to lead schools.
- 32 percent believed that there were too few people of color available who have the right training to be heads.
- 31 percent believed that an old boys' network still worked to hire and promote white men.
- 28 percent believed that professionals of color did not want to be heads of independent schools because the culture was predominantly white and unwelcoming.

Director of Diversity

For many reasons, the role of director of diversity is an important position in an independent school's effort to become more multicultural. First, if the director of diversity is representative of a marginalized group, he or she can literally be a "face" of diversity, which can benefit the whole community, regardless of cultural background (Bryant, 2000). Second, the director of diversity can maintain and sustain the motivation for creating a multicultural community even when there is an energy lull, systemic roadblocks, or if the general community interest is directed elsewhere. Third, the director of diversity can educate the community about the process of becoming multiculturally competent, while simultaneously supporting individual growth within the larger school community.

Placing a diverse individual in the role of director of diversity can impact positively the school climate for both students and adults (Bryant, 2000). Everyone in the independent school setting gains from seeing diverse adults in leadership positions. For example, if the director of diversity is a person of color, he or she visually represents nonwhite leadership. This challenges the traditional concept of organizational power structure and can be essential preparation for white students who will enter the diverse workforce of the future. Additionally, students of color benefit from seeing a nonwhite leader because of the potential for positive role-modeling. The positive impact on students of color to see an adult of color hold a position that represents leadership and community mobilization and transformation should not be underestimated. Directors of diversity are agents of change.

However, the role of the independent school director of diversity is challenging in many ways. As the face of diversity programming and climate change, he or she must be a cheerleader, a motivator, an educator, and a politician: "Diversity directors are simultaneously powerful and powerless, both leaders and followers, clear about their roles yet often lost in the larger organizational context" (Kaufman, 2003, p. 22). The director of diversity's multifaceted and complex role demands that he or she navigate, both assertively and diplomatically, numerous systems within the school climate, including those that are administrative, academic, residential, and programmatic. This is important because many critics argue that multicultural education does not address the structural inequities that support racism, and most likely other prejudices, such as power relationships, access to opportunities, and the continuation of oppression—despite multicultural efforts in education (Morelli & Spencer, 2000).

The director of diversity must always consider the ways in which his or her choices regarding diversity programming both affect and are affected by students and adults in the community. Above all, the director of diversity must be resilient. For example, one study revealed that students have difficulty expressing their resistance to diversity programming out of fear of appearing prejudiced (Whitehead & Wittig, 2004). If the community becomes resistant to multicultural change, the director of diversity carries the responsibility of remobilizing. He or she can do so in a way that respects adverse feelings, promotes dialogues of difference, and allows students and faculty to speak the "unspeakable," even when the feelings are in response to the program itself, and even when the director of diversity becomes the object of projections. This is easier said than done. One way the director of diversity can cope with adversarial reactions is by capitalizing on his or her understanding of difference. Educating and supporting the community on the deeper issues of cultural conflicts, social privileges, multicultural competencies of attitudes, knowledge, and skills, and cultural identity development, the director of diversity can potentially impact multicultural change at a significant level.

A person of color can face extra challenges when placed in the role of director of diversity. Bascia's (1996) examined some of the challenges faced by "Edgar," a black teacher advancing in a leadership position by heading a school diversity project within a white administration. First, Edgar perceived that his white administration coworkers had difficulty believing that Edgar would work on a project without the intention of advancing his own career. Next, Edgar reported that when he conducted classroom observations for his diversity project, the principal questioned the teachers, whose classes he visited, regarding Edgar's professional behavior. In particular, the principal wanted to know if Edgar "barged in" for the classroom observations. Bascia (1996) stated that Edgar perceived his administrative superiors to mean that as a black man, he had neither expertise nor authority and could, therefore, not contribute anything of professional or personal value to other nonminority educators. Edgar's beliefs were widespread among other minority educators who were involved in a similar diversity project as Edgar.

Bascia (1996) posited that most teachers who attempt to initiate community change within the academic setting are "not necessarily popular" (p. 155). This is true because often projects that initiate such change are seen as insignificant or potentially threatening to the school's status quo. However, there are additional factors that complicate the ability to mobilize change when the teachers initiating such change are minority individuals. Teachers' ability to advocate for school climate change is influenced largely by the school setting in which they work. If a school community does not endorse nor facilitate transformation, even the most eager and enthusiastic teacher will have difficulty mobilizing his or her stakeholders to support change. Furthermore, minority teachers may not have as much access to the ways and means of stakeholders, who can initiate climate change, simply because they are of a minority status. Minority teachers are highly susceptible to being affected by larger systematic and organizational influences of advantage and disadvantage, including limited policy and procedural information, decision-making authority, and legitimacy and status (Ball, 1987; Finley, 1984; Siskin, 1994.) Therefore, initiating and creating school climate change at the administrative level is difficult in general and can be more difficult for the minority teacher. Other research (Foster, 1992; Moses, 1989; Ortiz, 1982) reveals similar findings about minority educators working in roles involving macro-level organizational development and administration.

Up Close and Personal Effects of Faculty and Administrators' Cultural Identity

Alongside adolescent students' processes of coming to understand their cultural identity are the adults' processes of exploring their own cultural identity. Helms (1994) asserted, "Everyone with whom a child comes in contact in the school environment (including teachers, peers, support staff) is also at some stage of identity development" (p. 30), thereby underscoring the importance of adults knowing their own cultural identity, which also affects the cultural identity of the students. Holcomb-McCoy (2005) posited that Helms' definitions of dyadic racial interactions—parallel, regressive, or progressive—can be applied successfully to define the cultural interactions that occur between students and adult school personnel.

Parallel interactions occur when the adult and student are in the same stage of identity development. While not negative, this type of relationship is characterized as a sort of impasse, as the adult cannot contribute to the growth of the adolescent's cultural identity. The interactions that are defined as regressive result from the adult's being less developed in terms of his or her cultural identity than the child. Holcomb-McCoy (2005) pointed to causes, such as the adult's lack of awareness of his or her own worldview or a larger, more general discomfort with cultural diversity, as initially contributing to the regressive relationship. The regressive relationship is also marked by the adult's attempt to alter the student's belief system, which results in "disharmony, conflict, tension, and rebellion" (Holcomb-McCoy, 2005, p. 123). Finally, Holcomb-McCoy notes that the progressive relationship is the most desirable type of cultural interaction between the adult and the student. In this type of relationship, the cultural identity of the adult is more developed than that of the student. In the progressive relationship, the adult honors the student's cultural identity and helps the student develop further. The adult who has a well-developed cultural identity acts as a role model for the student and inspires the student to explore issues related to developing his or her cultural identity as well. Together, the adult and student in the progressive relationship can become catalysts for climate change on the school campus. As the independent school's adults develop their cultural identity, so, too, do the school's students.

FUTURE DIRECTIONS IN INDEPENDENT SCHOOLS' MULTICULTURALISM

Several interventions for improving multiculturalism of independent schools are presented here. Many can be easily implemented into the existing curriculum and climate.

Curriculum and Academic Climate

The curriculum should include voices and views of nondominant cultures. While the assumption is often that such courses as English, history, religion, and foreign language are naturally more conducive to implementing multiculturalism, there is no reason that science and math classes cannot find ways to incorporate diversity into the academic coursework and climate. For example, coursework could include studying the contributions of women or differently abled individuals to the field of mathematics. Similarly, classroom décor could be changed. Science teachers could arrange for students to change lab partners on an ongoing basis to create a natural, safe mixing of students across reference groups. Such immersion-type interventions involve creating subtle changes within the academic climate and curriculum that can reduce students' resistance and aversion to a "forced" diversification.

Diversity Day Programming

In an effort to improve their multiculturalism and diversity programming, schools offer isolated events, seminars, and trainings that are about addressing difference. Whether these programs are specific to one cultural group (e.g., an ethnic celebration) or about broader concepts such as tolerance and acceptance, they often leave their target audience with feelings of frustration or indifference and even further marginalization of minority individuals. While a Diversity Day is appreciated by some, in actuality it is another school day, only different in that there may be two assemblies, workshops instead of classes, ethnic food in the dining hall, and decorations displayed throughout the campus. If the climate and curriculum were multicultural in nature, there would be no need for such a day. The school's weekly assemblies could be modified to include diverse speakers and encourage student involvement in planning, execution, and follow-up activities. Material and activities around which Diversity Day workshops are based could simply become part of classwork and homework. For example, an economics class could incorporate the concepts of white privilege and social class into its curriculum. The dining hall should always offer food representative of its international students, and the school's art, wall displays, bulletin boards, museum, and chapel should be representative of an environment that values difference. An independent school might display multicultural flags on special occasions or on prospective student visiting days; these flags could be always displayed. Then the Diversity Day can be seen more as an enriching, celebratory experience—an exemplar practice day for an already multicultural climate and curriculum.

Student Voice in Climate Change and Policy

Independent school systems often operate in isolation and administrators tend to work closely with small groups of adult stakeholders. It is important that student voices are heard regarding school climate and policy. A school should provide an ongoing forum for students to express their thoughts and feelings about interpersonal and programmatic issues. Frequent dialogue and discourse should occur on a regular basis and be open to all community members, so that students may express their concerns publically. Because culturally and racially diverse students often experience prejudice, fearing retaliation should they express their concerns, the school should also implement an anonymous venue for student input. This could occur through utilization of school technology, such as read-only intranet surveys, forums, or message boards. Students should also be encouraged to report positive multicultural interactions or interventions within the school climate and curriculum. "Telling on people for doing well" allows policy makers to receive feedback as to what students perceive as effective interventions, so that they can then facilitate more of these interventions. By keeping open the multicultural dialogue, students can be part of community-wide multicultural infusion, best seen as a process rather than a product.

Multiculturalism and School Personnel

Actively recruiting and employing diverse school personnel not only challenges traditional institutional power structures, but also provides opportunity for students to see diverse individuals hold positions of power within the school setting. Aside from the director of diversity, most independent school faculty, staff, and administrators have had very limited training in managing diversity issues and multiculturalism (Hayes, 1996). As part of discovering their multicultural identity, teachers should be provided an ongoing forum to express their thoughts and feelings related to diversity. Anonymous intranet-based surveys that allow adults to be introspective and examine their own multicultural attitudes, values, biases, assumptions, challenges, and successes would be a good place to start. Such surveys should address teachers' ideas about themselves as individuals, the school climate and curriculum, policy, and most importantly, their interactions with students. The future directions envisioned above for a multicultural and diverse independent school are realistic and doable.

PUBLIC HIGH SCHOOLS

Public high schools are a very heterogeneous collection of institutions. Public high schools differ tremendously in terms of size, setting (urban, suburban/small town, and rural), structure, student population, and level of available financial support. Many well-resourced, suburban public high schools resemble private schools and have diversity issues similar to those of independent schools. Many inner city, small town, and rural high schools are afflicted with pernicious diversity issues and fewer resources to address these.

The most visible manifestation of failures to deal adequately with student diversity is seen in the achievement gap. With some notable exceptions, students of color typically show lower high school graduation rates, lower scores on standardized achievement tests, and lower rates of college attendance and graduation. For example, while 67 percent of whites between the ages of 18 and 24 are enrolled in two- or four-year colleges and universities, only 11.6 percent of same age African Americans and 9.8 percent of same-age Hispanics are enrolled in higher education (Snyder, Dillow, & Hoffman, 2007). The public school achievement gap results in unequal representation in higher education and diminished life outcomes (Murname, Willet, Braatz, & Duhaldeborde, 2001; Rothstein, 2004). Lack of a college education, for example, translates to lower earning potential. On average, high school graduates earn $30,000 per year, while those with just some college or a bachelor's degree earn beyond $45,000 per year (U.S. Census Bureau, 2000).

The No Child Left Behind Act (NCLB) of 2002 initiated an unprecedented level of federal influence on public education. Among the many provisions of the act were: (1) mandatory public reporting of qualitative indicators of schools' performance (related to disaggregated standardized test performance, attendance, and high school graduation rates), (2) documentation of yearly gains in both improving general academic achievement and reducing the achievement gap between white students and students of color, and (3) strong sanctions against schools that fail to meet adequate yearly progress expectations. Every public high school in the United States must publish achievement data for all major student subgroups in the school and is accountable to improve the outcome for all major student subgroups. NCLB has resulted in a clear documentation of the extent of the achievement gap in schools in the United States and increased urgency in schools to do something about the gap. While poor inner city schools may still be showing the largest achievement issues, it has become apparent that the achievement gap also exists in high schools that serve very affluent communities.

Addressing the Achievement Gap

The traditional explanations for the achievement gap situated the problem within students and their home communities (see Coleman et al., 1966) and suggested that schools were relatively powerless to overcome the powerful effects of poverty and restricted experience. However, research in the "effective schools tradition" has consistently demonstrated that some inner city high schools are able to dramatically outperform both neighboring schools and predictions based upon their demographic characteristics. In general, effective schools research suggests that school personnel's beliefs, attitudes, and behaviors interact to create a social environment—a school climate—that has a strong influence on students' achievement. In effective schools administrators, teachers, counselors, school psychologists, and special educators believe that all students can learn to high standards; they develop a shared consensus on school goals, values, and policy; and they work together to communicate their expectations and develop policies, approaches, and practices that support learning. These schools have a student-centered (rather than a custodial) orientation and have a democratic orientation with a few clear rules that are consistently enforced (Carey & Boscardin, 2003).

Schools in which all the professionals share the responsibility for initiating positive change are more likely to be more effective. The principal's "distributed leadership" practices and the creation of communities within school where the adult constituents are engaged in continuous learning and improvement can increase connectivity within the schools, improve pedagogy, and enhance internal capacity of the school to educate all children (Elmore, 2000; Halverson, 2003; O'Day, 2004). Schools that are student-centered promote student engagement, which fuels achievement (Borman, Hewes, Overman, & Brown, 2003; Elias et al., 2003). Evidence also suggests that intentionally empowering high school students to participate in school improvement initiatives leads to increased student engagement and achievement (Joselowsky, 2007).

While many approaches to redesigning public high schools exist to eliminate the achievement gap, three principles—*rigor, relevance,* and *relationships*—seem to underlie all successful initiatives (McNulty & Quaglia, 2007). All students need rigor, which is defined as access to challenging educational experiences and the supports that will allow them to achieve. All students need to be able to see the relevance of what they are being asked to learn. All students need to learn in the context of healthy, caring, and supportive relationships between (and with) both adults and peers. If school personnel can collaborate with each other to redesign a school to maximize the impact of rigor, relevance, and relationships, then increases in student engagement and achievement can be expected to follow. Typical strategies might include: (1) changing school policy so that all students are encouraged to take Advanced Placement courses and providing needed tutoring for students who need it (rigor), (2) implementing an explicitly multicultural English language arts curriculum that connects with students' culture and experiences (relevance), and (3) instituting advisory groups where students meet weekly with a school staff member in small groups to talk about how to improve the school (relationships).

Implications for School-Based Counselors and Psychologists

Too often school-based high school counselors and psychologists focus on the personal effects of ineffective schools on students' academic achievement and development without a concomitant focus on and participation in the systemic reform that is needed to promote high quality education for all students. Recently, the Education Trust has been leading a national movement to reinvent school counseling so that counselors are better able to help students by affecting the systemic factors that cause student problems. The Transforming School Counseling Initiative (TSCI) is aimed at transforming the role of school counselors to connect with school counseling education reform and to focus the profession of school counseling on eliminating the achievement gap. With funding from the DeWitt Wallace Foundation, the Trust first established a new vision for the school counselor role and function and then worked with six funded "lead" counselor education programs and a number of unfunded "companion" institutions to accomplish reform in the initial preparation of school counselors. Participating university-based preparation programs committed to revise their school counseling curriculum, review admission processes to create a more diverse counselor-trainee population, redesign their practicum experiences, and strengthen their partnerships with school districts and state education agencies.

The TSCI defines school counseling as "a profession that focuses on the relations and interactions between students and their school environment with the expressed purpose of reducing the effect of environmental and institutional barriers that impede student academic success" (Education Trust, 2005). The TSCI's new vision emphasizes an explicit focus on the school counselor's role in promoting academic achievement for all students and the elimination of the achievement gap. This model calls attention to the importance of interventions at the systemic level to promote change in the capacity of educational systems to educate all students and an explicit connection between school counseling and school reform. The TSCI places more emphasis on expanding the traditional role and function of school counselors to include distributed school leadership, student advocacy, collaboration, and participation in systemic change. House and Hayes (2002) have identified ways in which TSCI school counselors should expand their traditional roles to be more actively involved in promoting academic achievement for all students. They indicate that counselors should:

- Advocate to remove systemic barriers that impede student learning and success
- Lead and participate in school improvement initiatives
- Work to improve students' access to rigorous courses and curricula
- Collaborate on the development and implementation of needed supports for learning
- Collaborate with administrators, parents, and teachers to improve school processes and climate
- Help to build a school community that institutionalizes the beliefs that all students can learn and are capable of academic success

Several new skills have been identified by the TSCI as essential to this reformed school counselor role. In addition to leadership, advocacy, teamwork, and collaboration, these new skills include use of data and the effective use of technology (House & Martin, 1998; Martin, 2002). Both the explicit skills and methods for teaching them have been refined by the lead and companion institutions. Some specific processes for data-based decision making and using data to facilitate education reform emerged from the TSCI's new vision (see Dahir & Stone, 2003). Quantitative data skills are seen as necessary for counselors to track all students' academic performance, to use student achievement data to plan interventions, and to persuasively advocate for systemic changes in school policies, procedures, and practices. School counselors need data skills in order to effectively participate in and contribute to school level, systemic reform.

FUTURE DIRECTIONS IN PUBLIC SCHOOLS' MULTICULTURALISM

While it is important for public school based-counselors and psychologists to deliver quality services for students, it is equally important for them to be involved in advocacy for all students and advocacy for systemic change. In order to be an effective advocate, counselors and psychologists need to be knowledgeable about principles of systemic reform and be able to take a systemic view of student issues and problems. Counselors and psychologists need to be culturally competent and firmly committed to actualize their beliefs that all students can learn to high standards. Counselors and psychologists also need to become integral and influential members of the school community (e.g., serving on school leadership teams, leading task groups to revise curricula, and collaborating with teachers to find better instructional approaches). Counselors and psychologists need to be aware of school policies, practices, and routines that may be limiting student opportunity and contributing to the achievement gap and be able to document their impact using school data and work to replace them. In addition to being an advocate for students, counselors and psychologists will need to find ways to empower and include students in the process of improving their own schools.

CONCLUSION

Public high schools lack some of the flexibility that independent high schools have in terms of feasible organizational and curricular approaches to enhancing individual as well as institutional cultural competence. Both types of institutions, however, are similar in that the changes in the knowledge, beliefs, skills, and comfort levels of adults who hold power in the school are essential to systemic change that will enhance the capacity of the school to serve diverse students. In independent schools, changes are needed to improve the delivery of multiculturalism within a school's climate, curriculum, and leadership structure. Assessing the cultural competency of school personnel and of the school organization, as well as active utilization of student voice in policy change must also be put into place.

In many public schools, students (and their families) have little power to alter the power dynamics and interaction patterns of school personnel that result in dysfunctional policies and instructional practices. Counselors and psychologists need to first stop enabling a dysfunctional system by correctly attributing the cause of recurring achievement problems to the system rather that to the students (and their parents). Quality professional development can enable counselors and psychologists to achieve a "systemic perspective" on achievement that will enable them to recognize the debilitating effects of culturally inappropriate school practices and to envision culturally competent school practices. Counselors and psychologist then need to advocate on behalf of students (and their parents) for more appropriate policies and effective instructional practices. Counselors and psychologists must be in the vanguard of systemic school reform and provide genuine and meaningful ways for students (and their families) to be involved in shaping the institution that is educating them.

REFERENCES

American Psychological Association. (2003). Guidelines on multicultural education, training, research, practice, and organizational change for psychologists. *American Psychologist, 58*(5), 377–402.

Anderson, S. K., MacPhee, D., & Govan, D. (2000). Infusion of multicultural issues in curricula: A student perspective. *Innovative Higher Education, 25*(1), 37–57.

Ball, S. (1987). *The micro-politics of the school.* London: Methuen.

Banks, J. A., & Banks, C.A.M. (Eds.). (1997). *Multicultural education: Issues and perspectives* (3rd ed.). Boston: Allyn & Bacon.

Bascia, N. (1996). Teacher leadership: Contending with adversity. *Canadian Journal of Education, 21*(2), 155–156.

Bassett, P. F. (2001). Taking action on diversity. *Independent School, 61*(1), 7–9.

Boatright, S. I., & Little, S. S. (2003). The introductory psychology course forms a broader human perspective. In K. Ouina & P. Bronstein (Eds.), *Teaching gender and multicultural awareness: Resources for the psychology classroom* (pp. 15–31). Washington, DC: American Psychological Association.

Borman, G., Hewes, G., Overman, L., & Brown, S. (2003). Comprehensive school reform and achievement: A meta-analysis. *Review of Educational Research, 73*(2), 125–230.

Braverman, P., & Looney, S. (1999). Tomorrow is today. *Independent School, 58*(3), 32–37.

Bryant, R. (2000). You gotta' go there, to know there. *Independent School, 60*(1), 6.

Buckheit, J. E. (1992). Organizational vices: A cautionary tale. *Independent School, 51*(2), 27–30.

Carey, J. C., & Boscardin, M. L. (2003). Improving the multicultural effectiveness of your school in the context of state standards, accountability measures, and high-stakes assessment. In P. B. Pedersen & J. C. Carey (Eds.), *Multicultural counseling in schools: A practical handbook* (2nd ed., pp. 270–289). Boston: Allyn & Bacon.

Coleman, J. S., Campbell, E. Q., Hobson, C. J., McPartland, J., Mood, A. M., Weinfeld, F. D., et al. (1966). *Equality of educational opportunity,* 2 volumes. (OE-38001; Superintendent of Documents Catalog No. FS 5.238:38001.) Washington, DC: U.S. Government Printing Office.

Dahir, C. A., & Stone, C. B. (2003). Accountability: A M.E.A.S.U.R.E. of the impact school counselors have on student achievement. *Professional School Counseling, 6*(3), 214–221.

Education Trust. (2005). *Transforming school counseling initiative (TSCI).* Retrieved February 1, 2009, from http://www2.edtrust.org/EdTrust/Transforming+School+Counseling/Counseling+tsci.htm.

Elias, M. J., Arnold, H., & Hyssey, C. S. (2003). *EQ + IQ = Best leadership practices for caring and successful schools.* Thousand Oaks, CA: Corwin Press.

Elmore, R. (2000). *Building a new structure for school leadership.* Washington, DC: Albert Shanker Institute.

Finley, M. K. (1984). Teacher and tracking at a comprehensive high school. *Sociology of Education, 57,* 233–243.

Foster, M. (1992). The politics of race: Through the eyes of African-American teachers. In K. Weiler & C. Mitchell (Eds.), *What schools can do: Critical pedagogy and practice* (pp. 177–202). Albany, NY: SUNY Press.

Gonzalez, R. (2003). Reconciling academic and ethnic identity: Mexican-American adolescents' encounter experiences. *Dissertation Abstracts International, Section A: Humanities and Social Sciences, 64*(5-A), 1525.

Green, M. F. (Ed.). (1989). *Minorities on campus: A handbook for integrating diversity.* Washington, DC: American Council on Education.

Halverson, R. (2003). Systems of practice: How leaders use artifacts to create a professional community in schools. *Educational Policy Analysis Archives, 11*(37), 1–35.

Hayes, L. D. (1996). Differential perceptions of prospective administrators and non-administrative in-service teacher graduate students on diversity paradigms. *Dissertation Abstracts International, 56*(8-A), 3085.

Helms, J. E. (1994). Racial identity in the school environment. In P. Pedersen, & J. C. Carey (Eds.), *Multicultural counseling in schools: A practical handbook* (pp. 19–37). Needham Heights, MA: Allyn & Bacon.

Holcomb-McCoy, C. (2005). Ethnic identity development in early adolescence: Implications and recommendations. *Professional School Counseling, 9*(2), 120–127.

House, R. M., & Hayes, R. L. (2002). School counselors: Becoming key players in school reform. *Professional School Counseling, 5*(4), 186–191.

House, R. M., & Martin, P. J. (1998). Advocating for better futures for all students: A new vision for school counselors. *Education, 119,* 284–92.

Jay, M. (2003). Critical race theory, multicultural education, and the hidden curriculum of hegemony. *Multicultural Perspectives, 5*(4), 3–9.

Joselowsky, F. (2007). Youth engagement, high school reform, and improved learning outcomes: Building systemic approaches for youth engagement. *NASSP Bulletin, 91,* 257–276.

Kaufman, I. (2003). Directing diversity. *Independent School, 62*(4), 22–27.

Kozol, J. (2005). *The shame of the nation: The restoration of apartheid schooling in America.* New York: Crown Publishing.

Kuriloff, P., & Reichert, M. C. (2003). Boys of class, boys of color: Negotiating the academic and social geography of an elite independent school. *Journal of Social Issues, 59*(4), 751–769.

Martin, P. J. (2002). Transforming school counseling: A national perspective. *Theory Into Practice, 41,* 148–153.

McNulty, R. J., & Quaglia, R. J. (2007). Rigor, relevance and relationships: Three passwords that unlock the door for engaged high school students to learn at appropriate levels. *The School Administrator, 64,* 18–24.

Morelli, P. T., & Spencer, M. S. (2000). Use and support of multicultural and anti-racist education: Research-informed interdisciplinary social work practice. *Social Work, 45*(2), 166–175.

Moses, Y. T. (1989). *Black women in academe: Issues and strategies.* Washington, DC: Association of American Colleges, Project on the Status and Education of Women.

Murname, R., Willet, J., Braatz, M. J., & Duhaldeborde, Y. (2001). Do different dimensions of male high school students' skills predict labor market success a decade later? Evidence from the NLSY. *Economics of Education Review, 20,* 311–320.

Nichols, J. C. (2003). Changing what is taught: Hearing the voices of the underrepresented. *Innovative Higher Education, 27*(3), 195–208.

O'Day, J. (2004). Complexity, accountability, and school improvement. In S. H. Fuhrman & R. Elmore (Eds.), *Redesigning accountability systems for education* (pp. 15–46). New York: Teachers College Press.

Orem, D. (2002). Leaders: On leadership. *Independent School, 62*(1), 40–46.

Ortiz, F. I. (1982). *Career patterns in education: Women, men, and minorities in public school administration.* New York: Praeger.

Rothstein, R. (2004). *Class and schools: Using social, economic, and educational reforms to close the black-white achievement gap.* New York: Teachers College Press.

Roysircar, G. (2006). A theoretical and practice framework for universal school-based prevention. In R. Toporek, L. H. Gerstein, N. A., Fouad, G. Roysircar, & T. Israel (Eds.), *Handbook for social justice in counseling psychology* (pp. 130–145). Thousand Oaks, CA: Sage.

Roysircar, G., Arredondo, P., Fuertes, J., Ponterotto, J., & Toporek, R. (2003). *Multicultural counseling competencies 2003.* Alexandria, VA: Association for Multicultural Counseling and Development.

Roysircar-Sodowsky, G. & Frey, L. L. (2003). Children of immigrants: Their worldviews value conflicts. In P. Pedersen & J. C. Carey (Eds.), *Multicultural counseling in schools: A practical handbook* (pp. 61–83). Boston, MA: Allyn and Bacon.

Sciarra, D. (2001). School counseling in a multicultural society. In J. G. Ponterotto, J. M. Casas, L. A. Suzuki, & C. M. Alexander (Eds.), *Handbook of multicultural counseling* (2nd ed., pp. 701–728). Thousand Oaks, CA: SAGE.

Siskin, L. S. (1994). *Realms of knowledge: Academic departments in secondary schools.* Philadelphia, PA: Falmer.

Sleeter, C. E., & Grant, C. A. (1996). *Multicultural education as social activism.* Albany: State University of New York Press.

Smith, G. P. (2004). Desegregation and resegregation after Brown: Implications for multiculultural teacher education. *Multicultural Perspectives, 64*(4), 26–32.

Snyder, T. D., Dillow, S. A., & Hoffman, C. M. (2007). Digest of Education Statistics, 2006. Washington, DC: National Center for Education Statistics, U.S. Department of Education.

Tatum, B. D. (1999). *"Why are all the black kids sitting together in the cafeteria?" and other conversations about race.* New York: Basic Books.

Toporek, R. L., Gerstein, L. H., Fouad, N. A., Roysircar, G., & Israel, T. (Eds.). (2006). *Handbook for social justice in counseling psychology: Leadership, vision, and action.* Thousand Oaks, CA: Sage.

U.S. Census Bureau. (2000). *Earnings by occupation and education.* Washington, DC: Author.

Van Buren, E. (2005). School experiences among African American and Latino adolescents: Effects on ethnic and school adjustment. *Dissertation Abstracts International, Section B: The Sciences and Engineering, 65*(8-B), 4308.

Whitehead, K. A., & Wittig, M. A. (2004). Discursive management of resistance to a multicultural education programme. *Qualitative Research in Psychology, 1*(4), 267–286.

Willkinson, R. B. (2004). The role of parental and peer attachment in on psychological health and self esteem of adolescents. *Journal of Youth and Adolescence, 33*(6), 479–493.

CHAPTER 7

Experiences of Educators and Students in Integrative Diversity Training

*Kathleen A. Malloy, James E. Dobbins, Julie L. Williams,
Jeffery B. Allen, and Janeece R. Warfield*

According to the American Psychological Association's Code of Ethics (American Psychological Association [APA], 2002) psychologists are committed to using psychological knowledge and practice to improve the condition of individuals, organizations, and society, and to working to assure that all persons are offered equal access to high quality psychological services. There are forces within our broader culture that impede that access, including an unequal distribution of power and privilege, as well as the ongoing institutional oppression of marginalized groups. Psychology as a profession is in a position to challenge these forces and act as powerful agents of change on both individual and societal levels. Much change must start with the ways in which we train future psychologists. The recognition of the importance of training psychologists to be agents of change has required a major shift within the field. The impact of this shift has been so pervasive that it has led some scholars to conclude that it represents a "fourth force," along with humanistic, psychodynamic and behavioral schools of thought, in understanding how psychologists conceptualize personality and behavior (Pedersen, 1991). Essentially, diversity training adds a focus on context, ranging from individual context through cultural and political context, as an important variable that must be explored when attempting to understand how individuals and the external world interact.

Another paradigm shift that has changed the way in which we train future practitioners is the development of professional competencies that define training models and best practices in the psychology profession (Council of Chairs of Training Councils [CCTC], 2007; National Council of Schools and Programs of Professional Psychology, 2007). Core competencies that should guide training were developed as early as 1992 (Peterson et al., 1992). More recently, competencies were articulated at a joint conference sponsored by multiple organizations committed to training (Kaslow et al., 2004) and are being further developed by training councils that espouse various models of training, including, but not limited to, scientist-practitioner and practitioner-scholar models (CCTC, 2007; NCSPP, 2007). While there are some differences in the products being advanced by various groups, all have agreed that working with diverse individuals is one of the areas of competence that should be required of aspiring psychologists. The National Council of Schools and Programs of Professional Psychology (NCSPP) defined competence in diversity as requiring the ability to identify and understand issues of individual and cultural difference, as well as issues of power, privilege and oppression, and how these issues inform and influence all professional functions and activities, including assessment, conceptualization, intervention, consultation and evaluation approaches (NCSPP, 2002).

Another commonality among the various bodies addressing competencies is the recognized need to define competence in terms of the dimensions of knowledge, skills and attitudes (KSA) across critical developmental levels of training. The elaboration of these competencies has moved the educational taxonomy of knowledge, skills and attitudes (Bloom, 1956) to an operational standard never before realized in the sixty years of clinical psychology training and practice.

The first step in any training context is making clear the model within which that training is grounded. Thus, the first thing that we will do is describe the model that informs our approach to diversity training. We will then discuss ways in which the model informs student training, especially regarding the attitudes, knowledge, and skills necessary to develop competence in working with diverse individuals and communities. Next, we will address the challenges for instructors and organizations in providing that training. Finally, we describe desired outcomes of diversity training.

TRAINING FROM A DIVERSITY INTEGRATION MODEL

Integrative diversity is the term we are using to represent the model underlying our approach to diversity training. Underlying this model is an acceptance of the centrality of social responsibility in providing psychological services. The model focuses specifically on the interaction of several variables, namely, social construction, privilege/power/oppression, and cultural context. In addition, an understanding of the existence and interaction of multiple identities within individuals plays a central role.

Social Responsibility

A socially responsible approach to professional psychology accepts that the profession can be justified only if it meets the fundamental needs of the larger society (Peterson, Peterson, Abrams, & Stricker, 2006). It implies a commitment to the responsible use of and education about power, privilege and oppression on individual, professional, and sociopolitical levels. As stated by Peterson et al. (2006), professional psychology "values the sharing of power, equal access to opportunity, social justice, affirmation of differences and the prevention of marginalization as primary goals" (p. 32).

Interactions of Social Construction, Power/Privilege/ Oppression, and Cultural Context in the Formation of Identity

We take a postmodern, social constructionist approach to understanding diversity. A basic tenet of this approach is that the ways in which individuals experience identity variables such as race, gender, sexual orientation, age, disability, spirituality, and class are socially defined. For example, while the concept of race as a biological category has been discussed and challenged by many scholars, the fact remains that mainstream culture defines race as a primary component of identity (Smedley & Smedley, 2005). Many of the experiences that individuals have as a result of being a member of a specific racial group are not biologically defined, but rather are the result of how members of racial groups are expected to be within the cultural contexts within which those individuals live.

Part of the social definition of identity variables includes assigning differentiated levels of power and unearned privilege to various identities. Individuals from historically marginalized social groups (e.g., people of color, women, gays and lesbians, the poor, those with disabilities, etc.) are assigned less socially endorsed power and privilege, while those in more socially valued positions are assigned more. Though the power and privilege that one possesses, along with the oppression that results when power and privilege are not recognized and confronted, have a real impact on individuals' lived experiences, these qualities are often not named and are frequently not visible to those who possess them.

Cultural context includes the environmental forces and elements that shape and direct our motives, reactions and attitudes. It includes family, friends and community, as well as larger social and political entities. It is the external that interacts with the internal with sufficient potential to change our internal definitions, affective responses, coping behaviors, and overall worldview. Social context helps to organize our sense of well-being and of our "place" in the world. In the study and practice of psychology and diversity, cultural context is a dynamic variable that has led some scholars to assert that it is a force that operates consciously and subliminally in the lives of both the client and the clinician (Pedersen, 1991). Cultural context is inextricably related to identity, as it helps one to judge the meaning of one's function and roles in a given social setting. Thus, as context changes, our understanding of our own identities, as well as our way of being in the world, may also change. We assert that it is essential to be aware of and to help students appreciate the impact of cultural context in understanding both themselves and individuals whose context may vary from their own.

The interaction of social construction, power/privilege/oppression, and cultural context in the formation of identity simply means that each construct has a meaningful and reciprocal impact on each of the other constructs. Therefore, both cultural context and the allocation of power and privilege will impact how identity is socially constructed, just as social construction will affect the context within which individuals find themselves and the ways in which power and privilege are allocated. In addition, social context will affect the allocation and use of power and privilege, and the use of power and privilege will impact an individual's social context. Adding to the complexity of this model is the fact that each individual is more than one identity.

The Role of Multiple Identities in the Integrative Diversity Model

Competence in working with diverse individuals and communities encompasses an understanding that all individuals, including therapists and clients, have multiple identities and that those identities are interactive, dynamic, and fluid (Dobbins & Malloy, 2007; Malloy, 2008). Identities include, but are not limited to, age, ability, ethnicity, gender, language, national origin, race, religion, spirituality, sexual orientation and social economic status (NCSPP, 2007). Of the multiple identities possessed by each individual, some identities will carry more privilege while others will experience more oppression. For example, a white woman will be privileged based on her race, but will be less privileged based on her gender. Also, within individuals' lives and experiences, different identity variables will be more or less salient at different times in their lives and within different contexts. For example, an African American woman may find that when she was a student in her primarily African American high school, her gender had more impact on her every day life than her race. However, when she moved on to a predominantly white university, her race became more salient. At the same time, her race and her gender are interactive, meaning that her experience of being a woman is strongly impacted by her race and her race by her gender, so that even when her gender is most salient, she experiences being an African American woman, not a woman with no race. In other words, being a woman never occurs in a vacuum that is void of other identity variables.

Now let's consider another example: consider an individual who is an able-bodied, white, agnostic man for whom spirituality is not important. He is gay and currently of a low socioeconomic status. Each of these identities has a socially constructed meaning that impacts how he is perceived by others and, frequently, how he perceives himself. The construction of each identity is impacted by the ways in which that identity is given unearned privilege and power, which in turn determines the ways in which the individual may experience oppression or, perhaps, be in a position to oppress others. Thus, when race, gender and physical ability are more salient, he is in a more privileged position, but when sexual orientation and economic status are more salient, he is in a less privileged position. He may, either consciously or unconsciously, choose to oppress women, people of color, and/or individuals with disabilities while experiencing oppression from heterosexual and middle-class people. The context within which he finds himself at any given time impacts which identity is more salient for him. The interaction of his various identities also impacts how each individual identity is experienced, so that, for example, even when his identity as gay is salient, his experience of being gay will always be informed by the fact that he is white. His experience of being gay will differ from that of gay men of color in that he will not face the interaction of both heterosexism and racism.

CLASS PROCESS, CONTENT, AND ORGANIZATION: ATTITUDES, KNOWLEDGE, AND SKILLS

While the diversity competency is complex, it is also teachable. As noted earlier, it is commonly accepted that training in diversity requires addressing attitudes, knowledge, and skills (CCTC, 2007; NCSPP, 2007; Sue, Arredondo, & McDavis, 1992). In developing diversity competence, exploring attitudes begins with widening students' awareness of their own understanding of the world and how it may differ from others' understanding. Becoming aware of and confronting one's own attitudes is so fundamental that it forms the foundation of all successive stages and levels of cultural competency. As a result, we believe that it is the first element of instruction to be addressed. Without first expanding students' awareness of issues like power, privilege and oppression and their impact on the beliefs and attitudes that they bring to their training, they will not be able to openly explore experiences and cultures different than their own, to understand the role of social construction in the everyday lives of individuals, or to critically examine the ways in which cultural biases have impacted the knowledge base underlying the field of clinical psychology. Nor will they be able to build on that knowledge base to develop the skills necessary to provide culturally competent clinical services. Thus, the model that we are proposing as most effective begins by facilitating an awareness of the socially constructed nature of identity and the role of unearned privilege, power, and oppression related to that identity, as well as the impact of individuals' social context on their experiences and their understanding of their own identities. Helping students to apply that awareness to their own experience, beliefs, and understanding of self will stimulate and help to maintain attitudinal formation and change, as well as help them to better understand the experiences of diverse individuals. The next step is to help students to develop a solid knowledge base in diversity content and process, which can allow them to develop and apply the skills necessary to work competently with diverse individuals and communities. However, this process should not be seen as strictly linear. The process of challenging attitudes is never ending; thus, while the concept of attitudes is addressed as a separate construct here and is the first to be addressed in training, attitude formation is an ongoing process that should be embedded throughout training and in conjunction with the development of a knowledge base and intervention skill set. Similarly, knowledge acquisition can spur ongoing awareness and attitude exploration, as well as ongoing skill development. As skills develop, students will be confronted with the ever present need to address their own attitudes and biases, as well as the need to gather additional knowledge. Below, some content and methods for training regarding attitudes, knowledge and skills will be discussed.

AWARENESS AND ATTITUDINAL CHANGE

Probably no areas of professional training are more challenging than training geared toward attitude development and change. This part of our discussion will present ways that attitudinal training is linked to attitude definitions, illustrate how teaching methodologies are linked to issues of safety and process in diversity attitudes training, and how teaching methods can be used to develop and maintain this most fundamental part of diversity training.

Before discussing how to integrate attitudinal change into diversity education, we will first establish a working definition of "attitudes." Attitude has been defined by Eagly and Chaikin (1993) as a "psychological tendency that is expressed by evaluating a particular entity with some degree of favor or disfavor" (p. 1). Attitudes inform and interact with our affects, beliefs, and behaviors and consequently impact learning; positive attitudes can enhance learning experiences while negative attitudes can impede learning experiences. Finally, while attitudes certainly generate beliefs that are not necessarily forgotten, attitudes are not considered stable in that they can be changed or challenged when one is presented with new information (Albarracin, Johnson, Zanna, & Kumkale, 2005).

When students enter training programs they do so with a lifetime of attitudes and beliefs that will inform their learning, impact their acquisition of knowledge and ultimately shape future professional work. Those attitudes and beliefs were generally developed in a society that often renders invisible the ways in which various groups of people are disempowered while others are privileged, and the resulting impact on human experience. Consequently, those who choose to become psychologists, thus committing to working with individuals and communities that often differ from themselves in significant ways, must be challenged to not only identify their attitudes, but also to consider how those attitudes may include biases and blind spots that prevent them from truly understanding others and may lead them to, at least, offer less effective services and, at worst, cause harm to those with whom they work. Once they are aware of the attitudes that they are bringing to their work, it is their responsibility to modify those attitudes in ways that allow them to best understand the experiences of others.

The Process of Attitudinal Change

Depending on the nature of personal values that a student brings to diversity training, this process can be experienced as a challenge to one's sense of self that quickly leads to resistance in students. Exploring issues surrounding diversity requires the ability to participate in difficult discussions (Sanchez-Hucles & Jones, 2005; Young, 2003). In these discussions, students are asked to share their experiences and beliefs, and to express their own curiosity, thus acknowledging their own biases and limited understanding of the experiences of diverse people. As a result, they risk vulnerability, discomfort, and, at times, even hostility (Sanchez-Hucles & Jones, 2005). They are asked to break a cultural "code of silence" that reflects society's denial of the reality of an unequal distribution of power and opportunity that results in the oppression of marginalized groups of people (e.g., sexism, racism, ableism) and of the privilege experienced by members of socially empowered groups (e.g., whites, males, heterosexuals, etc.) (Young, 2003). For example, when asked to share their thoughts on their experiences with diversity training one student stated, "I knew a lot less than I thought I did when I first came in. You know, I'm like, 'Oh, I'm not prejudiced,' or 'You know, I get diversity, I understand these issues and those issues,' I had no clue. I really had no clue and I didn't have any clue about my power and privilege and how it affected me and other people."

Understandably, such discussion can result in a variety of responses. Another student described this experience: "It was really overwhelming ... Everyday I left that class physically and emotionally just exhausted." At times, students may feel excited by the challenge and the personal learning and growth that are occurring. On the other hand, difficult discussions often trigger feelings of anger, incompetence, fear, and even dread (Sue, Arredondo, & McDavis, 1992). Natural responses to such reactions can include emotional withdrawal, intellectualization, and highly emotional responding. Jackson (1999) views those responses as forms of resistance that operate to create silence, passivity, avoidance and anger as ways of maintaining social distance in the classroom. Such resistance is a normal part of the process of diversity training that results from requiring students to challenge their own previously unexplored beliefs and values. If not handled well, such discussions can lead students to remain emotionally withdrawn and angry. The first step in assuring that difficult discussions are productive is to establish a classroom climate that feels safe to the students and allows them to take the risks necessary to increase their own understanding of both their own beliefs and experiences and those of others.

Creating a Safe Space for Diversity Training

It is vital that a climate of respect is developed in the classroom in order for students to feel safe in exploring what is often very difficult material and to allow productive diversity-related discussions to occur (Buckley, Foldy, & Rivard, 2007). However, it should be emphasized that safety does not guarantee comfort. There is nothing easy or comfortable about a diversity dialogue. As a result, students will be expected to participate in discussions that may cause them discomfort. They should not, however, fear for their safety. Helping students understand the difference between "unsafe' and "uncomfortable" can help them to remain involved in difficult discussions instead of resorting to silence or directing their anger and frustration at others in the class and/or the instructor.

The primary "rule" that students seem to find helpful in maintaining a safe climate asks that everyone in the class maintains an awareness of the difference between "impact" and "intent." When having difficult dialogues, individuals sometimes say things that are not meant to be harmful to others, but which may indeed be heard as insensitive or hurtful. Thus, the impact is that some in the class may feel hurt, even though the intent was to not to cause harm, but rather the result of naiveté or an attempt to expand understanding. In a safe environment the person being impacted by the statement should feel free to express their feelings, while understanding that no harm was meant. The speaker has the responsibility to listen and to strive to understand how her or his comment could have been taken as offensive, but should feel safe in the understanding that others realize that she/he did not mean to offend or hurt anyone. Discussion should continue until both parties understand the other's intent and/or reactions. It is the role of the instructor to assure that, indeed, the speaker meant no harm. If harm was seemingly intentional, the instructor must intervene to hold the speaker accountable and to minimize negative impact on the other person(s) and the class process as a whole.

Students should be encouraged to use communication strategies that they have discussed in other classes, such as active listening and "I statements." They should be encouraged to accept the experiences of others as valid for that person, even when they would have interpreted what happened or responded to the event in different ways. Arguing with someone in a way that suggests that his/her response is incorrect serves to invalidate the individual reporting the experience and to stop conversation. For example, if a student shared an incident in which someone had whistled at her on the street and stated that she felt it to be demeaning and sexist, it would invalidate her experience if classmates argued that she should feel complimented. It is important to emphasize that there is no right or wrong way for individuals to react to their experiences. Rather, what is most productive is to strive to understand the reactions of others, especially when they differ from one's own.

Students must also be encouraged to accept their own reactions as theirs and not necessarily a "correct" reaction to what another has said. Accepting different ways in which individuals express emotions is particularly important. Within some cultures animated expression of emotion is acceptable, while in others it is seen as attacking or frightening. In other cultures either emotions are not to be expressed or are to be expressed in a measured, sometimes intellectual manner; this style of communicating emotion can lead others to believe that the speaker is detached from the issue being discussed. Maintaining an awareness of differences in styles of communicating emotion will both allow students to express strong emotion in the way that they are accustomed and help them to hear each other's emotions in the way they are intended. Remarked one student, "I think when I started to get some insight into what kinds of emotions the other people were having. . . . Once I could see past my emotions and not to get over there, that was when I was able to really start actually listening and making sense."

Silence as a form of communication must also be explored. Students who choose not to participate in class discussion should understand the impact of silence. They should understand that their silence carries meaning and that, without clarification, that meaning may be misinterpreted. For example, if each time racism is being discussed a student is silent the class may interpret that silence as the student not caring about the impact of racism or, even more damaging, that the student does not see the information and personal experiences being shared as valid. Reality may be that the silent student is listening intently and feeling such a range of emotion regarding what is being said that she or he feels overwhelmed. Much misinterpretation can be avoided if the silent student either pushes her/himself to share her or his feelings or, at least, briefly explains the reasons for her or his silence.

Finally, it is important to remember that the classroom is a microcosm of the larger society. As a result, the same socially constructed reality will be present. Students will have preconceived ideas about the ways in which various individuals "should" be based on the ways in which their multiple identities have been defined. Students will bring into the classroom the same levels of power and unearned privilege that they experience in their lives in general; they will also bring with them the results of oppression that they have endured. Instructors should be prepared to

handle the resulting dynamics that occur and to help students to understand the ways in which their beliefs and behaviors are not indicators of
negative intent, but rather have been shaped by their own social context.
The instructor can also help students to understand their own defenses
and how those defenses serve to protect individuals from feared harm,
as well as how they can inhibit group process and individual growth. By
establishing a safe, non-blaming, and empowering classroom climate, students can be challenged to become aware of their own individual processes, as well as the overall class process, and move toward awareness
and attitudinal change.

Teaching Strategies to Enhance Awareness and Attitude Exploration and Development

It is vital to develop course syllabi that clearly articulate the course
goals, objectives, and expectations to which students will be held. Objectives should address the need for students to be active participants in the
class process. An example of such an objective would be "finding and
demonstrating your voice in the diversity dialogue as evidenced by contributions made in class discussions and personal reflection journals."
Given the differences between classes designed to impact attitudes and
more traditional classes, it is especially important to include a specific ex-
planation concerning how progress will be measured and how grades will
be assigned.

During the first class, ground rules should be discussed and collaboratively agreed upon by students and instructors prior to the initiation of
other substantive discussions. They can be referred to as needed throughout training in order to maintain a climate that is conducive to exploration
and growth. Once ground rules have been established, students should be
encouraged to share their expectations of the class, including things they
may have heard about the class from students who have already taken it.
This helps the instructor(s) to begin to understand the level of openness or
defensiveness present in the class. Planning an activity that allows students
to understand what is expected of them in the class can be helpful. Using an
activity that encourages discussion but allows students to disclose only at a
level that they feel comfortable is a good way to decrease anxiety, increase
comfort and trust, and introduce students to the process of the class.

As attitudes become identified and challenged, emotions get activated
and related protective behaviors get exhibited. Anger, frustration, irrita-
tion and fear are common emotional reactions observed among students.
Reactions can also include such behaviors as raised voices, nervous laugh-
ter, or silence. An encouraging message that the instructor may need to
repeat is that students not only can tolerate this experience, but if they
actively participate they will benefit from it. This message should be used
when regression to unproductive ways of dealing with difficult dialogues

are evident. Students can be encouraged to name emotions they are experiencing and connect those emotions to related topics and/or process moments and, ultimately, to attitudes. They can also be reminded of the importance of diversity training, the goals of the class, and the rules they developed to assure safety in the class. For instructors it is important to remember that these incidents of overt reactance are potentially powerful teachable moments. "I felt really pushed at first" said one student, "and really, like, poked at and attacked and unhappy and as I moved forward it became less about, you know, my emotions and how I was feeling and more about learning what I needed to learn in order to appreciate differences and work with people who come from various backgrounds." Emotions and behaviors demonstrated should be acknowledged, validated immediately and normalized whenever appropriate. Students should not be "rescued"; rather, they should be challenged to bring their feelings and struggles to the class for discussion and feedback. Most importantly, students should be charged with the expectation that they will stay actively involved in the discussion.

Class assignments should include readings introducing the constructs of power, privilege and oppression. Class exercises can afford students opportunities to connect these concepts to their own lives, especially in identifying ways in which they are privileged and/or oppressed. One exercise, the Diversity Walk, begins with students standing on one side of the room. The instructor calls out an identity (e.g., man, African American, gay or lesbian, grew up poor, Christian) and asks students who identify with that identity to move to the opposite side of the room. Those students are then asked to list all of the things that they never want to hear again about that identity. Other students are to listen and, when the group that is speaking is finished, reflect back what they have heard. This exercise is powerful for a number of reasons. Since each student generally walks to the other side of the room more than one time, the existence of multiple identities is highlighted. Also highlighted is the fact that all students at one point are in both the more privileged and the more oppressed groups. It also allows the students in the more privileged groups to hear the emotions expressed by the more oppressed groups and allows the more oppressed groups to feel heard. The desired outcome of this exercise is increasing students' appreciation of their multiple identities and their awareness of long-held attitudes that informed their life experiences as both privileged and oppressed persons.

Another teaching method that can be highly effective is having students complete weekly reflection journals, the contents of which are not shared with the other members of the class unless the writer chooses to do so. The journal encourages students to continue processing their own feelings and reactions outside of class. It also allows a mechanism for one-on-one discussions with and feedback from the instructors. Throughout the course, students can also be assigned developmentally staged self-exploration questions that are related to class content and reviewed for inclusion of the constructs of power, privilege and oppression and attitude formation, as well as stereotypes, beliefs and prejudices held. Finally, students might be asked to engage in a biographical life review activity that encompasses family history and genealogy. The purpose of this assignment is to help students to identify beliefs held by their families that have impacted their own beliefs and worldviews.

As students become acclimated to the process of self-exploration and diversity discussions, their attitudes and those of others in the class become more clearly illuminated. At this stage in the process, students can be challenged to explore the impact of their attitudes on others and to make changes where warranted. As a consequence of coming to understand the gravity and pervasiveness of oppression, students often begin to feel guilty, overwhelmed and even hopeless, sometimes resulting in feelings of inertia. At this point, they should be encouraged to begin setting personal growth goals. They should also be introduced to the concept of becoming an ally to members of oppressed groups (Kivel, 1996). The term *ally* can be defined in reading materials and depicted in selected videos. Instructors can invite speakers to class who can authentically discuss the lived experience of oppressed individuals and can impress on students the need for allies in challenging their oppression. Immersion experiences may also be helpful.

Immersion experiences are experiences that allow students to enter into situations that allow them to experience the realities of individuals different from themselves. The experience involves students in the community and assures that they have the opportunity to interact and engage with others who are members of marginalized groups. For example, students may attend cultural events, visit a gay/lesbian/bisexual center, or experience everyday events with a person with a disability. In arranging immersion experiences it is important to assure that the student is prepared to respectfully enter new situations and that the community the student is entering is welcoming. It is highly recommended that an instructor or another individual who is comfortable in the community being visited accompany students to facilitate discussion and to process the experience with the students. In processing the experience, students should be encouraged to consider ways in which they can become allies to those that they visited. Students' responses to these experiences are often very powerful as they provide an opportunity for them to experience "real world" interactions and to understand the experiences of others different from themselves in a way that is not possible in the classroom.

KNOWLEDGE

As students become aware of the impact of power, privilege, and oppression on both themselves and others and of the attitudes and biases that they bring to diversity training, they are able to explore diversity-related knowledge with their minds open to understanding the experiences of diverse individuals and communities. As noted above, the focus on attitudes, knowledge, and skills is not a linear process. As a result, it is critical to be aware of how some of the same reactions, including defensiveness, can be triggered as knowledge is explored. The instructor should continue to monitor for attitudinal variables that impact learning and to address them as they arise.

The knowledge base that underlies an understanding of diverse individuals and communities is very broad. At this point in training, the acquisition of knowledge has actually already begun, as knowledge of variables such as power, privilege, and oppression are needed to help stimulate the attitudinal awareness and change that was discussed above. However, acquisition of knowledge as a primary objective begins only after students have developed attitudes that allow them to view much of what they are learning about psychology from a diversity-sensitive perspective. They can then critically examine such issues as the history of psychology; theories of personality, psychopathology, diagnosis and intervention; ethical decision making; the ways in which diverse individuals express distress; the impact of prejudice and stereotyping on individual experience; and potential bias in research, including evidence-based treatments, as it applies to diverse individuals and communities. For example, they can begin to explore the concept of diagnosis while considering the impact of power, privilege, and oppression on both client presentation and on the diagnostic system being used. They can be challenged to include social context in their understanding of individual behavior that leads to their diagnoses, as well as the socially constructed nature of the diagnostic system. Students should also learn how to incorporate both their ability to critically explore and their developing knowledge base into all of the competencies that they are developing as emerging clinical psychologists, including competencies that underlie their work not only in intervention and assessment, but also in consultation, education, management, supervision, and research (NCSPP, 2007).

In addition to critically exploring broad constructs within psychology, they should learn about how specific identities can impact individual experiences. Again, it is important to recognize the existence of multiple identities within individuals as students learn about diverse groups. One suggested way of approaching such learning is to take a "funneling" approach. In using this approach, the instructors first explore issues of spirituality and religion with students. Next, issues of race and ethnicity are explored, while incorporating what has been learned about spirituality and religion. After that, the impact of gender on individual experience is explored, incorporating an understanding of how religion/spirituality and race/ethnicity impact individuals' experiences of their gender. Next, sexual orientation is introduced, again incorporating how the lived experience of one's sexual orientation may be impacted by that individual's spirituality/religion, race/ethnicity, and gender. This process continues, adding socioeconomic status, disability status, and age into the mix. The fluid nature of identity is emphasized throughout the discussion.

Throughout the learning process, it is vital that students are cautioned against using the knowledge they are gaining to simply stereotype individuals in different ways. Rather, the knowledge they are gaining should help them to expand the hypotheses they develop in attempting to understand the experiences and resulting worldviews of diverse individuals. Like all hypotheses, some will prove relevant while others will not when tested in any given situation, with any given individual. A goal of diversity training is to help students to expand the possible hypotheses that they bring to any situation to include an array of variables that they may not have considered when viewing the client based on their own understanding of the world, an understanding that developed as a result of their own experiences and identities.

As instructors move their focus from primarily awareness and attitude change to development of a knowledge base, classroom technique may vary. As in addressing awareness and attitudes, discussions regarding relevant readings can be very helpful. At this point, however, additional emphasis can be placed on exploring the content of the readings, while continuing to maintain an awareness of process variables. Journaling can be helpful, but again more focus on critical discussions of important points emerging from the readings can be added. Reaction papers that require that they integrate what they are learning can be helpful. Videos that portray the experiences of those being studied can help students to apply what they are learning to personal experiences. An assignment that the authors have found to be particularly useful is having students write papers and present on specific cultures. In their work students are required to address how the experiences of individuals possessing the various identities addressed during the funneling process, including spirituality, ethnicity, gender, economic status, disability, sexual orientation, and age, are impacted by the ways in which the culture they are researching socially constructs those identities. It is not expected that students will be able to learn all there is to know about all cultures; that is not realistic. Rather, the goal of the assignment is to allow students the opportunity to immerse themselves in the knowledge base related to one specific culture so that they can have the experience of understanding the uniqueness and complexity of that culture. Hopefully, that process will highlight for them the importance of exploring each individual's unique cultural experiences and will give them the experience of having used existing literature to help them develop culture-specific knowledge that will help them to better understand diverse individuals and communities.

SKILLS

A vital step in diversity training is to work with students to translate their awareness, attitudinal growth, and knowledge base into the development of the skills needed to work competently with diverse individuals and communities. A student stated, "I think some of the biggest impact has really come from working with diverse clients and being able to bring that back to class. That really gave me some really solid real-life ideas about how it was to really have such a different experience from my clients and how that was going to impact our interaction." There are many ways in which classroom experiences can be designed to prepare students to accomplish this task. Instructors can present case conceptualizations and treatment plans that incorporate awareness of and knowledge about diversity issues, eventually requiring students to do the same. Role plays can be used to allow students to both observe competent interventions and to practice those interventions themselves in a supportive environment where they can receive feedback designed to improve their skills. For example, a role play could be used to help students develop skills in discussing issues such as race, gender, disability, and sexual orientation in initial sessions with clients. Other techniques that can help students to develop skills include watching videos of experts in the field addressing diversity variables in sessions (e.g., some of the APA psychotherapy series) and viewing actual therapy sessions performed by skilled therapists either live or on video. Instructors can use vignettes to help students understand the impact of diversity variables in providing various types of professional service, including therapy, assessment, supervision, consultation, management, education, and research.

While work in the classroom can begin to address skill development, without supervised practice diversity training will remain incomplete. Didactic trainings and case presentations within clinical settings can further diversity training, but the primary vehicle for helping students to strengthen skills in providing diversity-sensitive services is clinical supervision. It is the supervisors' responsibility to work with students to translate their awareness and knowledge into action (Porter, 1996). Supervisors must indicate both the willingness and the competency to discuss diversity issues early in the supervisory process (Constantine, 1998; Toporek, Ortega-Villalobos, & Pope-Davis, 2004). Part of their role as supervisors is to model for students how to analyze the impact of power, privilege, and oppression on clients, on the student, and on the supervisor. They should aid students in understanding how socially constructed roles and expectations impact clients, including the importance of understanding client context when doing case conceptualization and diagnosis. Supervisors should also help students to maintain an awareness of the multiple identities possessed by each client and how those identities interact with one another and with the context within which the client lives. They should be open to exploring both their own and their students' awareness and attitudes and how they affect work with diverse individuals and communities. Supervisors should also emphasize the need to turn to the literature for help in understanding diversity variables as they are presented by individual clients.

There are a number of supervision techniques that can help to facilitate a supervisee's personal growth and understanding of diverse populations, including modeling by the supervisor; initiating discussions related to diversity issues; discussing how cultural considerations can be integrated throughout the trainees work, including during intake, assessment, and intervention; and assuring that diversity issues are included in all case presentations, both in supervision and in agency staffings and case presentations. It is critical that supervisors use live observation or videotaped sessions with diverse clients so that they can observe and address with the student possible subtle, often unconscious, use of stereotypes and/or traditional role expectations on the part of the student. Supervisors should also help students to be aware of the ways in which unequal power and privilege can emerge and impact the relationship between the student and the client (Constantine, 2001; Porter, 1996).

INSTRUCTOR PREPARATION FOR FACILITATING DIVERSITY TRAINING

Because of the attitudinal issues that are central in diversity training, the interactions between students and instructors have more of a relational focus than is generally present in other types of classes. Instructors in diversity classes often serve as mediators, group facilitators, neutral observers, observer-participants, expert-learners, emotional support specialists, and administrators. In order for instructors to develop the competence and confidence necessary to teach diversity classes and to earn the trust of their students, they must be willing to undertake the same tasks that are being asked of the students. In other words, instructors must be willing to participate in vigorous self-appraisal prior to expecting a similar process from students. Before entering the multicultural classroom, instructors must take stock of weaknesses or blind spots within their own knowledge base, skill set, or attitudinal biases. Perhaps most critically, they must be willing to remain open to the divergent perspectives and phenomenological experiences of others, including colleagues and students. While most instructors approach their work with openness and a valuing of egalitarianism, in order to competently guide their students through diversity training, they must also acknowledge that they, too, are capable of unknowing complicity in institutional racism and cultural insensitivity. In order to do this, they must closely examine their own experience of power and privilege. Given the foundational role these concepts play in understanding the experiences of marginalized individuals, instructors must engage in personal exploration of how they have enjoyed the benefits of unearned power and privilege. Understanding ways in which one possesses or may have exploited societal power is as difficult and ongoing a process for instructors as it is for students. By watching instructors struggle with understanding their own attitudes, power, and privilege, students will be provided appropriate role modeling for the difficult self-examination that is part of ongoing growth toward cultural competence. Additionally, by performing the difficult work of examining their own experience of awareness and attitudinal change, instructors will better appreciate the time and psychological energy required of students attempting to make their own attitudinal shifts in these domains. Perhaps most importantly, if instructors fail to take on this difficult task for themselves, they may be unprepared to deal with the psychologically-charged experiences, reactions, and commentary from students who, as members of disempowered groups, have experienced, or are experiencing, oppression.

ORGANIZATIONAL SUPPORT FOR DIVERSITY TRAINING

A commitment to social responsibility and training students to work competently with diverse individuals and communities should be evident in all public information disbursed by programs, as well as in their mission statements. In achieving that mission, programs should strive to develop an environment in which it is safe to explore issues of power, privilege, and oppression. All members of the departmental community should understand the nature of training students regarding awareness and attitudes and should be prepared to support students as they experience emotional and/or defensive reactions. In addition to providing specific course(s) on diversity integration, information related to integrative diversity should be incorporated into all classes in the curriculum. Student evaluations of teaching should include items that assess how successful instructors have been in integrating diversity content into their courses. Any formal evaluations of students, faculty, and administrators should include attention to diversity issues.

Programs should also understand the ways in which teaching integrative diversity courses are stressful and provide appropriate support for instructors. In reviewing student evaluations of teaching, administrators should consider the strong possibility that some students will negatively evaluate instructors as a result of their own response to the material, rather than as a result of poor instruction. It is strongly recommended that integrative diversity courses, especially those focusing on awareness and attitudes, should be co-taught so that instructors can support one another, share the responsibility of holding students responsible for working through their own defenses, and to role model for students ways of productively having difficult discussions. The responsibility to teach the course should not rest with one or two faculty members; rather, all faculty who are willing to do the personal work necessary should be encouraged to teach. In terms of tangible resources, programs must make available necessary classroom resources, including texts, videos, and materials needed for exercises, as well as provide financial support for diversity-related programming outside of the classroom.

DESIRED TRAINING OUTCOMES

The outcomes related to integrative diversity training should be assessed at multiple levels. On a national level, outcomes are long-term issues that will likely be best observed in places like the APA employment surveys, the Association of Psychology Postdoctoral and Internship Centers (APPIC) internship match data, and the APA early career psychologists initiatives. These types of initiatives should be followed closely by training institutions and various training councils to determine ways of measuring diversity competence. Attention should be given to determining the long-term impact that attention to integrative diversity has on the field in general, including on values within the field, theories and research that are generated, and the arenas within which psychologists are employed.

On a program level, integrated diversity training should result in students exhibiting an expanded understanding of themselves, their own multiple identities, and how those identities have, at various times, both afforded them unearned privilege and led to experiences of oppression. They should be able to explore and confront how those experiences have contributed to the development of beliefs and biases that impact how they view others whose experiences differ from their own, leading them to approach working with diverse individuals and communities with an open and curious attitude. They should routinely seek out information regarding the context within which individuals live and apply that knowledge to all of their professional work. An impact on the overall climate should also be noted. Educational and recreational events designed to help students and faculty to better understand the experiences of diverse groups should be held regularly and should be open to all members of the community.

The issues addressed in integrative diversity training, including issues of power, privilege, oppression, social context, and social construction of identity, should be openly discussed in formal settings, including classrooms, clinical settings, and meetings. Such discussion should also be taking place in more informal settings, including "in the hall" discussions among and between students and faculty. It has been our observation that integrative diversity has had a profound effect on faculty expectations and student performance overall, including on dissertations and competency examinations. Students are able to apply integrative diversity concepts and considerations in ways that make their scholarly work and clinical conceptualization more relevant to work with diverse individuals and communities.

For many students, training in integrative diversity is a transformative experience in that it can result in their challenging and changing their own values, identities and understanding of the world. Throughout the integrative diversity course(s), instructors should strive to assist students in achieving such an experience. Here students share some of their thoughts on their experiences with diversity training.

The biggest barrier for me was myself. I don't know if it was my defensiveness, per se, as much as my courage to just admit what was going on inside of me and admit what I was realizing about myself openly with my colleagues, with my classmates. And it took me a long time to do that. What facilitated it—I can still remember the class, the person, and where she was sitting when she said, "I'm racist, and I hate it about myself." And just to hear another white student say that and say it openly and just to have the courage that occurred, it really helped me to see the process and to see what happened because of it. I think that is what helped me to locate my own courage. (white, gay man)

Without the training, I think I would be naive about my own biases. I think I'd go with the assumption of—I've had all of these experiences outside of academia. I'm not racist. I've got my separate adopted family, and they're all black. I've dated men of various cultures. I'm not racist. I couldn't be racist. If I was racist, I wouldn't have done this. Having the freedom to say that I have biases and that I'm racist and that I'm sexist and that I'm all these things. To identify it is to be able to control it—to be able to understand where it comes from and to challenge it with the things I know and learn and to keep that dialogue open. Otherwise I think it would be more of a closed door, and I would think, well I've got that under control I don't need to revisit that anymore. So this program has taught me the value of keeping those doors open and continuing to look at yourself, evaluate yourself. (white, heterosexual woman)

Words like oppression, sexism, white supremacy, they're not academic, they're personal. So when you talk to me outside of class, if I'm not at a desk, whatever, they're just implanted in my vocab—privilege—you know all of these words, they are just part of who I am. (African American, heterosexual man)

SUMMARY

Throughout this chapter we have presented a training model and discussed a number of techniques that may be used, as well as challenges that may arise, in preparing future psychologists to provide culturally competent services and to confront forces, such as oppression and unearned privilege, that may impede their efforts. We have addressed the role individual faculty, programs, and the field in general play in enhancing the ability of psychologists to serve as change agents on both individual and societal levels. The ongoing challenge to our field is to assure that the training that is being provided leads to action. We hope that our suggestions will lead to an enhanced ability on the part of psychologists to meet the goals noted in the APA Code of Ethics mentioned at the beginning of this chapter: to provide high quality services for all individuals. Given that the roots of integrated diversity training lie in social responsibility, such training can only be deemed successful when those trained are able to provide high quality services to all individuals, including those who are socially marginalized, in a manner that best meets the needs of those individuals.

REFERENCES

Albarracin, Z., Johnson, B. T., Zanna, M. P., & Kumkale, G. T. (2005). Attitudes: Introduction and scope. In D. Albarracin, B. T. Johnson, & M. P. Zanna (Eds.), *The handbook of attitudes* (pp. 13–19). Mahwah, NJ: Lawrence Erlbaum Associates.

American Psychological Association. (2002). *Ethical principles of psychologists and code of conduct.* Washington, DC: Author.

Bloom, B. S. (Ed.). (1956). *Taxonomy of educational objectives: The classification of educational goals.* New York: David McKAY Co.

Buckley, T., Foldy, E. G., & Rivard, P. E. (2007, February 15–16). *Multicultural training: Classroom context matters.* Paper presented at the Multicultural Roundtable at Columbia University, New York.

Constantine, M. (1998). Developing competence in multicultural assessment: Implications for counseling psychology training. *Counseling Psychologist, 26*(2), 922–929.

Constantine, M. (2001). Multiculturally-focused counseling supervision: Its relationship to trainees' multicultural counseling and self efficacy. *The Clinical Supervisor, 20*(1), 87–98.

Council of Chairs of Training Councils (CCTC). (2007). *Assessment of benchmark competencies.* Retrieved February 17, 2009, from http://www.psych trainingcouncils.org/pubs/Comptency%20Benchmarks.pdf.

Dobbins, J. E., & Malloy, K. A. (2007). *An integrated identities approach to teaching diversity.* Paper presented at the Annual Conference of the American Psychological Association, San Francisco, CA.

Eagly, A. H., & Chaikin, S. (1993). *The psychology of attitudes.* Orlando, FL: Harcourt Brace Jovanovich.

Jackson, L. (1999). Ethnocultural resistance to multicultural training. *Cultural Diversity and Ethnic Minority Psychology, 5*, 27–36.

Kaslow, N. J., Borden, K. A., Collins Jr., F. L., Forrest, L., Illfelder-Kaye, J., Nelson, P. D., et al. (2004). Competencies conference: Future directions in education and credentialing in professional psychology. *Journal of Clinical Psychology, 6*, 699–712.

Kivel, P. (1996). *Uprooting racism: How white people can work for racial justice.* Gabriola Island, BC, Canada: New Society Publishers.

Malloy, K. (2008). *Integrative diversity an emergent competency in professional psychology.* Paper presented at the National Council of Schools and Programs of Professional Psychology Mid-Winter Conference, Austin, TX.

National Council of Schools and Programs in Professional Psychology (NCSPP). (2002). *Diversity competency statement.* Retrieved February 17, 2009, from http://ncspp.info/div.htm.

National Council of Schools and Programs in Professional Psychology (NCSPP).
(2007). *NCSPP competency developmental achievement levels.* Retrieved December 1, 2007, from http://www.ncspp.info/pubs.htm.

Pedersen, P. B. (1991). Multiculturalism as a generic approach to counseling. *Journal of Counseling and Development, 70,* 6–12.

Peterson, R. L., McHolland, J. D., Bent, R. J., Davis-Russell, E., Edwall, G. E., Polite, K., et al. (1992). *The core curriculum in professional psychology.* Washington, DC: American Psychological Association.

Peterson, R. L., Peterson, D. R., Abrams, J. C., & Stricker, G. (2006). The National Council of Schools and Programs of Professional Psychology educational model. *Training and Education in Professional Psychology, 1,* 17–36.

Porter, N. (1996). Supervision of psychotherapists: Integrating anti-racist, feminist, and multicultural perspectives. In H. Landrine (Ed.), *Bridging cultural diversity to feminist psychology: Theory, research, and practice* (pp. 163–175). Washington, DC: American Psychological Association.

Sanchez-Hucles, J., & Jones, N. (2005). Breaking the silence around race in training, practice, and research. *The Counseling Psychologist, 33,* 547–558.

Smedley, A., & Smedley, B. D. (2005). Race as biology is fiction, racism as a social problem is real: Anthropological and historical perspectives on the social construction of race. *American Psychologist, 60*(1), 16–26.

Sue, D. W., Arredondo, P., & McDavis, R. J. (1992). Multicultural counseling competencies and standards: A call to the profession. *Journal of Multicultural Counseling and Development, 20,* 64–88.

Toporek, R. L., Ortega-Villalobos, L., & Pope-Davis, D. B. (2004). Critical incidents in multicultural supervision: Exploring supervisees' and supervisors' experiences. *Journal of Multicultural Counseling and Development, 32,* 66–83.

Young, G. (2003). Dealing with difficult classroom dialogue. In P. Bronstein & K. Quina (Eds.), *Teaching gender and multicultural awareness: Resources for the psychology classroom* (pp. 347–360). Washington, DC: American Psychological Association.

CHAPTER 8

Teaching Diversity to the Oppressed: Understanding and Engaging Students of Color

Kumea Shorter-Gooden

In the past three decades, there has been a clarion call for graduate training programs to develop the capacity of psychologists to provide culturally congruent and effective therapeutic services to people from diverse cultures and backgrounds (Ridley & Kleiner, 2003). The multicultural movement in psychology has been fueled primarily by three factors: (1) the recognition that traditional American psychology is Eurocentric in focus and poorly attuned to the cultural differences and realities of people from diverse cultures and backgrounds, (2) the awareness of prejudice and discrimination in the lives of those from marginalized and underserved groups and the need to understand power and privilege dynamics in order to effectively serve these communities, and (3) the rapidly changing demographics in the United States, which by mid-century will be majority "minority" (Daniel, Roysircar, Abeles, & Boyd, 2004).

The call for a multicultural perspective has become a mandate for psychology: The American Psychological Association's (APA, 2002) *Ethical Principles of Psychologists and Code of Conduct* now addresses the importance of cultural diversity in psychological practice, and a number of guidelines for culturally competent practice have been developed over the years, including *The Guidelines on Multicultural Education, Training, Research, Practice and Organizational Change for Psychologists* (APA, 2003). Moreover, APA accreditation guidelines, first in 1979 and more substantially in 1997, indicate that programs need to address issues of cultural and individual differences in the curriculum as well as in the composition of the student and faculty bodies (Altmaier, 2003).

To address the need for culturally competent psychologists, many graduate psychology programs have developed courses that focus on enhancing students' cultural attitudes and awareness, knowledge, and skills, in alignment with Derald Sue's tripartite model of multicultural competence (Sue, Arredondo, & McDavis, 1992). In order for trainees to become culturally competent, it is especially important for them to focus on the foundational leg of the mode—awareness—and to explore and examine their awareness, attitudes, and beliefs related to cultural identity and cultural differences (APA, 2003; Daniel et al., 2004; Vázquez & García-Vázquez, 2003). As a result, many graduate programs now include a required diversity course (Hills & Strozier, 1992) that is partly or mostly experiential and process-oriented (see, for example, Adams, 2002; Taylor et al., 2002).

Multicultural courses were initially developed to help majority-group students become more aware of the realities of cultural differences and to become sensitive to their own power and privilege. These courses often aimed to help white students become aware of their own biases and prejudices, and thus their cultural countertransference, which might impede their ability to develop rapport with and to effectively serve marginalized clients. There are numerous anecdotal reports of diversity courses in which white students, and white males in particular, felt that the primary aim of the class was to shake them up or even to "beat them up."

The focus on the training needs of white students is understandable given that they are the beneficiaries of white privilege in a society that diminishes other races (Tatum, 2000a). Moreover, as members of a dominant group, whites have typically not had to confront their cultural encapsulation and their biases (Sue & Sue, 2008). Furthermore, whites comprise 79 percent of the graduate students in psychology (APA, 2004), and thus, they provide a substantial portion of the mental health services that people of color receive (Daniel et al., 2004).

But what about graduate students of color? Has there been an implicit assumption that students of color don't really need these courses? That they don't have biases and prejudices? That they're just along for the ride? That they are already attuned to diversity issues and to the need to be culturally responsive? For example, Jackson (1999) reports that students of color often feel pressure to be experts on their racial/ethnic group and to informally assist the instructor in teaching the diversity class.

Though there is evidence that both participants of color as well as majority-group students benefit from multicultural education (Smith, Constantine, Dunn, Dinehart, & Montoya, 2006), we know much more about the experiences of white students who participate in multicultural training than that of participants of color (see, for example, Brown, Parham, & Yonker, 1996; Neville et al., 1996; Parker & Schwartz, 2002; Spanierman, Poteat, Wang, & Oh, 2008). Yet, there is some evidence that graduate students of color may be less satisfied than majority-group students with the quality of multicultural training that they receive (Kaplan, 2001).

Moreover, we know that multicultural courses, particularly those that focus on awareness and attitudes, are emotionally challenging and can stir up resistance for both majority-group (Reynolds, 1995; Young & Davis-Russell, 2002) and minority-group students (Jackson, 1999; Ridley, Mendoza, & Kanitz, 1994). Yet with the exception of Jackson's valuable paper on the resistance of students of color, there's been little exploration of the particular challenges of this group—a group that is typically additionally burdened because of their numerical minority status (APA, 2004), and often marginalized status (Vasquez et al., 2006), both within the multicultural course and within the graduate program.

In addition, whereas the original paradigm for multicultural training was often focused on race and ethnicity only (see, for example, Ridley, 1985), the contemporary paradigm has expanded to take account of multiple identities, including gender, sexual orientation, socioeconomic status, religion, ability, and age (APA, 2003; Daniel et al., 2004; Tatum, 2000b). This expanded perspective embraces the intersection of identities and the complex patterns of power and privilege that emerge when, for example, a white gay male from a poor rural background is the therapy client of a black heterosexual woman from an upper-middle-class urban family. When the lines between the dominant and the subordinate, the oppressor and the oppressed are not so clear cut, it becomes apparent that students of color have to attend to their own work. Sometimes the work has to do with acknowledging and exploring their dominant identities; sometimes the work has to do with examination of their target identities and related internalized -isms; often the work has to do with the intersection therein. But how easily and readily can this work be done?

This chapter will describe and discuss the particular challenges and needs of graduate students of color in process-oriented multicultural psychology courses, and it will recommend strategies to more effectively engage students of color in these courses. These perceptions derive from approximately a dozen years of experience as an instructor and several as the coordinator of a team of instructors teaching a required first-year clinical psychology graduate course, entitled "Intercultural Processes and Human Diversity," at the California School of Professional Psychology, Los Angeles (CSPP-LA), Alliant International University. While CSPP-LA has a fairly diverse student body, the largest demographic group is white women, who typically make up about half of each cohort.

The year-long course, which typically has a dozen students per section, meets once a week for three hours. The first semester is primarily experiential and process-oriented, with an emphasis on facilitating students' awareness of their own cultural identity and of their assumptions and biases about others, related to multiple dimensions of identity. The second semester continues the process emphasis but is more knowledge-focused, with specific attention to: (1) core multicultural mental health concepts, like racial identity and acculturation, (2) cultural characteristics and values of historically oppressed and underserved groups within the United

States, and (3) the implications of this material for understanding help-seeking behaviors and for effective therapeutic engagement.

FIVE COMMON STANCES OF STUDENTS OF COLOR

In my years as an instructor of this required core multicultural training course, I have tried to stay attuned to and make sense of the reactions and responses of students of color. Because one's standpoint affects one's perceptions, it is important to note that I am an African American woman. I have noted five common stances that capture how students of color often respond to these courses. The five stances are: (1) Already Enlightened, (2) Internalizer, (3) Idealizer, (4) Guarded, and (5) Silenced. I posit that these stances reflect different strategies, often unconscious, sometimes conscious, for managing the understandable and expected anxiety of the multicultural course, particularly when the focus is on often-taboo topics that are tough to dialogue about in our society. The stances often serve a defensive function, helping to protect the student from emotional harm. These five positions will be described and specific examples will be offered.

But first, a caveat: these five stances are seen as a heuristic device to help us think about the experiences and needs of students of color. Clearly, students of color—an incredibly diverse group with respect to race, ethnicity, socioeconomic status, acculturation status, and innumerable other factors—cannot be sorted neatly into five discrete categories; at the same time, my belief is that these five types do reflect some shared experiences and ways of being in the world that are typical of graduate students of color in multicultural courses. Also, it is important to note that these five labels are not being used to suggest characterological impairment on the part of the students. The message, in fact, is quite the contrary. While some minority-group students (which is true for some majority-group students as well) face characterological challenges, it is critical to use a contextual or ecological perspective (see, for example, Levine & Perkins, 1997) and to consider the impact of being a student of color who is likely in the numerical minority in the diversity course as well as in the graduate program. These five stances are offered as ways to better understand this person-environment interaction.

Already Enlightened

Already Enlightened students believe that they know all there is to know about oppression. They may believe that they as well as others from the same racial/ethnic group and all people of color have clearly and definitively experienced more victimization than all members of the mainstream group. Because they have suffered with ongoing societal discrimination and because they are sure that they "get it," Already Enlightened students are often not willing to use the diversity course as a way to explore their own assumptions, biases, and privileges. As far as they are concerned, they have already done the work, and it is time for their class-mates to do theirs. Sometimes the Already Enlightened student relates in a very intellectualized way, sharing lots of relevant and valuable information, but impersonally and almost devoid of affect.

These students may, in fact, be very knowledgeable about multicultural issues and may have done lots of personal work around experiences of oppression. However, they may present themselves in a self-righteous way, as if they own the truth, with little tolerance for classmates who are naïve and unsophisticated with respect to these issues. Sometimes this is because the Already Enlightened student is in the Immersion-Emersion phase of their own racial identity development process (Cross, 1995), a time when people withdraw from and completely devalue the dominant culture and become immersed in and idealize their own racial/ethnic culture. This student's view of the world may be very "black and white," both literally and figuratively, with little room for nuance or complexity with respect to multicultural issues. As a result, Already Enlightened students may be dismissive of and easily angered by other students' perspectives and concerns. They may question the value of the course, deeming it impossible for their classmates to really face their racism and to learn and grow.

At times, as Jackson (1999) describes, this student presents as a co-instructor, helping the designated instructor do his or her job. The junior or naïve instructor, who feels anxious about his or her own capacity to facilitate and lead the class, or, alternatively, the instructor who is yearning for students who can speak with considerable understanding about oppression and power and privilege may collude with the Already Enlightened student and encourage them to serve as a fellow teacher. While the aim of experiential courses is for all participants to serve as teachers of each other, the danger here is that the Already Enlightened student may be rigidly cast in the instructor role and may not be supported and pushed to also assume the role of learner.

An additional difficulty is that if a student early on presents himself or herself publicly to the class as highly sophisticated and enlightened, the need to "save face" can make it difficult to drop that stance later on. Thus, it can be particularly problematic when students assume the Already Enlightened stance early on in the term and then find themselves stuck there.

As alluded to earlier, the Already Enlightened student often acts as if racism is the only -ism worthy of attention and that all else pales in comparison. One example was an African American male student who was very knowledgeable about the history of racism and its continued manifestations, but who was very reluctant to explore or address his own sexist and homophobic attitudes. He seemed to use the reality of racism and racial oppression as a way to hide out from other areas of difference and -isms. It was as if his views on women and gays and lesbians were unassailable because, as a black man, he had endured so much racism.

The Already Enlightened stance can also get in the way of examining within-group biases. A Mexican American female student had a rather aloof, above-it-all attitude in the class, and she rarely seemed engaged or contributed to the dialogue. At times she would jump in with very intellectualized comments about the history of oppression; alternatively, she would gently chastise others for their biases and prejudices; however, she never acknowledged any of her own. Then, one day, she described in her journal how her encounter with a Latina custodian on campus pushed her to begin to explore her class privilege, something that she had never considered. As a result, her Already Enlightened stance began to crumble and she was able to engage more fully and personally in the learning process.

Internalizer

The second stance is the Internalizer, who struggles with maintaining a positive racial identity, who may harbor feelings of self-hatred toward his or her own racial/ethnic group and toward his- or herself, and who, as a result, often feels uncomfortable in a multicultural class. Whereas the Already Enlightened may see the course as an opportunity to finally school ignorant classmates, the Internalizer may feel threatened by the focus on difference, racism, power and privilege. Because of ambivalence about their own identity, they may want to hide out, blend in, and not draw attention to themselves. They may experience shame when the characteristics, challenges, and difficulties of their own group are discussed. They may collude with those majority-group classmates who see the course as unimportant or unnecessary.

If, during the course, the student becomes aware of internalized negative self-views, they may experience new feelings of shame in connection with this budding awareness. The student may have no place to go with these feelings—no place to process or make sense of them—as he or she may be very reluctant to share them with classmates or even the instructor. A Latina woman who had been relatively active in the class discussion early on became quieter and quieter as time went by. In the first few weeks of the semester, she had openly identified herself as Salvadorian and had talked about her pride in her culture and heritage. I later learned, however, that as the class progressed, she became aware of her tremendous shame with respect to her uneducated and illiterate immigrant father— feelings that negatively tinged her view of Salvadorians and that had propelled her in many ways during her lifetime to distance herself from her cultural roots. The growing awareness of her own internalized negative views made it increasingly difficult for her to participate in the class.

Idealizer

The Idealizer is a third stance that students of color sometimes assume. The Idealizer is often, though not always, an international student or first-generation immigrant, who has difficulty engaging in the course because he or she has not faced the reality of oppression, privilege and injustice in the United States. Idealizers have limited "lived" experience of how privilege and power dynamics work in the United States, and they may, for example, have very little formal education about U.S. history, about the near-genocide of Native Americans, the lynching of African Americans from the late nineteenth century well into the twentieth century, the incarceration of Japanese Americans during World War II, and the anti-Chinese sentiment and legislation post-World War II. In my experience, instructors of multicultural courses typically make an assumption that students know something about the history of race relations in the United States, and since these are not history courses, this material is not usually directly taught.

Moreover, the Idealizers may be in a honeymoon relationship with the United States, and they may be clinging to it furiously. Because of the need to manage any cognitive dissonance related to the immigration experience, and thus to see the harsh times as worthwhile, these students may have particular difficulty seeing the reality of the U.S. experience. Idealizers may need to hold onto their idealized view of the United States for defensive reasons.

Moreover, many international students and immigrants come from nations where opportunities for advancement are virtually nonexistent and where abuses of human rights are much worse than in the United States, making it more difficult to see what may be more subtle power and privilege dynamics here. During class discussions, a Filipina international student's frequent refrain was: "But things are so much worse in my country." This stance made it difficult for her to fully engage in the course, to explore her own role in the process of oppression, and to consider how culturally diverse clients in the United States might perceive her. As was true in this example, there are often elements of the Internalizer in the Idealizer; the student idealizes the United States and concomitantly devalues their native country.

Guarded

The fourth stance that students of color often take is that of the Guarded participant. The Guarded student is highly defended, often very intellectualized, unexpressive of feelings, and often withdrawn. The reality is that most students are somewhat guarded in discussing diversity issues and topics, as these discussions often generate discomfort, anger, and shame (Jackson, 1999; Reynolds, 1995; Young & Davis-Russell, 2002). If we add to this the fact that students are also being evaluated, there are lots of good reasons to be on guard.

Moreover, people of color are often socialized to be guarded, particularly around majority-group members, to contain their individual feelings in the service of the family or the group and not to "air their dirty laundry" in public (Sue & Sue, 2008). Furthermore, many people of color have learned to be stoic, cool, or strong in an untrustworthy environment as a survival mechanism (see, for example, Majors, Tyler, Peden, & Hall, 1994; Romero, 2000). To openly and assertively interject one's personal reactions may be culturally inappropriate.

In my experience, it is not uncommon for white students to feel frightened and overwhelmed in experiential diversity courses; however, when the class time is up, many will walk out the door and regain a sense of power, entitlement, and control. Students of color, on the other hand, often cannot escape from issues that are stirred up in class once they leave the classroom.

For example, on the second day of class, a Mexican American male student participated in an exercise where students were assigned to groups, given a task to complete, and offered differential resources in order to complete the task. In his journal that week, the student expressed his outrage about having to participate in this exercise. He had been in the group allocated the least resources; and he was angry that he was forced to experience in class the very thing that he struggles with in the world everyday—being poor. Although he tried to keep his guard up, it was difficult because the exercise was powerful and he felt vulnerable during the first weeks of his doctoral program.

In another example, an African American and openly gay male, was never able to climb out of the Guarded stance. He was the only African American student in a class with little ethnic diversity. He seemed to shut down from the outset and never really engaged in class discussions. When his classmates looked to him to represent both the black and gay experiences, he retreated further. As the instructor, I was able to forge a one-on-one relationship with him, but he never felt safe enough to really join the class.

Guardedness serves a function. Even though it gets in the way of deeper exploration and learning, it can allow the person to hold onto a modicum of safety in a threatening situation (Young & Davis-Russell, 2002), and thus not have to face situations that may aggravate preexisting wounds.

Silenced

Sometimes the Guarded student becomes the Silenced student—the fifth type. The Mexican American male who was just mentioned was not silenced; the fact that he was able to immediately share his feelings and reactions with me, his instructor, boded well for his not shutting down. Silenced students, on the other hand, are withdrawn and uninvolved in the class discussion. They may be emotionally engaged or disengaged, but they do not let others in on what is going on internally for them. They may feel invisible. They rarely speak and efforts to get them engaged are often unsuccessful. Their position in society is mirrored in class—they are voiceless. Rather than the multicultural course serving as an opportunity for a new, healthier, more validating experience with those who have white privilege, the course recapitulates the status quo power dynamics that the student lives with on a daily basis.

In one class that I taught of 12 students, which included 4 women of color, 3 of the 4 were the least participatory students in class discussions. The rest of the class was comprised of 6 white women, 1 man of color, and 1 white man. Toward the middle of the first semester, I asked the class to consider whether there was a pattern of who spoke and who did not speak in class. The class was able to identify the pattern and talk about how the pattern of participation echoed patterns of oppression outside the class. The women of color actively engaged in this discussion and were able to share some of what got in the way of their speaking up. (Not surprisingly, they each had somewhat different thoughts and feelings about this.) This discussion helped to sensitize the rest of the class as to their complicity in silencing the women of color. For example, the class discussed why other students did not actively create space for the women of color or invite them to join in, and what it was about the "culture" of the class that might have contributed to the women of color feeling silenced. This proved to be an excellent opportunity for me to talk with the students about the importance of a contextual approach to understanding, that is, instead of asking the question, "Why don't the women of color participate much in classroom discussions?" we are better served asking, "What is it about the intersection of these women's experiences with the classroom culture that contributes to their silencing?" While this discussion did not radically change the pattern of participation, it had some impact and deepened the sense of connection within the class.

IMPLICATIONS AND RECOMMENDATIONS
FOR MULTICULTURAL TRAINING

Multicultural graduate courses in psychology, particularly if they are focused on the development of awareness and attitudes, are emotionally challenging for many students (Jackson, 1999; Reynolds, 1995; Young & Davis-Russell, 2002). Students of color, who are typically in the minority in these courses and in their programs, may be particularly at risk for being emotionally overwhelmed. I posit that students of color often assume one of five stances as a way of managing their anxiety related to the course material and course process. The problem, of course, is when the strategies to tame one's anxiety get in the way of openness to learning.

It is important to keep in mind that the five proposed stances—Already Enlightened, Internalizer, Idealizer, Guarded, and Silenced—are not pure types; many students of color may have characteristics from more than one category or will shift between stances. Moreover, I expect that there are numerous students of color who do not fit into any of these categories. Nevertheless, these stances are offered as a tool to consider the needs of students of color with respect to multicultural training and to reflect on how the broader context—including the course, the graduate program, and the broader society—contributes to their emergence.

What are the implications of this discussion for how we teach multicultural courses in graduate programs? I offer several recommendations to more effectively engage students of color in multicultural courses:

Group Students of Color

If at all possible, it is helpful to have two or more students of color, and ideally two or more students from each racial/ethnic group in each class. This can reduce the pressure on the lone black student or the lone Asian student to have to represent and serve as the expert on his/her entire group, which can contribute to the Already Enlightened stance. This strategy also often allows students of color to feel less isolated and threatened, and thus to be less Guarded. Moreover, this helps in the surfacing of within-group differences and thus provides a healthier, more differentiated and realistic picture for majority-group students.

At CSPP-LA, since we have multiple sections of the first-year required diversity course, we assign students to sections, based on their racial and gender identification during the admissions process. We do this in order to prevent students from being the only one from their broad racial/ethnic group. For example, we might have one class section with three Asian American students, two Latinos, two students of Middle Eastern heritage, and five white students, and another section with two African Americans, two Asian American students, two students who identify as multiethnic, and six white students.

Focus on Multiple Identities

It is important to explicitly frame the course as focusing on multiple aspects of identity and the -isms related to them, rather than focusing solely on race and ethnicity (Jackson, 1999). The notion of "agents" and "targets" is very valuable—the idea that almost all of us have identity dimensions that are targeted or devalued and that almost all of us simultaneously have identity dimensions where, consciously or unconsciously, we are agents of or collude with oppression (Tatum, 2000b). This framework can help students of color to look more broadly at areas of victimization as well as areas of privilege.

Recognize That the Course Expectations
Are Not Culture-Free

It is important for instructors to carefully induct students into the course—to share with students their expectations for the course and to elicit students' feedback on what is being asked of them. The typical awareness-oriented graduate multicultural class fits well with Western white upper-middle-class culture. The expectation that students will talk openly and candidly about their feelings, that they will teach each other, that the instructor is more of a facilitator than a lecturer, all reflect a flatter, more individualistic culture, in contrast to a more hierarchical, authority-centered, collectivistic culture (Sue & Sue, 2008). Our teaching approach is not culture-free, and it is important to acknowledge this and to consider ways to broaden the cultural parameters of our pedagogical approach. As an example, what does it mean if class participation is a substantial part of the evaluation and the student is Guarded or Silenced? There are no easy answers here, but I advocate cultural sensitivity and flexibility in the grading process, so that we avoid recapitulating the status quo, where those students who are the most comfortable speaking up are privileged and automatically evaluated more positively than those who are not as comfortable.

Use Journal Entries

Requiring weekly or periodic journal entries is an excellent way for the instructor to learn more about what is going on under the surface with students of color. Often what students of color do not feel comfortable sharing in class may get addressed in journals and shared with the instructor. The instructor is then able to be empathic and supportive, and to gently coach the student to share their concerns and feelings with the class as a whole. Requiring journal entries also addresses the concern raised in the previous section about how to evaluate students who are less engaged in class discussions, as it provides students with an alternate venue in which to demonstrate their learning.

Help Students to Identify Growth Edges

It can be useful to encourage sophisticated students of color, who have done significant personal work around diversity issues and who are very knowledgeable about these issues, to identify an area where they themselves want to grow. In particular, when many of their classmates are naïve, I have pushed more highly developed students to recognize this work as lifelong learning and to own an area of growth so that their learning (and tuition!) is not sacrificed. It is not uncommon for multiculturally sophisticated students of color to be most mature with respect to issues of race and ethnicity, but less advanced with regards to gender, sexual orientation, socioeconomic status, religion, and/or ability. Course assignments can be constructed so as to allow some flexibility in what students read, what experiences they engage in, and what they write about.

Process, Process, Process

To be effective, an experientially oriented multicultural course must be skillfully facilitated by an instructor who is not only a knowledge expert, but who, even more importantly, can thoughtfully attend to and manage what can often be a very difficult process. Some of the instructor's core responsibilities are to work to create an environment of relative safety (Jackson, 1999); to model open, nondefensive engagement around tough issues; to balance both challenging and supporting students (Jackson, 1999); and to convey and model a process orientation. Not all content experts have the skills to effectively attend to the process. It is important for graduate training programs to recognize that teaching multicultural courses requires a particularly rich and varied skill set and to commit to engaging appropriate instructors in this important work.

CONCLUSION

These recommendations are offered as a way of more fully engaging students of color in multicultural courses; however, it is likely that these strategies will not only improve the experiences and learning of students of color, but also that of majority-group students as well. Additional research that explores the experiences of students of color in multicultural courses is sorely needed—research that examines not only whether their awareness, knowledge, and skills are enhanced, but also what the "lived" course experience is like for them.

The numbers of psychologists of color is sorely limited and is far from being reflective of the broader U.S. population. To put diversity into effective action, both dominant-culture students and students of color need to be well-trained in addressing a wide diversity of clients and an array of multicultural issues. This paper argues for specific attention to the course experiences of graduate students of color and for consideration of the different stances that these students take in response to experiential diversity courses. Additionally, this paper provides recommendations for strategies to enhance the learning of students of color. If these strategies help in strengthening the education and training of students of color, then they ultimately will enhance the quality of psychological interventions and research that is available to increasingly diverse, yet still direly underserved, communities.

Moreover, this proposed typology may have broader applicability. I have received feedback that the five proposed postures might also characterize the day-to-day attitudes and behavior of students of color in the context of their graduate programs. In other words, it may be that it is not just the specific multicultural course experience, but also the overall experience of being a graduate student of color that induces these stances. It would be useful to explore the applicability of this typology not only to graduate psychology training programs, but also to other settings. The various stances that students of color assume in diversity courses may mirror postures taken by people of color in educational, work, and community settings when they are in the numerical minority or feel threatened. The better we understand these dynamics, the more capable we will be to address the challenges of living effectively in a multiracial society.

REFERENCES

Adams, D. (2002). A metastructure for multicultural professional psychology education and training: Standards and philosophy. In E. Davis-Russell (Ed.), *The CSPP handbook of multicultural education, research, intervention, and training* (pp. 20–36). San Francisco: Jossey-Bass.

Altmaier, E. M. (2003). Multicultural competence and accreditation in professional psychology. In D. Pope-Davis, H.L.K. Coleman, W. M. Liu, & R. Toporek (Eds.), *Handbook of multicultural competencies in counseling and psychology* (pp. 303–312). Thousand Oaks, CA: Sage.

American Psychological Association. (2002). Ethical principles of psychologists and code of conduct. *American Psychologist, 57*(12), 1060–1073.

American Psychological Association. (2003). Guidelines on multicultural education, training, research, practice, and organizational change for psychologists. *American Psychologist, 58*(5), 377–402.

American Psychological Association. (2004). *Race/ethnicity of newly enrolled students in doctoral-level departments of psychology, 2002–2003.* Retrieved June 12, 2008, from http://research.apa.org/race01.html.

Brown, S. P., Parham, T. A., & Yonker, R. (1996). Influence of a cross-cultural training course on racial identity attitudes of white women and men: Preliminary perspectives. *Journal of Counseling &Development, 74,* 510–516.

Cross, W. E. (1995). The psychology of Nigrescence: Revising the Cross model. In J. G. Ponterotto, J. M. Casas, L. A. Suzuki, & C. M. Alexander (Eds.), *Handbook of multicultural counseling* (pp. 92–122). Thousand Oaks, CA: Sage.

Daniel, J. H., Roysircar, G., Abeles, N., & Boyd, C. (2004). Individual and cultural-diversity competency: Focus on the therapist. *Journal of Clinical Psychology, 60*(7), 755–770.

Hills, H. I., & Strozier, A. L. (1992). Multicultural training in APA-approved counseling psychology programs: A survey. *Professional Psychology: Research and Practice, 23*(1), 43–51.

Jackson, L. C. (1999). Ethnocultural resistance to multicultural training: Students and faculty. *Cultural Diversity and Ethnic Minority Psychology, 5*(1), 27–36.

Kaplan, D. A. (2001). Towards an examination of multicultural competency training in clinical psychology doctoral programs. *Dissertation Abstracts International, 61*(11-B), 6138.

Levine, M., & Perkins, D. V. (1997). *Principles of community psychology: Perspectives and applications* (2nd ed.). New York: Oxford University Press.

Majors, R., Tyler, R., Peden, B., & Hall, R. E. (1994). Cool pose: A symbolic mechanism for masculine role enactment and coping by black males. In R. G. Majors & J. U. Gordon (Eds.), *The American black male* (pp. 245–259). Chicago: Nelson-Hall.

Neville, H. A., Heppner, M. J., Louie, C. E., Thompson, C. E., Brooks, L., & Baker, C. E. (1996). The impact of multicultural training on white racial identity attitudes and therapy competencies. *Professional Psychology: Research and Practice, 27*, 83–89.

Parker, W. M., & Schwartz, R. C. (2002). On the experience of shame in multi-cultural counseling: Implications for white counselors-in-training. *British Journal of Guidance & Counseling, 30*(3), 311–318.

Reynolds, A. L. (1995). Challenges and strategies for teaching multicultural counseling courses. In J. G. Ponterotto, J. M. Casas, L. A. Suzuki, & C. M. Alexander (Eds.), *Handbook of multicultural counseling* (pp. 312–330). Thousand Oaks, CA: Sage.

Ridley, C. R. (1985). Imperatives for ethnic and cultural relevance in psychology training programs. *Professional Psychology: Research and Practice, 16*(5), 611–622.

Ridley, C. R., & Kleiner, A. (2003). Multicultural counseling competence: History, themes, and issues. In D. Pope-Davis, H.L.K. Coleman, W. M. Liu, & R. Toporek (Eds.), *Handbook of multicultural competencies in counseling and psychology* (pp. 303–312). Thousand Oaks, CA: Sage.

Ridley, C. R., Mendoza, D. W., & Kanitz, B. E. (1994). Multicultural training: Reexamination, operationalization, and integration. *The Counseling Psychologist, 22*, 227–289.

Romero, R. (2000). The icon of the strong black woman: The paradox of strength. In L. C. Jackson & B. Greene (Eds.), *Psychotherapy with African American women: Innovations in psychodynamic perspectives and practice* (pp. 225–238). New York: The Guilford Press.

Smith, T. B., Constantine, M. G., Dunn, T. W., Dinehart, J. M., & Montoya, J. A. (2006). Multicultural education in the mental health professionals: A meta-analytic review. *Journal of Counseling Psychology, 53*(1), 132–145.

Spanierman, L. B., Poteat, V. P., Wang, Y-F., & Oh, E. (2008). Psychosocial costs of racism to white counselors: Predicting various dimensions of multi-cultural counseling competence. *Journal of Counseling Psychology, 55*(1), 75–88.

Sue, D. W., Arredondo, P., & McDavis, R. J. (1992). Multicultural counseling competencies and standards: A call to the profession. *Journal of Counseling & Development, 70*, 477–486.

Sue, D. W., & Sue, D. (2008). *Counseling the culturally diverse: Theory and practice* (5th ed.). New York: John Wiley.

Tatum, B. D. (2000a). Defining racism: "Can we talk?" In M. Adams, W. J. Blumenfeld, R. Castañeda, H. W. Hackman, M. L. Peters, & X. Zúñiga (Eds.), *Readings for diversity and social justice* (pp. 79–82). New York: Routledge.

Tatum, B. D. (2000b). The complexity of identity: "Who am I?" In M. Adams, W. J. Blumenfeld, R. Castañeda, H. W. Hackman, M. L. Peters, & X. Zúñiga (Eds.), *Readings for diversity and social justice* (pp. 9–14). New York: Routledge.

Taylor, S., Parks, C. W., Shorter-Gooden, K., Johnson, P. B., Burke, E. A., Ashing-Giwa, K. T., et al. (2002). In and out of the classroom: A model for multicultural training in clinical psychology. In E. Davis-Russell (Ed.), *The CSPP handbook of multicultural education, research, intervention, and training* (pp. 54–66). San Francisco: Jossey-Bass.

Vasquez, M. J. T., Lott, B., García-Vázquez, E., Grant, S. K., Iwamasa, G. Y., Molina, L. E., et al. (2006). Personal reflections: Barriers and strategies in increasing diversity in psychology. *American Psychologist, 61*(2), 157–172.

Vázquez, L. A., & García-Vázquez, E. (2003). Teaching multicultural competence in the counseling curriculum. In D. Pope-Davis, H. L. K. Coleman, W. M. Liu, & R. Toporek (Eds.), *Handbook of multicultural competencies in counseling and psychology* (pp. 546–561). Thousand Oaks, CA: Sage.

Young, G., & Davis-Russell, E. (2002). The vicissitudes of cultural competence: Dealing with difficult classroom dialogue. In E. Davis-Russell (Ed.), *The CSPP handbook of multicultural education, research, intervention, and training* (pp. 37–53). San Francisco: Jossey-Bass.

CHAPTER 9

Navigating Diversity in Leadership Roles of Higher Education

Mildred García

Imagine having been a proponent of social justice and equality all your life and finding yourself ready to enact those values in a new leadership role. As a student and/or employee, you fought for underrepresented groups and wanted a just society for all. Having navigated the higher education maze for years, you have reached a new level: you have become a leader at one of the many colleges and universities in the country. You are known for your fierce commitment, and people are looking to you to take charge and act on your convictions. As you enter this new leadership role, how can you serve in a way that ensures that your commitment to diversity becomes central to your institution? As a college or university president, how can you advocate for diversity in higher education without losing your credibility as a leader or being seen as someone with only one cause?

In this chapter, the key aspects of leadership for diversity in higher education will be addressed. The importance of several components of inclusive leadership will be discussed: understanding personal cultural context, appreciating institutional context, transitioning from the historical past to the present, building a learning community, inclusion of all voices, planning for institutional change, and assessing your personal progress as you enter new leadership roles.

UNDERSTANDING PERSONAL CULTURAL CONTEXT

Our journeys in navigating diversity are always grounded in our experiences and realities. How we view the world is based on our vantage point. To deepen our personal knowledge, we must continuously question our values. For me, this means always interrogating my own reality as an urban first-generation Puerto Rican/Latina student and questioning whether my actions truly include everyone, as my definition of diversity would require. I am one of the fortunate ones whose education has provided me and my family the opportunity to leave poverty behind. But how do I learn more about the migrant worker and others whose cultural experiences are different from mine? How can I include their realities in my thinking? Where are my blind spots—for example, do I unintentionally exclude immigrants who are not black or brown? How can I learn about their struggles? Now that I am president of a higher education institution in Los Angeles, how can I learn more about the diversity of the West Coast and the lives of its people?

Diversity work requires each person to delve into his or her soul and acknowledge that everyone has biases—including oneself. The ability to expand one's lens to acknowledge that personal biases exist, even while looking beyond and overcoming them, is critical to navigating the journey. I found my own sense of enlightenment when I realized that achieving true appreciation for diversity in ourselves, in our institutions, and in our nation begins with the understanding that this appreciation is a journey, not a destination. It is a journey that begins from within and involves continuous self-reflection about one's own development.

As we deepen our knowledge, it is also critical that we find ways to step outside of our comfort zones and experience the world as others see it. One experience that was transformative for me occurred at an institution of higher education in Bemidji, Minnesota. Through a faculty development grant, faculty and staff worked collaboratively with Ojibwe tribal elders toward the goal of increasing the number of Native American students to enter college. The local Native American tribes invited these faculty and staff members to visit the reservations and learn about the Ojibwe culture from the elders themselves. Participating as a consultant, I learned from college personnel that even though they lived in the local area, they had never visited the reservation before this experience. While initially apprehensive about the training, these faculty and staff members walked away with new knowledge and understanding of a culture different from their own, and new excitement about the partnership's potential. Such experiences lead to the development of true partnerships and promoted a culture of learning exchange. This experience led the higher education institution to create faculty and elder team teaching courses, pair student affairs personnel and tribal members for student advising, and offer an Ojibwe language course for students.

Faculty members who had participated in the training recounted how their personal and professional development had shifted course because of this experience. They transformed courses that were entirely unconnected to the grant as they began to see the world differently. For me, the experience of moving outside of my comfort zone was transformative. It allowed me to deepen my knowledge of other cultures and more effectively promote diversity as I entered new leadership roles.

UNDERSTANDING INSTITUTIONAL CONTEXT

With over four thousand institutions of higher education in the United States, each campus has followed a different history, found a different level of success, and reached a different stage of progress in its journey toward inclusiveness. While we can assert that diversity within our institutions is critical for the social good of a diverse society, before we can pursue any plans to support diversity, we must understand the particular historical context. Is the institution like Oberlin, proud of its forerunner status as one of the first colleges in the country to admit African American students? Is it like Kent State, where civil rights struggles have left anguish impressed on the depths of its institutional soul? Is it a Historically Black College or University (HBCU) like Howard University, or a women's college like Mills College, whose creation symbolized a progressive stance in opposition to the establishment? Or is it like my own institution, California State University, Dominguez Hills, founded in 1960 by state legislators to serve the affluent Palos Verdes neighborhood in Los Angeles, but built instead in the diverse community of Carson after the Watts race riots changed everything?

Historical context provides insights into the cultural foundation and values of each institution. Knowledge about this context can help a college or university leader shape the direction of diversity initiatives. Questions to ponder include: Who were the institution's early leaders, and for what values were they fighting? What were the original demographics of the student body, how have they changed? What characterized former faculty and presidents: for what were they known, and what issues gained prominence on campus during their tenure? How has the institution grappled with diversity in its student body, faculty, climate, and curriculum, both qualitatively (as in matters of course content) and quantitatively (as in conversations about student demographics)? What is the diversity in the institution's vicinity, and has it changed over time? Does the student body reflect the community, and has the institution truly served that community? Through these questions, a picture emerges of how the institution has addressed diversity within its historical context.

Setting a new diversity plan in motion begins with evaluating this historical journey. It requires a comprehensive plan for gathering information and identifying goals, including trajectories of goals and expectations charted over time. Scholars in the field have provided models adaptable to individual institutional contexts. The bibliography at the end of this chapter identifies some resources developed by the Association of American Colleges and Universities (AAC&U) as pragmatic tools to help practitioners begin the journey toward discovering their campus's historical foundation. The first step is selecting the mechanism for your plan and engaging community members in understanding the institutional context.

BUILDING A LEARNING COMMUNITY

After researching the historical context, you are ready to begin establishing a learning community. As you take the first steps in this direction, remember that your diversity goals cannot be conceived of as separate from your institutional mission; nor is your leadership separate from or reducible to only diversity issues. The campus community should view you and your diversity work within the parameters of your designated leadership role. How you use this role to mobilize support for diversity will form the core of the institution's journey toward becoming an inclusive learning community. Whatever your position, your role can enable the institution and promote its capacity to support change.

If, for example, you are in academic affairs and planning for faculty hires, you can utilize data on applicant composition—those interviewed, those hired, and those retained—to help deans and department chairs understand and track progress toward diversity goals. At one institution planning for the retirements of baby boom faculty (those born between 1946 and 1964), the senior administrative team examined faculty data to establish historical hiring patterns before approving new hiring positions. The academic affairs team began by reviewing the data by age, ethnicity, and gender, reading *Scholarship Reconsidered* (the latest literature on changing faculty roles), and reviewing monographs on diversity published by the AAC&U to develop an understanding of the obstacles to creating a diverse faculty.

During a one-day retreat, the team reviewed the data on faculty composition and compared it to the demographic characteristics of the students they served. The team also identified a set of experiences and skills necessary for every faculty member to be successful at that particular institution. They agreed to include in the job description for each new faculty position these skills and experiences: engagement within the local community, demonstrated experience with a diverse student body, experience with or the willingness to learn teaching technology, and the ability and desire to engage students in their research. The deans implemented these criteria for recruitment within their individual colleges across the institution. The provost's office approved all positions that met these criteria, and all job descriptions came to reflect the institution's collaborative agreement to value such faculty characteristics. This proactive recruitment process profoundly affected the institution's diversity over time. Over a six-year period, the institution increased women hires by 30 percent and faculty of color hires by 25 percent.

The lessons learned from this promising practice included:

1. Shared Planning and Action: The academic team moved faculty recruitment from an individual departmental responsibility to responsibility shared by an administrative team whose values supported institutional needs and student success.
2. Data-Driven Assessment: Data provided quantifiable ways to understand the institution's successes and shortcomings (such as patterns of faculty departures) within the historical context. The team developed new capacities to use data to hold units accountable for institutional improvement.
3. Educational Development: The inclusion of women and faculty of color in higher education transformed the curriculum because different perspectives enrich analysis, research and knowledge. Thus the process educated campus faculty, students, staff and administrators about the role of diversity in achieving educational excellence.
4. Modeling Inclusiveness: The team modeled decision-making that included a range of voices: the senior academic team, the department chairs, and the faculty. The process fostered shared responsibility and consensus-building and created a mechanism based on shared values for replacing, recruiting, and retaining faculty.

MOVING BEYOND THE BLACK AND WHITE PARADIGM

Before World War II, U.S. college and university students were predominantly white males from the upper socioeconomic stratum. Higher education catered to the country's elite, the only sector of the population that could afford a bachelor's degree. The G.I. Bill of 1944 changed the educational landscape, providing U.S. veterans an opportunity to pursue higher education with federal financial support. At the same time, diversity in the United States was widely perceived in terms of black and white, seeing how the country struggled with the vestiges of slavery and the civil rights movement had not yet reached its peak. Public discourse, and higher education with it, paid little attention to Native Americans, the true first inhabitants of the United States. Nor did it acknowledge Latinos and Asian/Pacific Islander Americans, populations that helped build America by working as farm laborers, servicing the white elite, and building the transcontinental railroads.

In the twenty-first century, higher education occupies a much different space. Population demographics in the United States have changed, with growing racial and ethnic diversity that is mirrored in our colleges and universities. By 2010, the Latino population will be the largest ethnic group in the country, a phenomenon already evident in states like California. Asian Americans will continue to be the fastest growing group, while the African American population will maintain stable numbers even as the European American population decreases. These racial and ethnic demographic shifts will accompany similar socioeconomic changes. Students

are no longer solely from the upper class: our campuses are now popu-
lated with students from low- and middle-income families. These students
understand that education is a route to upward mobility. But they lack
sophisticated knowledge of the culture of higher educations institutions,
whose values still mirror those of earlier populations. Until institutional
cultures have shifted to reflect the diverse global world in which we live,
these students will face the challenge of navigating uncharted territory.

We thus find ourselves at an historic crossroads. As more persons of
color enter leadership roles in higher education, they will shift the educational conversation, bringing new cultural contexts and views to their
institutions. A new consciousness is on the rise as leaders navigating
twenty-first-century diversity focus their efforts on educating future generations for life in a multicultural, globally interdependent, and democratic society. As we reach this crossroads, Barack Obama, a biracial man
born of a black father and a white mother, made history as the first person
of color elected president of the United States. Yet we have not moved
beyond the black/white paradigm. During the presidential campaign,
media coverage of then Senator Obama glossed over his biracial background and posited him as the first black candidate for president. Senator
Obama himself lost an opportunity to educate citizens about racial complexity when he delivered his famous speech on race during the primary
campaign (Obama, 2008). The speech reflected the classic double bind
placed on persons of color: any defense of race seems "too black," while
denial of race seems "too white." While some voters accused Obama of
playing "the race card," mistrusted him for his Muslim-sounding name,
and judged him for his ties to the sometimes-inflammatory Reverend
Jeremiah Wright, others accused him of elitism (based on his Columbia
and Harvard education) and charged that he was out of touch with black
Americans. With these constraints, it's little wonder that his speech rein-
forced the black/white paradigm.

Still, although Senator Obama was correct in identifying "this nation's
original sin of slavery" as the heart of the black/white conflict, he lost
an opportunity to deepen the dialogue about race to reflect the country's
true diversity. The nation has many "original sins" that Americans must
acknowledge: the forced relocation of the country's true first inhabitants,
the Native Americans, from their land to the barren Indian reservations
and related attempts to erase their cultural roots; the disenfranchisement
of Mexicans and the appropriation of their lands; the legislation and assault against Chinese Americans, who built the transcontinental railroads.
When Obama spoke of America's segregated neighborhoods and churches,
of the pervasive educational achievement gaps between black and white
students, of legalized discrimination against blacks in housing and hiring,
and of the lack of economic opportunity for black Americans, his observations reflected his own experience. But they failed to expand the conversation to include people of all groups of color whose unjust treatment is

also part of our country's history. His omission reverberated among those excluded from the paradigm, Americans whose realities were invisible until the final quarter of his address, when Obama attempted to capture the entire audience and engage them in the message.

I refer to this example because it has rich implications for diversity in higher education and its leaders. The United States must become a nation able to see beyond the black/white paradigm to recognize the intersections of multiple races that characterize twenty-first-century America and even characterize Barack Obama himself—no matter how invisible these intersections have been. Media coverage that defines race as black or white to the exclusion of other groups creates false dichotomies and harks back to the 1960s, when those who were gay/lesbian, multiracial, Native American, Latino, and/or Asian American or Pacific Islander stood at the margins. It returns us to an oversimplified and outdated paradigm simply because it is easy to codify and easy to label. But diversity is never simple. Leaders in our colleges and universities must use their bully pulpits to educate the nation and our students about the complexity of diversity and its multiple and intersecting faces of identity.

TRANSFORMING CONCEPTIONS OF DIVERSITY THROUGH LEADERSHIP

When I arrived at California State University, Dominguez Hills, an emeriti faculty member gave me a very important gift: *City of Promise: Race and Historical Change in Los Angeles* (Schiesl & Dodge, 2006), to which he and his wife had contributed chapters on Asian American history. Divided into two sections (before and after World War II) and including chapters on Asian Americans, Latino Americans, and African Americans, the book encapsulates deep knowledge of the diversity within as well as between groups. In Los Angeles, people of Chinese and Japanese descent were the first Asian immigrants, followed by Koreans and Filipinos; early Latino immigrants were predominantly Mexican, while early African American settlers originated primarily from the South. These complex histories confirm the importance of disaggregating within and between groups, illustrating that both similarities and differences play a role in defining identity and collective experience.

As I tried to understand this history and its effects on CSU, Dominguez Hills, I broadened my lens and avoided the tendency to view each ethnic group as monolithic. I saw that when we limit ourselves to the federal government's census categories or media sound bites about race and ethnicity, we fail to appreciate the complexity of diversity. When we describe our student bodies, we must challenge ourselves to broaden our language beyond the traditional categories of African American, Hispanic American, Asian-Pacific Islander, and white if we are to promote true diversity in our recruitment and retention efforts. By disaggregating within groups, we can examine in greater detail whether or not we are serving our underserved students.

In Los Angeles, for example, the underserved South Bay region is popu-lated by Koreans, Vietnamese, Hawaiians, Samoans, and Tongans. While all these groups are labeled Asian American, each has its own unique his-tory and culture. Medgar Evers College in Brooklyn, New York, provides another excellent example of the importance of within-group differences. While a visitor might initially assume that a majority of the student body is African American, students hail from cities in locales as widespread as Africa, Jamaica, Trinidad, the Dominican Republic, and Haiti. These stu-dents' multiple cultures form the richly interwoven fabric of the institution and have influenced its climate. By embracing its cultures, the institution has enabled students to explore their differences and similarities while learning how to work together in a multiracial context. Similar examples exist within institutions serving Native American, Latino American, and white groups as well.

Other dimensions of difference—socioeconomic status, number of fam-ily generations in the United States, or geographic region, to name only a few—are equally important factors to consider when addressing student body diversity. Understanding these cultural parameters enables an insti-tution to decide where to focus its efforts to support and recruit students from underrepresented areas. Leaders must also recognize how institutional mission can affect demographic profile: for example, some public institu-tions are mandated to serve specific geographic counties or regions, while private institutions with religious traditions may have limited religious di-versity. Attention to these restrictions and their limitations is essential if we are to move our institutional cultures beyond dichotomies and exclusions. By understanding all these complex factors, a university can provide the best and most nurturing academic environment for its students.

At CSU, Dominguez Hills, our mission as a public university is to serve our local community and the greater Los Angeles region. Some have said that as a place where no one single ethnic group is in the majority, we are the most diverse institution west of the Mississippi. But with South Bay in our backyard, we must make a stronger effort to reach out to and recruit from the Tongan and Samoan communities. These communities have some of the lowest educational and socioeconomic levels in contrast to the high educational levels, as a group, of Asian Americans. We at CSU, Domnguez Hills, must analyze our data to understand why Samoan and Tongan students are not enrolling at our institution and to identify ways to open CSU's doors to these students, whether through community part-nerships, collaboration with community elders, or other methods. If we truly wish to serve the public, we must recognize and honor all our re-gion's populations, from the South Bay's Asian populaces to Caucasian groups at the beach cities, to understand and address their educational needs.

ASSESSING FOR INSTITUTIONAL CHANGE

After taking stock of personal and environmental context, our work to ensure the creation of an inclusive learning community is still incomplete. Context and history may guide leadership, but without planned, comprehensive assessments, they will not create institutional change. Assessment measures cannot be an afterthought. They must be deliberatively designed and implemented from the beginning of the change process to evaluate progress and buttress institutional improvement.

This is an era of accountability in higher education, and when financial resources are limited, diversity initiatives will require justification. Assessment measures can fulfill this need. Measures of success might include whether a university has attracted diverse students or students from the local community. They might include proof of desired learning outcomes amongst graduating students, such as improved attitudes toward difference and diversity. They might include increased retention rates among underrepresented student groups or postgraduation measures of success, such as successful employment.

The AAC&U's *Assessing Campus Diversity Initiatives* (Garcia et al., 2003) lays out 10 steps for evaluating campus diversity:

1. Define the purpose
2. Determine the audience
3. Assemble the evaluation team
4. Identify the context
5. Target the topic
6. Formulate the Questions
7. Obtain the data
8. Assess the data
9. Analyze the data
10. Report the findings

Within these processes, assessing diversity initiatives means bringing all voices to the table. Successful institutional diversity work engages all individuals throughout the campus, and assessment work is no exception. All stakeholders in an institution must collaborate to affirm what has worked and reform what hasn't, as we strive to provide strong learning environments for our students. In our journey toward the goals of recruitment, retention, and graduation for all, identifying our collective strengths and weaknesses is a necessary first step.

CHALLENGES FOR A DIVERSE PRESIDENT

A president who is different from his or her predecessors, whether because of race, class, gender, or sexual orientation enters the leadership role with additional challenges to overcome. If you are the first person of color appointed as president, you will face high, even unrealistic, expectations.

Some who share your background will expect you to singlehandedly change the injustices of the past. Some from other backgrounds might question your credibility or believe that you will address only the needs of your identity group. If you are the first woman, some may expect you to behave like a woman, but act like a man—or at least exhibit male-coded styles of leadership. Others may criticize you for taking "masculine" actions—the same actions that a man might take without inviting comment. Some may have unrealistic expectations for change, holding you to a higher standard or expecting you to understand "where they come from." Others may withhold judgment—and support—until you "prove yourself" through the changes you make. Even simple and innocent statements like "our senior team does not reflect the student body we serve" may be misinterpreted—in my case, understood to mean that I would fire everyone who wasn't Latino.

Given these pressures, the message you send in the very beginning is crucial. When I began my tenure at CSU, Dominguez Hills, I defined diversity as including everyone at the center and pushing no one to the margins. That message garnered respect. From your first days in office, you must work to establish your presidency as fair and equitable to all. For the first year, you will live in a fishbowl as everyone watches to see whether you "walk the talk." Your constituents will have many questions: What does your senior team look like? Who are you appointing? Which stakeholders do your appointed committees reflect? Who are you meeting with? What communities are you embracing? In the face of this elevated scrutiny, you must honor the institution's past before recommending changes, working to recruit all members to support your plans for institutional transformation.

CONCLUSION

The role of a leader in higher education today is complex. We are witnessing a tremendous and unprecedented confluence of differences emerging on our campuses. With leadership roles comes the responsibility of ensuring that our institutions honor the complexity and diversity that different groups bring—and the responsibility of offering all students the best academic experience possible. These changes require a leader who can take assertive action that first and foremost includes a commitment to personal development. They require leaders who understand historical contexts, build a learning community, and assess institutional change when implementing diversity initiatives. As leaders, we must model the change we want to see as we collaboratively transform our institutions into inclusive environments. In promoting diversity, we demonstrate a commitment to social justice that may require substantial and proactive institutional change. At the same time, we must understand and honor each institution's history as we formulate these changes. Mishaps are inevitable, but we must learn from them. Creating institutions centered on social justice and inclusivity is a constant and continuing process: we will peel away layer after layer of intolerance before reaching the social justice goals that lie at the core of our work. But when we boldly move forward in partnership, dialogue, and risk-taking, we recognize that change, although never easy, is possible. With committed leadership, we can transform our institutions to educate all who enter their doors, regardless of race, creed, or origin.

REFERENCES

Association of American Colleges and Universities. (2008). *More reasons for hope: Diversity matters in higher education.* Washington, DC: Author.

Boyer, E. L. (1997). *Scholarship reconsidered: Priorities of the professoriate.* Princeton, NJ: Carnegie Foundation for the Advancement of Teaching.

Clayton-Pedersen, A. R., Parker, S., Smith, D. G., Moreno, J. F., & Teraguchi, D. H. (2007). *Making a real difference with diversity: A guide to institutional change.* Washington, DC: Association of American Colleges and Universities.

Garcia, M., Hudgins, C., Musil, C. M., Nettles, M., Sedlacek, W., & Smith, D. (2003). *Assessing campus diversity initiatives: A guide for campus practitioners.* Washington, DC: Association of American Colleges and Universities.

Kuh, G. D. (2008). *High-impact educational practices: What they are, who has access to them, and why they matter.* Washington, DC: Association of American Colleges and Universities.

Musil, C. M., Garcia, M., Moses, Y., & Smith, D. G. (1995). *Diversity in higher education: A work in progress.* Washington, DC: Association of American Colleges and Universities.

Obama, B. (2008). *Speech on race.* Retrieved March 18, 2008, from http://www. barackobama.com.

Schiesl, M., & Dodge, M. M. (Eds.). (2006). *City of promise: race and historical change in Los Angeles.* Claremont, CA: Regina Books.

Smith, D. G., Garcia, M., Hudgins, C., Musil, C. M., Nettles, M., & Sedlacek, W. (2006). *A diversity research agenda.* Washington, DC: Association of American Colleges and Universities.

CHAPTER 10

Racial Microaggressions in the Workplace: Manifestation and Impact

Derald Wing Sue, Annie I. Lin, and David P. Rivera

People of color continue to be the most underemployed and unemployed when compared to their white counterparts in the workforce (U.S. Department of Labor, 2006). For example, in the 20 years and older age group, 9.5 percent of African American men as compared to 4 percent of white men were unemployed. Additionally, the percentage of racial minorities at higher levels of employment is much lower than whites for every racial minority group except Asians: 35.5 percent of whites hold management, professional and related occupations, 46.4 percent of Asians held similar positions while only 26 percent of African Americans and 17 percent of Latinos were employed at the same levels. Even when the presence of Asian Americans in the upper echelons of management is considered, there is evidence to suggest that they must possess higher levels of education, training and experience than their white counterparts to attain these positions (Sue, Sue, Zane, & Wong, 1985). In general, influential and high-paying positions, such as chief executives, include the lowest percentage of racial minorities. Out of all the chief executives in the United States, 4.6 percent are Latino, 3.9 percent are Asian, and 3.1 percent are African American. As the positions get lower in the workplace hierarchy, the gaps between the racial groups that make up this population begin to close. For example, statistics for occupations categorized as office/administrative support show that this portion of the workforce is 13.5 percent white, 16.5 percent African American, 12.1 percent Latino and 11.7 percent Asians. More African Americans (23.9%) and Latinos (23.8%) are employed in service occupations than whites (15.2%) or Asians (15.7%). Disparities also seem to exist for type of occupations as well. The U.S. Equal Employment Opportunity Commission (2002a, 2002c) reports few racial minorities are employed in media and law. In radio and TV broadcasting, 11.4 percent are reported to be African American, 8.5 percent Latino, and 2.3 percent Asian American, while none of the racial minority groups have more than 6 percent of representation in the field of law.

These figures are disturbing for two reasons. First, it is projected that within several short decades, people of color will become a numerical majority in the United States (U.S. Census Bureau, 2004). Already, approximately 75 percent of those entering the labor force are persons of color or women, and by the time the so-called baby boomers begin to retire, those contributing to the social security and pension funds will be predominantly visible racial/ethnic minorities (Sue & Sue, 2008). If persons of color continue to occupy the lower rungs of the employment ladder as the most undereducated, underemployed, unemployed, and underpaid, it bodes poorly for the economic health of future retirees, businesses and the nation. Second, a society that continues to allow unfair disparities to exist between certain groups compromises its moral integrity, failing to provide equal access and opportunity to all. Thus, we believe that economic and moral-ethical reasons demand commitment to the eradication of barriers that continue to oppress and deprive citizens of color from attaining their full potentials.

Though reports from the U.S. Department of Labor (2006) and the U.S. Equal Employment Opportunity Commission (2002a, 2002b, 2002c) highlight the inequities that exist in various sectors of the workplace, these statistics do not explain the reason for these disparities. Given the historical role of race and racism in the United States and its manifestation in all areas of life, including work, we believe these statistics are not so much the result of overt racism as we know it, but of the detrimental impact of invisible forms of racial microaggressions in the workplace.

RACIAL MICROAGGRESSIONS AND SUBTLE RACISM

Increasingly, the concept of "racial microaggression" has been used to describe everyday forms of racism that occurs subtly and usually outside the level of awareness of perpetrators (Solórzano, Ceja, & Yosso, 2000; Sue, Capodilupo, et al., 2007). Racial microaggressions are conceived as "brief and commonplace daily verbal or behavioral indignities, whether intentional or unintentional, that communicate hostile, derogatory or negative racial slights and insults that potentially have harmful or unpleasant psychological consequences on the target person or group" (Sue, Capodilupo, et al., 2007, p. 273). Due to the "subtle, stunning, often automatic, and non-verbal" nature of racial microaggressions, these daily racial encounters are experienced as invalidating and demeaning to individuals of color (Pierce, Carew, Pierce-Gonzalez, & Willis, 1978, p. 66).

Racial microaggressions are not simply verbal or nonverbal, but can occur environmentally (visual and auditory) as well.

Many racial microaggressions are delivered outside the awareness of perpetrators because most white Americans experience themselves as good and moral people who believe in equality and democracy, and would never consciously discriminate against others because of their race (Dovidio & Gaertner, 2000; Dovidio, Gaertner, Kawakami, & Hodson, 2002; Fredrickson, 1988; Sue, 2003). According to multicultural scholars, many of the biased attitudes and beliefs of white Americans are deeply entrenched in American culture and handed down through the generations (Fredrickson, 1988; Sue, 2003; Sue, Capodilupo, et al., 2007). It has been found that unconscious and aversive forms of racism can be predicted from certain belief systems that are not in themselves considered racist in nature, but foster unintentional racial microaggressions (Brief, Dietz, Cohen, Pugh, & Vaslow, 2000; Monteith, 1996). Thus, many of the racial microaggressions are committed automatically and unconsciously through biased attitudes.

Racial microaggressions can be conveyed verbally, nonverbally, or environmentally as subtle snubs, dismissive looks, slighting gestures, trivializing tones, or a hostile climate. In many instances, the victims of racial microaggressions are placed in an unenviable position of attempting to interpret whether the act was racially motivated or simply an innocent nonracial incident. As a result, these biased comments or acts are often excused or explained away as being innocent or misinterpretations. The recipients, however, are often left to wonder whether microaggressions really occurred. The task of identifying the act is particularly difficult when the "excuse" given appears perfectly valid. The sense that they have been slighted or disrespected without substantial or concrete evidence can be particularly unsettling and disconcerting for the recipients of racial microaggressions (Sue, Capodilupo, et al., 2007; Sue, Bucerri, Lin, Nadal, & Torino, 2007). The insidious, unintentional and subtle nature of microaggressions have been found to be harder to deal with than overt and obviously racist behaviors (Salvatore & Shelton, 2007; Solórzano et al., 2000; Sue, Capodilupo, et al., 2007).

Microaggressive encounters have been found to affect the racial anger, frustration, self-esteem, and cognitive functioning of the recipient more than traditional forms of racism (Salvatore & Shelton, 2007; Solórzano et al., 2000). Focus groups conducted in examining racial microaggressions against African Americans reveal that victims of such aggressions experience several psychological consequences: powerlessness, invisibility, forced compliance/loss of integrity, and pressure to represent one's group (Sue, Capodilupo, & Holder, 2008). Adverse reactions to these racial experiences were described by Asian American participants in a related study (Sue, Bucceri, et al., 2007). Feelings of being invalidated, belittled, trapped, unrecognized, and invisible, in addition to anger, rage, frustration, and alienation were reported (Sue, Bucceri, et al., 2007). Initial studies on racial microaggression strongly suggest that they create injurious consequences for the recipients. Though the concept of racial microaggression is not a new one, empirical research on the precise nature of this subtler form of racism is in a nascent stage (Sue, Capodilupo, et al., 2007). Despite the dearth of research on racial microaggressions in the workplace, a survey of literature supports the operation of such phenomena in employment decisions and work-related interactions.

Hidden messages conveyed by racial microaggressions have a detrimental effect on people of color (Solórzano et al., 2000; Sue, Bucceri, et al., 2007; Sue, Capodilupo, et al., 2007; Sue, Nadal, et al., 2008). Employees of color who believe they are being "watched over" more carefully by their supervisors than their white peers are sent messages that they are not trustworthy or competent. These messages are consistent with findings that indicate people of color may be treated like criminals or intellectually inferior based on racial microaggressive interactions (Sue, Nadal, et al., 2008). Additionally, an employee of color might be complimented on how articulate they are after giving a work-related presentation. On the surface this appears to be a compliment. However, people of color may take this as a back-handed compliment to mean that their performance is an exception to what is typically expected of someone from their racial group. Racial microaggressive encounters take many forms in the workplace and send subtle messages to people of color indicating that a separate list of rules and norms apply to them when compared to their white counterparts. The accumulation of these daily encounters creates an uninviting and hostile work environment.

RACIAL MICROAGGRESSIONS IN THE WORKPLACE

Discussions of racism in the workplace typically involve acts of discrimination that are considered outright unlawful or analyzed from a legal perspective (Coleman, 2004). Many scholars, however, indicate that racial microaggressions that occur frequently in the workforce and create many forms of inequities are seemingly difficult to prove and, thus, immune from legal action (Deitch et al., 2003; Hinton, 2004; Rowe, 1990; Stallworth, McPherson, & Rute, 2001). Those who write and conduct research about racial microaggressions in the workplace use other names to describe these phenomena: "microinequities," "subtle discrimination" (Rowe, 1990), "everyday discrimination" (Essed, 1991), and "unconscious discrimination" (Stallworth et al., 2001). Regardless of the particular label being used, descriptions of these concepts yield characteristics that mirror those of racial microaggressions.

Mary P. Rowe, a diversity trainer, is recognized as the first person to apply Pierce et al.'s (1978) conceptualization of microaggressions to workplace settings (Stallworth et al., 2001). These subtle forms of racism in the workplace often go overlooked or ignored because, as with the general nature of microaggressions, they often occur at the unconscious level (Stallworth et al., 2001). Complicating the issue even further is the possibility that most of these "microaggressive" interactions go unchecked by superiors because they are not necessarily considered infractions of the law (Deitch et al., 2003) due to their unintentional and automatic nature. Furthermore, Rowe (1990) argues that ambiguity adds to the complexity of microaggressions, making the existence of these incidents hard to prove.

Evidence of racial microaggressions can be found in every aspect of work life, whether in the employment stages of recruitment and evaluation or in everyday interactions at the worksite. The recruitment, retention, and promotion model for cultural diversity training provides a framework for understanding the manifestation and impact of racial microaggressions on employees of color in the workplace (Sue, 1991).

Recruitment

Racial microaggressions can infect hiring decisions made by the organization, especially since they reflect a worldview of "superiority-inferiority" or "inclusion-exclusion." During the recruitment phase, racial microaggressions occur when recruiters deem white candidates more qualified than candidates of color, even though both groups possess comparable qualifications (Dovidio & Gaertner, 2000). As pointed out earlier, well-intentioned white recruiters might operate under the belief that they are making a decision because the "most qualified candidates should get the job," thereby justifying a biased action. These individuals tend to display their racist beliefs in situations or environments where "guidelines for inappropriate behavior are vague" (Gaertner & Dovidio, 2005, p. 620). Thus, even organizations and institutions that are required to abide by equal opportunity laws are susceptible to breaking or "bending" these laws in cases when racial microaggressions operate to encourage management to favor whites over people of color. This type of racial microaggression is particularly apparent in the recruitment process through comments such as: "There just aren't enough qualified minorities." Inherent in such a statement is that minority candidates are not as competent as white candidates, thereby justifying hiring white applicants over applicants of color. Further, when the selection standards and processes are closely examined, minority candidates may be at a disadvantage if the criteria are based on white definitions of being qualified (Sue, 1991), or if those in hiring authority are simply more comfortable with white employees.

However, racial microaggressions in the workplace do not solely occur in the context of human interactions. They are also found in institutional policies, practices, and structures, as well as the general physical climate of the workplace, and may discourage applicants of color in applying for a position at a particular company. Manifestations of environmental racial microaggressions can be found in the prominently displayed framed pictures of an all-white board of directors and in the "informal" practice of "hiring from within," which results in a predominantly white male management team. Candidates of color may be deterred from applying for a position in a company when they notice only white men at the upper echelons of management/leadership, low numbers of employees of color throughout the organization, or minority clustering at the lower levels of employment. These environmental racial microaggressions communicate hidden messages to prospective candidates: "You are not qualified, so don't waste your time applying," "You are not welcome here," "You will not feel comfortable here," "If you choose to stay, there is only so far you will advance in our organization."

Companies must be aware of potential environmental microaggressions and make a conscious effort to effect changes in recruitment policies and practices and the physical environment and image of the company so that qualified applicants of color will have the desire to work at their company and be encouraged to apply.

Retention

Once hired, however, many companies may experience difficulty in retaining employees of color (Sue, 1994). Efforts to increase minority representation in an organization without effecting real changes to the company culture will cause employees of color to feel uncomfortable, unvalued, and unfairly treated, leading to low retention of minority employees. At this stage of employment, racial microaggressions may be delivered through racially biased evaluations when superiors deem the work of employees of color as lesser in value than that of similar work accomplished by white employees (Hinton, 2004), or when supervisors maintain a mindset that black employees may need closer supervision to prevent them from making mistakes or "being lazy."

On a daily basis, workplace encounters of racial microaggressions could also be seen through failure to provide professional assistance, mentoring, or being avoided and excluded from both formal and informal networks (Pettigrew & Martin, 1987). If employees are continually surrounded by subtle reminders in the workplace environment that people of color are not valued by those in positions of power, all employees will be more likely to engage in behaviors and practices that will encourage and maintain the status quo. It is important to understand that this change in belief and attitude of the company culture must involve all employees, beginning with the employers. These everyday practices become normalized by members of the dominant group and thus are not questioned (Essed, 1991). In order to avoid fostering a racially microaggressive environment, employers will need to be willing to examine their own beliefs and attitudes and communicate clearly to their employees about the types of behaviors and practices that are appropriate in the workplace.

There are various work relationships that could complicate the expressions of racial microaggression and affect the retention rate of employees of color. A peer-to-peer racial microaggression occurs between employees who hold similar positions on the organizational chart in their company. This type of microaggression can be very difficult to handle or avoid because of the amount of communication one usually has with their coworkers. Experiencing "subtle and often unconscious manifestations of racism in the form of incivility, neglect, humor, ostracism, inequitable treatment" (Fox & Stallworth, 2004, p. 3) can cause serious distress for the receiver of this type of treatment. Most tasks at work involve the input, assistance, or collaboration of fellow coworkers, and if one is made to feel uncomfortable working with other individuals because they have experienced a microaggression, it can impede the progress of the task. Studies reveal, for example, that racial microaggressions sap the spiritual energies of the recipients, cause psychological distress, and disrupt cognitive problem solving and performance (Dovidio & Gaertner, 2000; Salvatore & Shelton, 2007). While racial microaggressions may be invisible to whites, the resulting lower work productivity by employees of color is glaringly obvious. This leads coworkers to falsely conclude that minorities are less capable and competent.

Racial microaggressions also make their appearance in the superior-to-subordinate relationship, resulting in increased attrition rates of employees of color. Without having experienced a microaggression, it has been suggested that relationships between racial minority workers and nonracial minority supervisors had a stronger impact on their levels of stress and health as compared to their relationships with nonracial minority peers (Fox & Stallworth, 2004). When a racial minority has experienced a racial microaggression from their superior, the experience has been demonstrated to negatively impact employees and their organizations in areas such as job and life satisfaction, justice perceptions, organizational commitment, work-family conflict, turnover and psychological distress (Fox & Stallworth, 2004). Racial microaggressions from superiors can leave minority subordinates frustrated and angry, leading to work withdrawal, isolation in the office, lack of motivation to be productive, decline in the quality of work produced, and working only the required minimum hours regardless whether work is completed or not (Fox & Stallworth, 2004). Supervisors hold higher positions, wield more weight in the company, and are usually deemed more credible than subordinates, especially in cases where supervisors are white and subordinates are people of color, making the situation difficult for employees of color. Given that racial microaggressions are difficult to prove and that an existing power differential exists between superiors and subordinates, supervised employees are left with feelings of helplessness. They are caught in a catch-22 about whether to raise the issue with superiors and risk negative consequences (e.g., isolation, lower evaluations, being fired) or to suffer in silence. Working under these conditions will likely induce the employee of color to perform less productively or to resign.

Promotion

When the microaggressions come from supervisors, they can skew subordinates' perception of the motives of their bosses. Subordinates will most likely associate anything negative that occurs to them at work, such as not being promoted, with their racial microaggression experience. One salient consequence of racial bullying from superiors is employees' perceptions of procedural injustice (Fox & Stallworth, 2004). Fox and Stallworth continue by stating that "ongoing and condoned supervisory abuse implies that the organization has done little to develop or enforce procedures to protect employees from such abuse" (p. 4).

On a social level, peer-to-peer microaggressions can lead to aggressed individuals becoming social pariahs. When employees go on lunch breaks, attend after-work happy hours and other social activities affiliated with their place of work, they usually do so with their peers. Socializing with colleagues can also be a forum for networking, which can possibly lead to career advancement. If employees of color are left outside of the social loop based on their race, they may be prevented from reaching higher level positions more so than their white counterparts. An example of the effect microaggressions have on a social level as it relates to possible career advancement is documented in an article in which physicians of African descent working in various settings within six New England states were asked about their experiences dealing with race in the workplace (Nunez-Smith et al., 2007). According to the authors, the black physicians interviewed felt that they are never invited to certain information networking and social gatherings. One of the black physicians was quoted as saying, "We won't get invited to the picnic or to the dinner parties . . . and that is where those jobs come up. . . . We're not in the corridors of power" (Nunez-Smith et al., 2007, p. 47).

Causes of Racial Microaggressions in the Workplace

The fact that racial microaggressions exist in the workplace is not a surprise because places of employment are reflections of race-relations in the United States. If racism exists in the United States and selected inhabitants of this country experience racial microaggressions in various capacities of everyday life, it is safe to say that if a potential target is employed, then this unique racial experience will also occur at their place of employment. Individuals who hold racist views, unconsciously or consciously, carry these views with them in all avenues of life, including the workplace. One does not simply drop their beliefs at the door before they enter an office building. Because racism is not politically or socially acceptable and because there is a fear of the legal ramifications of putting their beliefs into action, proprietors of racist thought either mask their true feelings or diminish them to a very subtle level once they enter an environment that does not support this type of thinking. It has been established that this form of subtle racism is present in the workplace (Fox & Stallworth, 2004; Jackson & Stewart, 2003; Virtanen & Huddy, 1998) but the possible causes of this racial phenomena in a professional setting have yet to be explored.

One possible reason for the occurrence of racial microaggressions in the workplace can be linked to the need of the dominant race to affirm their rank in the organization, though it is usually at a higher level. Many non-administrative positions require a degree, certifications, job experience, and so on. As the number of college graduates who are people of color increases, they progressively make the traditionally white-dominated positions more competitive to acquire. With their entrance into these positions, racial minorities are sometimes viewed by the dominant race as a threat to their own job security or advancement in the company or organization. The manifestation of racial microaggressions in the workplace solidifies a professional racial caste system that maintains the current power system; people of color are placed at lower levels of organizations. This racial hierarchal structure is supported by microaggressions that remind employees of color about their "proper place."

Consequences of Racial Microaggressions in the Workplace

Since most of the microaggressions that occur at work go unnoticed or unchecked, the cumulative effects of these interactions are argued to be extremely damaging (Sue, Capodilupo, & Holder, 2008). These more subtle forms of racism, rather than unlawful acts of discrimination, are primarily responsible for the maintenance of unequal opportunity for racial minorities and women in the workplace (e.g., Rowe, 1990). The more subtle and unconscious forms of prejudice and discrimination help to maintain unequal opportunity in the workplace more than overt forms of racism because they are not necessarily actionable in a court of law (Stallworth et al., 2001). Though these individual actions may appear to only affect the targeted victim, the actions taken cumulatively can have system-wide effects in the workplace (Rowe, 1990). Rowe presents the example of how glass ceilings and glass walls preserve "occupational segregation" in the workplace and posits that they are maintained by subtle discrimination. The glass ceilings and walls that exist to keep racial minorities and women out of certain positions provide a prime example of how researchers have used microaggressions to explain unequal opportunity in the workplace.

The psychological consequences of racial microaggressions could be inferred from research investigating the damaging effects of racism and racial discrimination on the psychological well-being of those who endure these phenomena (Chakraborty & McKenzie, 2002; Kessler, Mickelson, & Williams, 1999; Williams, Neighbors, & Jackson, 2003; Williams, Yu, & Jackson, 1997). These researchers suggest that those who endure racism and racial discrimination have an increased likelihood of developing psychological impairments such as depression, anxiety, substance abuse, psychosis, and anger issues. The focus of this line of research tends to be on the overt types of racism experienced by people of color in a general context. Several studies have also found that the impact of subtle discrimination in the workplace on black Americans (Deitch et al., 2003; Salvatore & Shelton, 2007) has a negative personal and work performance impact. Others suggest that racial microaggressions are detrimental experiences to people of color because the inequities created can impair performance in the workplace (Franklin, 2004; Hinton, 2004; Sue, Capodilupo, & Holder, 2008). More information is needed on how the association between racial discrimination and well-being manifests in the workplace, especially in interactions involving racial microaggressions.

Some speculate that the psychological consequences of racial discrimination can actually lead to a reduced level of productivity in the workplace (e.g., Rowe, 1990). Steele's (1997) work on how stereotypes negatively affect the academic performance of women and African Americans can lend a framework for how racial microaggressions in the workplace influence the productivity of employees. Steele found that stereotyping decreases the stereotyped individual's identification with the domain (i.e., an academic environment). Many social psychologists support the theory that individuals internalize stereotypes and make these a part of their personality (e.g., Allport, 1954). A contextual application of Steele's work to the workplace may help empirically validate the posited psychological effects of racial microaggressions on individuals.

The intensity of the emotional reactions to racial microaggressions in the workplace depends on the nature of the relationship between the individuals in which the microaggressive interaction takes place (Deitch et al., 2003; Rowe, 1990; Stallworth et al., 2001). Most of the incidents and examples in the workplace concentrate on superior to subordinate interactions (Deitch et al., 2003; Rowe, 1990; Stallworth et al., 2001). Rowe gives many examples of how superiors (supervisors, managers, etc.) exhibit microaggressive behaviors towards subordinates (employees, supervisees, etc.). When a subordinate experiences a racial microaggression, he or she may feel that there is no room to express their true reaction for fear of further persecution, such as future retaliatory acts. In an effort to keep the job, the subordinate will most likely have to internalize the microaggression and simply move on with their day. Additionally, since the threat of microaggressions is common in nearly all contexts, situations, and interactions, those in the workplace will also deal with microaggressions from peer-colleagues as well as those who may be in positions subordinate to their position. As stated before, the true effect of racial microaggressions may not be seen from individual incidents, but from the accumulation of these events over time in the daily life of an individual (Solórzano et al., 2000).

In reaction to the psychological effects of racial microaggressions in the workplace, those who experience the microaggression may develop ways to cope with it so that they can continue their employment. As mentioned earlier, one way to deal with microaggressions in the workplace, which is probably very common, is to internalize each microaggressive event. Internalizing the event can occur in several different ways. A person can internalize an event by making up excuses for why the interaction occurred, such as interpreting the act as unintentional. The problem with this tactic is that it unconsciously invalidates the employee's experiential and racial realities. Since microaggressions often occur at the unconscious level, dealing with the microaggression by calling it unintentional is an easy way to remove oneself from the damaging nature of the physical interaction, but this does not imply psychological costs to the victim. If, however, an individual acknowledges that the interaction was indeed intentional, they will then need to deal with reconciling more negative emotions associated with being purposefully insulted, assaulted or invalidated. Since the nature of racial microaggression is rather ambiguous, the intentionality of the microaggression is interpreted at the discretion of the aggressed (Sue, Lin, Torino, Capodilupo, & Rivera, 2008; Sue, Rivera, Capodilupo, Lin, & Torino, 2008).

The Costs of Racial Microaggressions to Perpetrators

The psychological consequences of racial microaggressions in the workplace have primarily been discussed in relation to those who experience the microaggression but not to the aggressor of the microaggression. In the American workplace, the principle aggressors of racial microaggressions are whites. As with overt racism (Fredrickson, 1988), it could be postulated that whites are likely to experience some psychological consequences from their involvement in these microaggressive encounters. At this point in the investigation of racial microaggressions, little is known about exactly how whites experience and process these events. Research is needed to investigate the psychological consequences on whites who are the aggressors of racial microaggressions, as well as on whites who are bystanders and witnesses in racial microaggressive encounters. If racial microaggressions, however, are conscious and unconscious reflections of white superiority and their inclusive and exclusive nature, then there is evidence to suggest that whites suffer from a distorted sense of racial reality, reduced empathic ability, callousness toward others, and feelings of guilt and shame over their complicity in the unfair treatment of others

(Feagin, 2001; Spanierman, Armstrong, Poteat, & Beer, 2006; Sue, 2003). White Americans, as a result, experience extreme discomfort when topics of race are raised in situations that involve public disclosure. Their emotive reactions run the gamut from feelings of guilt and helplessness to defensiveness, anger, and outright fear or anxiety (Sue, 2005; Young & Davis-Russell, 2002). These negative emotions and the ensuing discomfort act as a major impediment to whites honestly confronting issues of race, racism and unfair biases. Since they hold the power and influence, the tendency to avoid racial issues and to deny the racial reality of people of color ultimately means maintaining the unfair white advantages of the status quo.

IMPLICATIONS

Scholars have recently begun to see the importance of racial microaggressions in the everyday life of racial minorities, and as a result, a number of studies have been conducted to explore their manifestations and impact (Sue, Bucceri, et al., 2007; Sue, Capodilupo, & Holder, 2008; Sue, Nadal, et al., 2008). Since research on racial microaggressions is still in an infant state, studies investigating the forms these microaggressions take when they occur in the workplace are still lacking. The prevalence of everyday discrimination, the elusive nature of racial microaggression, and the fear of being frank are all issues inherent in conducting workplace discrimination research, making it difficult to obtain consistent and representative results (Deitch et al., 2003). In addition, lack of such reports does not necessarily imply that these incidents do not have an impact on the recipients (Deitch et al., 2003). Therefore, it is vital that some methodological ingenuity be used when assessing such phenomena in the workplace.

Aside from empirically examining specific microaggressions that employees of color experience at work, coping strategies that they develop and employ in maintaining their dignity and sense of well-being need to be investigated so as to assist future generations to better deal with the modern face of racism (Sue, Capodilupo, & Holder, 2008). Without conceptual analysis and empirical documentation, the perilous nature of workplace racial microaggressions could not be elucidated and the pernicious effects they invoke could be easily downplayed (Solórzano et al., 2000).

Due to their subtle and often unconscious nature, microaggressions in the workplace often go overlooked, if not blatantly avoided (Rowe, 1990). Since these events are most likely to go unnoticed by management and internalized by the aggressed, the establishment of formal mechanisms in the workplace may be necessary for the aggressed to cope with the occurrence of racial microaggressions. Creating a forum for frank discussions amongst employees of color regarding the importance, nature, and consequences of racial microaggressions alongside discussion on how these issues could be addressed within the company should be instituted by management (Hinton, 2004). Due to the automatic and subtle nature of racial microaggressions, typical single-session diversity training courses may do little to eradicate such incidents in the workplace. Thus, the concept, possible manifestations, and perilous consequences of racial microaggressions should be included in traditional diversity training to raise awareness.

In response to the subtle forms of discrimination and microaggressions that occur in the workplace, Rowe (1990) and Stallworth et al. (2001) have suggested ways to remedy these situations. Rowe argues against the use of legislation or formal policy in dealing with microaggressions in the workplace. Instead, she believes employees should be given safe spaces to individually speak about these types of incidents. Rowe also suggests that employers "encourage responsible networks of minorities and women to support each other in discussing such problems" (p. 163). Stallworth et al., however, suggest the use of formal mediation procedures to deal with these issues. Stallworth and fellow researchers present the benefits of mediation and also, unlike Rowe, suggest that legislation is needed to enforce the systematic use of mediation in dealing with issues involving subtle discrimination in the workplace. Although scholars may disagree on the particular measures that should be taken to address issues of racial microaggression in the workplace, the consensus is that they need to be addressed.

In conclusion, racial microaggressions serve as barriers in the workplace that promote the maintenance of racial inequality in employment. Racial microaggressions operate in countless forms, are found in every phase of employment, and occur between all types of employees. Given that racial microaggressions inhibit the development of a truly diverse workforce in which people of color have equal opportunity to reach top managerial positions, it is impossible to expect industry to respond to the needs of an ever growing diverse society. The problem of racial inequality in the workplace extends beyond the work setting and adversely affects all areas of society. In essence, the problem of racial microaggressions in the workplace is a societal problem. In order to affect workplace and, ultimately, societal change, leaders need to directly address racial microaggressions in the workplace. Managers can learn how racial microaggressions are maintained by recognizing the experiences of people of color. Those in top managerial positions need to be conscious of environmental factors that can exclude the presence of people of color in the workforce. Leaders can create a culture that promotes racial diversity by overtly sending the message that racial microaggressive behavior will not be tolerated. The cultural norms for behavior and expectations must change in order to minimize the affects of racial microaggressions on the maintenance of racial inequality in the American workforce.

REFERENCES

Allport, G. (1954). *The nature of prejudice.* New York: Doubleday.

Brief, A. P., Dietz, J., Cohen, R. R., Pugh, S. D., & Vaslow, J. B. (2000). Just doing business: Modern racism and obedience to authority as explanations for employment discrimination. *Organizational Behavior and Human Decision Processes, 81*(1), 72–97.

Chakraborty, A., & McKenzie, K. (2002). Does racial discrimination cause mental illness? *British Journal of Psychiatry, 180*(6), 475–477.

Coleman, M. G. (2004). Racial discrimination in the workplace: does market structure make a difference? *Industrial Relations, 43*(3), 660–689.

Deitch, E. A., Barsky, A., Butz, R. M., Chan, S., Brief, A., & Bradley, J. C. (2003). Subtle yet significant: The existence and impact of everyday racial discrimination in the workplace. *Human Relations, 56*(11), 1299–1324.

Dovidio, J. F., & Gaertner, S. L. (2000). Aversive racism in selection decisions: 1989 and 1999. *Psychological Science, 11,* 315–319.

Dovidio, J. F., Gaertner, S. L., Kawakami, K., & Hodson, G. (2002). Why can't we all just get along? Interpersonal biases and interracial distrust. *Cultural Diversity and Ethnic Minority Psychology, 8,* 88–102.

Essed, P. (1991). *Understanding everyday racism.* Newbury Park, CA: Sage.

Feagin, J. R. (2001). *Racist America: Roots, current realities, and future reparations.* New York: Routledge.

Fox, S., & Stallworth, L. E. (2004). *Bullying, racism, and power: An investigation of racial/ethnic bullying in the U.S. workplace.* Paper presented at the SIOP Conference, Chicago, IL.

Franklin, A. J. (2004). *From brotherhood to manhood: How black men rescue their relationships and dreams from the invisibility syndrome.* Hoboken, NJ: John Wiley and Sons.

Fredrickson, G. (1988). *The arrogance of race: Historical perspectives on slavery, racism, and social inequity.* Middletown, CT: Wesleyan University Press.

Gaertner, S. L., & Dovidio, J. F. (2005). Understanding and addressing contemporary racism: From aversive racism to the common ingroup identity model. *Journal of Social Issues, 61*(3), 615–639.

Hinton, E. L. (2004, March/April). Microinequities: When small slights lead to huge problems in the workplace. *DiversityInc, 79–82.*

Jackson, P. B., & Stewart, Q. (2003). A research agenda for the black middle class: Work stress, survival strategies, and mental health. *Journal of Health and Social Behavior, 44,* 442–455.

Kessler, R. C., Mickelson, K. D., & Williams, D. R. (1999). The prevalence, distribution, and mental health correlates of perceived racism in the United States. *Journal of Health and Social Behavior, 40*(3), 208–230.

Monteith, M. J. (1996). Contemporary forms of prejudiced-related conflicts: In search of a nutshell. *Personality and Social Psychology Bulletin, 22,* 461–473.

Nunez-Smith, M., Curry, L. A., Bigby, J., Berg, D., Krumholz, H. M., & Bradley, E. H. (2007). Impact of race on the professional lives of physicians of African descent. *Annals of Internal Medicine, 146*(1), 45–51.

Pettigrew, T. F., & Martin, J. (1987). Shaping the organizational context for black American inclusion. *Journal of Social Issues, 43,* 41–78.

Pierce, C., Carew, J., Pierce-Gonzalez, D., & Willis, D. (1978). An experiment in racism: TV commercials. In C. Pierce (Ed.), *Television and education* (pp. 62–88). Beverly Hills, CA: Sage.

Rowe, M. P. (1990). Barriers to equality: the power of subtle discrimination to maintain unequal opportunity. *Employee Responsibilities and Rights Journal*, 3(2), 153–163.

Salvatore, J., & Shelton, J. N. (2007). Cognitive costs of exposure to racial prejudice. *Psychological Science, 18*(9), 810–815.

Solórzano, D., Ceja, M., & Yosso, T. (2000). Critical race theory, racial microaggressions, and campus racial climate: The experiences of African American college students. *Journal of Negro Education, 69*(1/2), 60–73.

Spanierman, L. B., Armstrong, P. I., Poteat, V. P., & Beer, A. M. (2006). Psychosocial costs of racism to whites: Exploring patterns through cluster analysis. *Journal of Counseling Psychology, 53*, 434–441.

Stallworth, L. E., McPherson, T., & Rute, L. (2001). Discrimination in the workplace: How mediation can help. *Dispute Resolution Journal, 56*(1), 35–44, 83–87.

Steele, C. M. (1997). A threat in the air: How stereotypes shape intellectual identity and performance. *American Psychologist, 52*(6), 613–629.

Sue, D. W. (1991). A model for cultural diversity training. *Journal of Counseling and Development, 70*, 99–105.

Sue, D. W. (1994, Winter). U.S. business and the challenge of cultural diversity. *The Diversity Factor*, 24–28.

Sue, D. W. (2003). *Overcoming our racism: The journey to liberation.* San Francisco, CA: Jossey-Bass.

Sue, D. W. (2005). Racism and the conspiracy of silence. *The Counseling Psychologist, 33*(1), 100–114.

Sue, D. W., Bucceri, J. M., Lin, A. I., Nadal, K. L., & Torino, G. C. (2007). Racial microaggressions and the Asian American experience. *Cultural Diversity and Ethnic Minority Psychology, 13*(1), 72–81.

Sue, D. W., Capodilupo, C. M., & Holder, A. M. B. (2008). Racial microaggressions in the life experience of black Americans. *Professional Psychology: Research and Practice, 39*(3), 329–336.

Sue, D. W., Capodilupo, C. M., Torino, G. C., Bucceri, J. M., Holder, A.M.B., Nadal, K. L., et al. (2007). Racial microaggressions in everyday life: Implications for clinical practice. *American Psychologist, 62*(4), 271–286.

Sue, D. W., Lin, A. I., Torino, G. C., Capodilupo, C. M., & Rivera, D. P. (2008). *Racial microaggressions and difficult dialogues on race.* Manuscript submitted for publication.

Sue, D. W., Nadal, K. L., Capodilupo, C. M., Lin, A. I., Rivera, D. P., & Torino, G. C. (2008). Racial microaggressions against black Americans: Implications for counseling. *Journal of Counseling and Development, 86*(3), 330–338.

Sue, D. W., Rivera, D. P., Capodilupo, C. M., Lin, A. I., & Torino, G. C. (2008). *Racial dialogues and white student fears: Implications for education and training.* Manuscript submitted for publication.

Sue, D. W., & Sue, D. (2008). *Counseling the culturally diverse: Theory and practice* (5th ed.). Hoboken, NJ: John Wiley & Sons.

Sue, S., Sue, D. W., Zane, N., & Wong, H. Z. (1985). Where are the Asian American leaders and top executives? *P/AAMHRC Review, 4*, 13–15.

U.S. Census Bureau. (2004). *U.S. interim projections by age, sex, race, and Hispanic origin.* Retrieved April 11, 2008, from http://www.census.gov/ipc/www/ usinterimproj/.

U.S. Department of Labor, Bureau of Labor Statistics. (2006). *Household data annual averages.* Retrieved February 16, 2007, from ftp://ftp.bls.gov/pub/special. requests/lf/aat11.txt.

U.S. Equal Employment Opportunity Commission. (2002a). *Diversity in law firms.* Retrieved February 16, 2007, from http://www.eeoc.gov/stats/reports/ diversitylaw/index.html.

U.S. Equal Employment Opportunity Commission. (2002b). *Diversity in the finance industry.* Retrieved February 16, 2007, from http://www.eeoc.gov/stats/ reports/finance/index.html.

U.S. Equal Employment Opportunity Commission. (2002c). *Diversity in the media: A chart book for selected industries.* Retrieved February 16, 2007, from http:// www.eeoc.gov/stats/reports/media/index.html.

Virtanen, S. V., & Huddy, L. (1998). Old-fashion racism and new forms of racial prejudices. *The Journal of Politics, 60*(2), 311–312.

Williams, D. R., Neighbors, H. W., & Jackson, J. S. (2003). Racial/ethnic discrimination and health: Findings from community studies. *American Journal of Public Health, 93*(2), 200–208.

Williams, D. R., Yu, Y., & Jackson, J. S. (1997). Racial differences in physical and mental health. *Journal of Health Psychology, 2*(3), 335–351.

Young, G., & Davis-Russell, E. (2002). The vicissitudes of cultural competence: Dealing with difficult classroom dialogue. In E. Davis-Russell (Ed.), *The California School of Professional Psychology handbook of multicultural education, research, intervention, and training* (pp. 37–53). San Francisco, CA: Jossey-Bass.

CHAPTER 11

Incorporating Internationalism into Diversity Training
Elaine A. Burke

The educational system in the United States has historically been limited in terms of both multicultural considerations and international issues. In order to address the increasing numbers of racial/ethnic populations within American society, there has been more of an emphasis on multicultural issues within the past few decades. Many educational programs have begun to include diversity training in their curriculum and have included considerations of African Americans, Native Americans, Asian Americans, and Latinos, as well as gender and sexual orientation. More recently, a number of diversity programs have expanded the topics that are covered to include Middle Eastern Americans, religious oppression, ageism, ableism, and classism. The field of psychology has been rooted in Western culture, but its perspective is limited as it does not include alternative views. It is important to increase the understanding of psychological issues worldwide in order to address international issues and to help people adapt to various forms of modernization (Marsella, 2007; Stevens, 2007). American psychologists might work with their colleagues internationally in order to address complex global issues with a psychological basis in the next century. There is a need for psychologists to become internationally competent in order to work effectively with these challenging global issues.

INCREASING INTERNATIONAL COMPETENCY

In order to become multiculturally competent in America, a person needs to understand the issues of dominance and oppression in the United States and begin to dismantle the hierarchy that forms the structure of

American society. The political majority exerts its power and maintains its privilege by establishing the standards for society and determining what is normal and acceptable. Individuals in the political minority are judged by their ability to conform to the majority-dominant perspective based on beliefs, behaviors and appearance. In the United States people from a European background comprise the mainstream culture and benefit from "white privilege." Individuals from this group must recognize their own privilege, albeit invisible, and their own complicity in perpetuating this stratification of society. Likewise, there are a number of other types of majority privilege, such as being male, Christian, heterosexual, middle or upper class, young, able-bodied, and so on, all of which intersect to determine who is given affirmation (or conversely, denigration). The basis for developing international competency is to become aware of the dominance of Western cultural beliefs and, more specifically, American privilege.

An individual might consider world history in order to gain an understanding of the dominance of Western culture. Beginning in the sixteenth century, England and Spain "discovered" and colonized the Americas. England also colonized Singapore, Hong Kong and India on the Asian continent, as well as Australia. Spain, meanwhile, claimed the Philippines. Perhaps the most striking example of imperialism and colonization was in Africa. Almost the entire continent was under European rule until the late twentieth century. Its resources were taken and its people were forced to produce goods for the colonizing country. In fact, its very people were taken by force as property and made to work in inhumane conditions. In the United States slavery was not formally abolished until the late nineteenth century. The United States, a former colony itself, was not a colonizer in Africa, and yet it reaped the benefits of slavery while claiming to be a land where immigrants were welcomed, had inalienable rights, and all "men" were equal. Unfortunately, these rights did not extend to people of color or women. While Europe had dominated the world in centuries past, during the twentieth century the United States became a world power and engaged in similar hegemony. Slater and Taylor (1999) believe that during the last century the historical narrative consisted of a description of American power. In order to become more aware of American privilege, it may be important to consider American identity and how Americans are perceived internationally.

In some ways, describing what it means to be an American for a person from the United States is almost as difficult as having European Americans describe what it means to be "white." People are usually the most adept at defining their own culture when they are different from the mainstream. Part of American privilege is that Americans often view their culture as the "norm" and other cultures as different. In some ways there is truth to that belief, as American music, television, and movies have permeated most of the world, and popular culture within the United States is also popular culture in many other countries. Americans are usually more able to describe their own culture when they have either lived abroad or worked with immigrant populations within the United States.

Most Americans, regardless of ethnic background, share a complex set of American values and beliefs that comprise an American identity. According to Kohut and Stokes (2006) Americans compared to Europeans are more individualistic, more action-oriented and more negative toward government interference. Americans believe that people who are not successful are responsible for their own failure. They want personal freedom rather than justice and are less likely to think that the government should help those people who cannot help themselves. Schidkraut (2007) describes a number of American values, two of which are that America is a land of freedom and opportunity (liberalism) and that it tends to primarily consist of white Protestants (ethnoculturalism). Other American values are that America is a democracy with participation by its citizens (civic republicanism) and that it is a diverse country of immigrants (incorporationism).

The perception of Americans has been steadily declining. In 2001 support of America was 40 to 70 percent in the Middle East, Northern Africa, and South Asia, but in 2004 less than 5 percent of this population supported the United States (Schweitzer & Schweitzer, 2006). The Pew Research Center (2005) found that while the positive image of the United States has decreased since 2000, many countries still rate America positively, with the exception of the Muslim nations in the Middle East and Central Asia. While there is general support for the war on terrorism worldwide, there is the belief that the United States disregards the welfare of others in its foreign policy (Nakaya, 2005; Pew Research Center, 2005). Generally, countries are negative toward policies rather than values, even in the Middle East (Pew Research Center, 2005). However, not surprisingly, in the Middle East people are against the U.S. war on terrorism. Another reason for negative perceptions about the United States is that the culture is seen as wasteful, decadent, and harmful to the rest of the earth (Nakaya, 2005). American movies, television shows, books and music, as well as the Internet, all contribute toward the perception of an American lifestyle that many view as negative. While most Americans think that the transmission of its ideas and the behaviors of the American government benefit the world, the majority of the world disagrees. Americans are often unaware and surprised by the reactions of the rest of the world (Pew Research Center, 2005).

After an examination of American identity and privilege, diversity classes might explore perspectives on international topics such as worldwide racism, women, sexual orientation, ageism, ableism, classism, and religion.

INCORPORATING GLOBAL PERSPECTIVES INTO DIVERSITY CLASS CURRICULUM

Ethnic/Racial

Contemporary racism is connected to the European quest for expansion, which included colonization, slavery of Africans, and imperialism imposed by countries such as England, Spain, and Belgium (Mullings, 2005).

A number of countries in the world have a history of colonization, and some may have a relatively recent period of independence (Kenya in 1963, Botswana in 1966, Bahamas in 1973). The history of colonization continues to impact these countries. According to Adi and Sherwood (2003), the colonizing country used the work and resources of the colonized country to develop its wealth and improve the lifestyle of its people. The culture of the colonized people was destroyed, and the people were controlled and used for the benefit of the colonizer. People of the indigenous culture were made to feel inferior and became apathetic. Views on the hierarchy of race and the importance of being racially pure were also perpetuated by the countries that colonized in the past, which primarily was Europe (Cornwall & Stoddard, 2001).

Race has been the foundation for the development of the current world system in terms of how it has emerged and how it functions. According to Persaud and Walker (2001), race has had a position "in dividing the world into various binary opposites such as civilized/uncivilized, modern/backward, rational/superstitious, developed/undeveloped, and so on" (p. 374), which "have involved both subtle and very unsubtle practices of infantilization" (p. 375). The memories of displacement and migration of many African and Asian people continue to have an impact on the world's perception of identity and difference (in which people of European background are considered the "norm" and people of color are considered different). Racialized beliefs in supremacy and the allowance of economic exploitation of the populations perpetuate the current system in the world. Societies have developed by identifying who is in power and who is "the other." The "other" is subject to discrimination or sometimes even more severe forms of treatment such as death.

Countries that have been defined by wars or colonization may define themselves as nations for purposes of world trade and economy, but the people may continue to identify themselves according to historical subgroups, sometimes known as tribes (Cornwall & Stoddard, 2001). Since these groups share a minimal national identity and a strong ethnic, tribal, or religious identity, struggles over political power or resources can result in interethnic conflict, followed by violence and sometimes even genocide, as occurred in Rwanda (Chirot & Seligman, 2001).

Historically different events, such as the fight against colonization, the movement for civil rights, and the struggle against apartheid have sought to undo historic racism. But the advent of global capitalization has created a different type of contemporary racism (Mullings, 2005). Global capitalization occurs when corporations in wealthier countries develop factories in poorer countries where the cost of labor is significantly lower. The most well-known event to bring awareness of this current form of worldwide racism was the United Nations World Conference against Racism, Racial Discrimination and Other Forms of Intolerance, which met in August, 2001, in Durban, South Africa. At this conference, people from countries impacted by global racialization wanted to confront the unequal relationship with people from Europe and the Americas and promote the dismantling of global racialization by a more equitable distribution of resources.

Global capitalism has produced new consequences for racialization (Mullings, 2005). When industries seek labor in non-Western countries, these countries accumulate national debt, adjust policies, and continue colonial manifestations in many countries that are postcolonial. Indigenous populations are displaced in order to obtain natural resources in the areas where they live and then need to seek employment as a way to survive. A number of these people migrate to more industrialized countries, where they encounter racism and are blamed for racial problems and sometimes for the high levels of unemployment and the occurrence of recession in the host country, which occurred in the United States. Resentment of the immigrants by the middle-class population allows for the maintenance of racism in society. In addition, the media promotes racialized views through the export of U.S. movies, television shows, and music (e.g., rock music and rap). While overt forms of racism have declined, the attempt of some countries and individuals to be color-blind allows for both the invisibility of racial inequities and the perception that legislative or institutional practices (such as affirmative action and antidiscrimination laws) are unnecessary. When minority people do not advance, historical beliefs that they are culturally deficient, uneducated or have individual shortcomings, such as a lack of motivation, reemerge. These beliefs provide a basis for stating that antiracist practices are not advantageous and are, in fact, a rationalization for the inequities. The only way that these inequalities are perpetuated is through the consent of the dominant population, which in most cases are people of European descent.

Women

Women's issues internationally are complex because economic issues are very much related to legal issues, and both of these issues are also influenced by cultural considerations. Women's labor in the home is unpaid and not seen as valuable, and even when they work outside of the home, they work longer hours for less pay and benefits. They are taught that they are dependent upon men, and men are the leaders. These beliefs remain even in countries where women have achieved more equality, as these beliefs are often part of most, if not all, cultures and religions. These beliefs allow men to dominate women's lives, setting the stage for domestic violence. Burn (2005) believes that psychological and economic dependence make it difficult for women to leave men, and in some countries they are not allowed to get a divorce, or if they do, they are not entitled to any assets from the marriage, sometimes not even permitted to have their own children.

These psychological and economic problems are compounded by legal problems. A number of countries did not have laws against domestic violence until recently, such as Japan in 2001, Kenya in 2002, and Pakistan in 2003 (Burn, 2005). Laws have no effect, however, unless police are willing to intervene. Other international women's problems include culture-specific issues such as dowry death (India) and honor killing (Middle East), as well as more global problems like the sexual victimization of women through rape and prostitution (Burn, 2005). Burn suggests that sexual victimization might be an issue for women worldwide and could serve as an agenda to unite women.

Western feminism may not be appropriate for cultures with different social and economic situations, and the feminism of developing countries may be connected to other challenges such as poverty, racism, and imperialism (Burn, 2005). Women in Western countries are from countries that have been imperialistic, and Western feminism may be seen as an attempt to apply Western values, such as in some Middle Eastern countries like Iran and Iraq. While Western women are focused on equal rights, equal opportunity, and equal pay with men, women in developing countries are more concerned with starvation and ethnic discrimination, directing their efforts more toward the survival of their community rather than themselves as women. Aguilar (2004) recommends an approach that combines gender, race, class, and other forms of oppression within a framework of capitalist national relations.

Heterosexism

Being gay or lesbian is often considered to be unnatural, sinful, not normal, and/or criminal in many of the world's societies (Dorf & Perez, 1995). These perceptions allow governments to persecute gay or lesbian individuals without feeling the need to defend such an action. Dorf and Perez found legal statutes from the 1990s stating that gay men and lesbians in Nicaragua and Romania can be incarcerated, while in Iran they can be executed. People who are not heterosexual can be seen as undermining the social structure and the continuation of the population and thus face significant discrimination within societies across the world. Rights for gay individuals can sometimes be perceived as a Western (neo-imperialist) concept and therefore should not be imposed on other countries (e.g., Singapore). Many government leaders, in India for example, believe that people in their culture are all heterosexual; therefore, the need to consider gay and lesbian rights does not apply to their respective societies. There are no consequences for people who perpetuate violence, especially when it is enacted by government officials. What's more, private citizens who are gay or lesbian have no recourse to the law, since very rarely does specific legislation include hate crime behavior. People who are not heterosexual can have their children removed from them, be arrested and jailed, tortured, forced to receive psychiatric treatment (in the form of in-voluntary hospitalization, electroshock and aversion therapy), and even be executed (Dorf & Perez, 1995; Herdt, 1997).

There have been some advances in support toward the gay and les-bian population. Gay-friendly places emerged in the 1950s in some of the larger cities in Europe and the United States. In the later part of the twentieth century people began to identify themselves as gay or lesbian, and the media followed by spreading the concept of sexual orientation to other cultures, even those that denied alternative forms of sexuality ex-isted, such as cultures in Africa and Asia (Adam, Duyvendak, & Krouwel, 1999). While some Western societies have made significant progress in becoming more tolerant of gay and lesbian individuals, unfortunately the same level of tolerance does not exist worldwide.

Ageism

Some societies have believed that older people should be respected and that their children should care for them. However, the attitudes toward and roles of older people are changing. In Africa, for instance, because many parents are afflicted with HIV/AIDS, many older people are caring for grandchildren; in Asia modernization has caused many young people to work in the cities, lessening the value of filial piety, the practice of chil-dren caring for the elderly; and in Latin America developing nations are focusing on the needs of infants and children to such an extent that support for elderly people is in question (Takamura, 2001). In more industrialized nations, older people may receive supplemental income. In developing nations, poor elderly individuals may be fighting for survival.

Public pension issues are receiving considerable attention, becoming a challenge in many countries around the world due to the increasing el-derly population (Hokenstad & Johansson, 2001). It is anticipated that the policies of many countries will change during the twenty-first century. The population is continuing to live longer, while a number of people are retiring earlier, resulting in a longer period of time in which they are un-employed and needing to withdraw retirement savings and corporate and public pensions. In contrast to industrialized countries, many developing countries, such as Pakistan, do not have a pension system for older citizens who cannot work and do not have family to support them (Clark, 2001). Most developing countries have mandatory retirement ages, and many people are poor and do not have adequate resources for older age. There is a need for countries to determine ways to assist older individuals. A num-ber of these countries were former colonies and lack the financial means to provide governmental pensions. Not only that, there may be political problems in instituting a Western-style system of income for older people.

Internationally, there are differences regarding the care of elderly in-dividuals. Americans believe in the value of an individual and helping people that need assistance; however, there is also a belief in individualism and one's responsibility for caring for one's self. These contrasting beliefs challenge projected responsibility for caring for the elderly. Despite the perception (held by many people outside the United States) that Americans frequently place older people in nursing homes, Cox (2001) found that most elderly people and their caregivers do not use a formal support system, probably because of price, but if they do use it, it is only temporary. Though the American government has been uninvolved for the most part, the United Kingdom and Israel support the role of the community and the government in assisting in elder care. While programs must consider culture, they may be helpful in providing a better level of care to older people and a better quality of life for caregivers.

In both Japan and the United States, placing the elderly in an institution such as a nursing home is low. In Japan elderly citizens prefer to live with their children and prefer that a female relative cares for them, while in the United States older people prefer to live on their own (Silver, 1998). However, in Japan, despite the advantage of reducing feelings of isolation when older people live with children, at times the small, shared environment and reduced privacy results in elder abuse (Ajima, 2005). Also in Japan, there is a social structure that carries an obligation for caring for the elderly without outside assistance, and it cannot be assumed that caretaking for the elderly is due to feelings of caring for the individual. Americans are more likely to be willing to make sacrifices for parents as compared to Japanese; at the same time, Americans indicated that they are less likely to care for parents if the burden was too great. It may be beneficial for psychologists to explore some of the advantages and disadvantages of different types of elder care internationally in order to better meet the needs of this growing population.

Ableism

Priestley (2001) estimated that there are half a billion people with disabilities worldwide, and it is expected that the population of people with disabilities will increase in both technologically advanced and developing countries. Unfortunately, internationally there are only a limited number of legal protections for people with disabilities. In 1990 the Americans with Disabilities Act provided a number of opportunities that included access to services, transportation, and educational and occupational accommodations. Other countries have begun their own process of assisting people with disabilities. People with disabilities have low social power and can be considered a minority worldwide. In India they are not included as part of the national census and thus are not even counted as people (Ghai, 2001). Unfortunately, in many parts of the world people with disabilities are subject to a great deal of discrimination.

Some societies (e.g., Jordan) have negative perceptions of those with disabilities, especially severe disabilities, and the negative perceptions extend to the appropriateness of disabled people having sex (Turmusani, 2001). As they are not able to access higher education, they become financially dependent upon others. Access is often seen as less important in developing countries, as compared to financial concerns, shelter, education, medical services and sexuality.

People with disabilities in developing countries are particularly affected by class. Those with adequate means can procure assistants and devices that allow the functional impact of their disability to be minimized (Charlton, 1998; Ghai, 2001). In developing countries, work is not only an important aspect of a person's identity, but generally also to their survival. In some developing countries, they may participate in all activities (including work tasks) of the community to the extent they're able, but they are generally not included in more industrialized employment (Ingstad & Reynolds, 1995). People in Westernized societies may receive some income or pension from the government, yet Turmusani (2001), based upon his research in Jordan and United Nations reports, found that people in developing countries often either receive assistance from their families or beg to survive.

Religion

There has been a long history of oppression in the world because of religion. The group with the longest history of oppression is the Jewish population, seeing how anti-Semitism began three thousand years ago (Adams, 2000). Throughout history they were at times assimilated into the dominant culture and were successful, and then at other times they were forced to work as slaves, expelled from the community and killed. There were even attempts by the government to destroy the culture through genocide. The most horrific example was in the mid-twentieth century, when 6 million people of Jewish descent were killed in Nazi Germany. Anti-Semitism continues to be a significant global concern.

The Muslims are another religious group that has encountered significant religious discrimination (Hassan, 2006). However, since the 9/11 attack on the United States, there has been a substantial increase in discrimination toward this group. Hassan believes that the media perpetuates racism by allowing anti-Muslim cartoons in widely distributed newspapers at the same time it claims the right of free speech and that racism against Muslims is supported by governments. He thinks that European countries are joining the United States in promoting religious hatred and indicates that this behavior in Europe is similar to the behavior exhibited toward the Jewish population in the past. There have also been indications of anti-Muslim discrimination in other countries, such as China and Kenya (Filkens, 2002; Roberts, 2001).

Classism

According to Marsella (2007), 20 percent of the world's population lives in complete poverty, lacking adequate water, food, and housing. People in the lowest 20 percent in terms of income have 1.4 percent of the world's total wealth. There is an increasing gap between the incomes of the wealthy and the poor, and there is also increasing disparity between nations, with some much wealthier than others. Many worldwide believe that the United States perpetuates the divide between the rich and the poor (Pew Research Center, 2005).

Inequities arising from slavery and colonialism have produced great differences in living conditions, wealth, life expectancy and the power to impact governmental institutions (Booker & Minter, 2001). History has produced an assumption that different populations have different expectations when it comes to quality of life, thus legitimizing the inequities. For example, European refugees were given $1.23 a day and African refugees were given $0.11 a day because, state Booker and Minter (2001), "You must give European refugees used to cappuccino and CNN a higher standard of living" (p. 15). These disparities are not limited to issues of race; they are also about access to economic and political power and privilege. There is no single world government, but various organizations (such as the United Nations, the World Bank, and the World Trade Organization) do have considerable impact on world decision-making policies and possess the power to determine global direction. Representation and leadership in these organizations correlates with race (Booker & Minter, 2001). Based upon these differences, it is not surprising that people from the wealthiest countries wish to restrict the free flow of immigrants from the world's poorest countries to its richest. Some world leaders do not make decisions that are in the best interests of their citizens and these leaders' actions may result in increased emigration, which has global implications. A number of the world's poorest countries (e.g., Africa) were former colonies. While these countries are no longer colonized, there are rewards for conforming to outside pressures rather than to pressures of the country's own people. Leaders may ease policies to allow multinational corporations set up industries, reduce the minimum wage and devalue currency that promotes the widespread poverty. This new world order is a manifestation of neo-imperialism, which has in the past been described as modernization, development and growth (socially acceptable terms to justify oppression). While some people in these countries may be able to work in factories (although at very low wages and extremely long hours), others are no longer able to do the type of work they did in the past because their lands have been taken over to export crops. As a result, they are forced into poverty. Governments might assist in addressing this issue by considering how to best reduce poverty when allowing international migration. The discrepancies in the economies of different countries has been an important factor in the immigration of people from poorer, less developed countries to wealthier, more affluent ones. This issue will be further explored in the next section, which will address global concerns.

GLOBAL CONCERNS

Recent Immigration Patterns

Between 1850 and 1950 there were large groups of immigrants comprised of people of color (the Chinese immigrating to the United States, for instance); however, the vast majority of migration was either within Europe or between Europe and North and South America. Beginning in the 1950s, there were three main groups of immigrants from Latin America and the Caribbean, from southern and eastern Asia, and from northern Africa, the Middle East, and southern Europe (Marger, 2006). These groups migrated to North America, northwestern and western Europe, and Australia—an instance in which people from less industrialized countries migrated to more industrialized ones. Not only was there a change in direction, but the number of people migrating greatly increased. The two main reasons for the vast increase and change in immigration were disparate economic development and political conflicts within and between countries.

The dramatic change in immigration patterns produced a change in the racial complexion of Europe, North America and Australia, formerly comprised of people with European backgrounds. These individuals were not only the dominant culture (e.g., in the United States and Australia) but also the numerical majority. It is beneficial to consider different types of ethnic integration in order to explore how different ethnic groups might combine to form a greater society.

There are some people who believe that greater ethnic diversity within a country results in greater conflict. The group that is dominant may exert its power, physically or through a belief system, over minority groups that resist, accommodate or submit to the dominant population. Marger (2006) defines different models of ethnic integration. Societies with different ethnic groups can pursue either assimilation (in which the groups become more similar and regularly interact) or pluralism (in which the groups retain their distinct culture and are separated). In cultures where there is a belief in assimilation, ideally there are no ethnic groups, although this type of integration is rarely achieved and usually there are varying degrees of assimilation. (However, people of color in a European American-dominant society are generally never perceived as assimilated, unless there is considerable intermarriage and the groups are physically indistinguishable.) In contrast, pluralism is a model of integration in which cultural differences are maintained and sometimes become even more pronounced. Cultural pluralism occurs when there is retention of some cultural beliefs within the dominant cultural framework. In the United States this is known as multiculturalism. Structural pluralism describes distinct ethnic communities and organizations for its members that may mirror the organizations of the mainstream group.

While the United States may currently view itself as multicultural, as least historically, it has been seen as a "melting pot" in which assimilation into a national identity was promoted. The push for multiculturalism was instituted because its proponents believed that people of color would not be viewed as part of the mainstream, and therefore would not be accepted, unless there was a greater understanding of different cultures. In addition, while people from European backgrounds needed only to adapt to another type of "white culture" to assimilate, immigrants who were nonwhite needed to lose their culture, only to fail to be perceived as American. Other countries, such as Canada, have perceived themselves as having more than one national identity (English and French), so immigrants generally assimilate to one of the two dual national identities (Marger, 2006). Another model of integration is to develop an entirely new culture from the integration of a number of cultures (e.g., Brazil), resulting in a common culture described as ethnic assimilation. The belief is that the society will be improved if people from different ethnic and racial backgrounds can be rapidly merged into one overall culture. Some people have argued that a nationalistic identity may cause ethnic fragmentation and international conflicts and prefer using the term *cosmopolitan*, which signifies a person who is a citizen of the world united with others in a common humanity (Cornwall & Stoddard, 2001).

Role of American Superpower

Another important consideration is how superpowers impact the world. By the end of the twentieth century, it was believed that America was the superpower, and today it is believed that the political, economic and cultural power of the United States determines the structure of racial beliefs worldwide (Bonnett, 2006). This power allows the United States to perpetuate the belief that people from European backgrounds and white cultures are superior. The United States developed based on the belief that everyone is equal and has equal opportunity. This belief in antihierarchy is currently perceived as a sign of modernization. After 9/11, when U.S. foreign policy became more militarily aggressive, Bonnett (2006) believes that marginalized groups perceive themselves as being unable to resist American interests. American actions have a significant influence on everyone on earth, and its perception as a symbol of modernization is transnational.

Indigenous populations often indicate an attachment to their culture, pride and education, and their goals may not include increasing industrialization in their country and becoming part of the global market (Bonnett, 2006). The indigenous population are being encouraged to rid themselves of poverty by becoming more developed, however, this development might place them in significant danger of losing their culture. In significant danger of losing their culture, the indigenous are being encouraged to rid themselves of poverty by becoming more developed. The United States does not need to impose its views on the world because it has already been able to achieve that, symbolizing wealth, freedom and a good way of life. The United States is seen as a way for people who have been marginalized in the past to gain an opportunity for emancipation.

America is guilty of cultural imperialism. Indeed, its movies, books, and music have permeated the world's cultures (Kohut & Stokes, 2006). These exports have been seen as converting the rest of the world to its ideals, which were the founding principles of limited government, individualism, equality and liberty. The belief system is known as Americanism. Americans may not perceive their own imperialism because they may consider every person to be a potential American. American nationalism is based upon American ideals, not racial or ethnic superiority. It also looks to the future rather than the past and sees the future as being even more positive. Others believe that America is the land of opportunity, where immigrants can become successful, on account of its economic, educational, political and psychological attitudes.

Schweitzer and Schweitzer (2006) think that the present and future leaders of other countries might encourage their people to have a more positive image of America if the American people are conciliatory and engaging rather than utilizing military force. Policies must be developed that not only recognize American interests, but also the interests of people in other countries. One goal is to change the Muslim jihad to mutual cooperation and respect. In order to achieve this respect, there is a need to share resources, limit use of military power, and embrace attitudes of respect for all people and the many positive beliefs of the Muslim people. The alternative is bloodshed, fear and a depressed economy, even in wealthy nations. Because America has such a huge amount of power, some people may worry about that power being maintained (Bonnett, 2006). But perhaps it is better to acknowledge the dominance of the United States and then think about how racial and ethnic viewpoints are recognized and addressed. Because of its global domination, the United States has a responsibility to attend to the dynamics of social, political and economic change.

CONCLUSIONS AND RECOMMENDATIONS

A number of different types of oppression have been described, and while only some countries were used as examples, most of these types of oppression exist in many countries. The culture of each country impacts the form and expression of oppression. While some individuals believe that people in Westernized cultures are more liberal and accepting of differences, non-Westernized cultures are much more accepting of certain types of differences. For example, in less industrialized societies, people with disabilities are involved in all activities (including work) to the extent that they are able to participate (Ingstad & Reynolds, 1995). Some cultures, such as the Sambia of New Guinea and some Native American tribal groups, are more accepting of same-sex behavior (Herdt, 1997).

In addition to culture, economic and political power affects the hierarchal stratification both within and between nations across the globe. The United States has achieved significant economic and political power, due in part to its history of exploiting people of color and immigrant populations, its current transnational capitalization, and its values, which promote individual achievement and opportunity. Historically the people of the United States have also viewed the country as a land able to incorporate immigrants from diverse backgrounds. The fairly recent adoption of multiculturalism is an extension of the value of incorporation, which promotes the acceptance and appreciation of different cultures and the integration of a range of perspectives. Incorporation might further be extended to include internationalism.

In a world that is becoming increasingly more global (perhaps due to the Internet and the prevalence of transnational corporations and alliances), employment opportunities in the future will most likely include more international involvement. Students entering the workforce will have to compete for those positions. They might either promote what has been perceived as predatory cultural imperialism and capitalism, or they might consider the interests and values of countries that may be economically poorer but rich in culture. They might be able to make a more informed choice by the inclusion of internationalism in their educational training.

Schools and training programs can assist students in developing an awareness and knowledge of global issues by including international perspectives in their diversity classes. Instructors for diversity classes can include books on international topics (including personal experiences and perspectives), films, videos, music, and perhaps even live satellite broadcasts. Yet in order for students to become internationally competent and capable of working in a multicultural environment, schools need to incorporate an international perspective throughout their curricula. The diversity class can serve as a basis for understanding international issues; however, there is a need for integration in foundation classes (understanding human behavior from many contexts), as well as more advanced classes in research, interventions, and applications in the global environment. In order to gain applied experience, students can work with recent immigrants (or individuals who are not acculturated) and take a foreign language class concurrently. Students may also engage in practicum experiences in other countries.

By helping students to obtain a more global perspective, they may become competent to address some of the world's most complex issues and can later be successful in an international environment. The international psychologist faces many challenges, but also many opportunities. There are a number of problems in the world, such as poverty and war, which could be addressed by international psychologists and other social scientists in conjunction with world leaders. As psychologists become more globally competent and work in international collaboration with other professionals, they will be able to have a significantly positive impact not only on their country of origin, but throughout the world.

REFERENCES

Adam, B., Duyvendak, J., & Krouwel, A. (1999). *The global emergence of gay and lesbian politics: National imprints of a worldwide movement.* Philadelphia: Temple University Press.

Adams, M. (2000). Anti-Semitism. In M. Adams, W. Blumenfeld, R. Castaneda, H. Hackman, M. Peters, & X. Zuniga (Eds.), *Readings for diversity and social justice* (pp. 133–137). New York: Routledge.

Adi, H., & Sherwood, M. (2003). Frantz Fanon. In *Pan-African history: Political figures from Africa and the diaspora since 1787* (pp. 64–68). New York: Routledge.

Aguilar, D. (2004). Introduction. In D. Aguilar & A. Lacsamana (Eds.), *Women and globalization* (pp. 11–24). New York: Humanity Books.

Ajima, S. (2005, January 6). Intervention faces obstacles, efforts underway to stem abuse of elderly. *Kyodo News* [Japan]. Retrieved June 8, 2008, from www.globalaging.org/elderrights/world/2005/eldobstacles.htm.

Bonnett, A. (2006). The Americanisation of anti-racism? Global power and hegemony in ethnic equity. *Journal of Ethnic and Migration Studies, 32*(7), 1083–1103.

Booker, S., & Minter, W. (2001, July 9). Global apartheid. *The Nation,* 11–17.

Burn, S. (2005). *Women across cultures: A global perspective* (2nd ed.). New York: McGraw-Hill.

Charlton, J. I. (1998). *Nothing about us without us: Disability oppression and empowerment.* Berkeley: University of California Press.

Chirot, D., & Seligman, M. (2001). *Ethnopolitical warfare: Causes, consequences, and possible solutions.* Washington, DC: American Psychological Association.

Clark, G. (2001). Pakistan's zakat system: A policy model for developing countries as a means of redistributing income to the elderly poor. In F. Ahearn (Ed.), *Issues in global aging* (pp. 47–76). New York: The Haworth Press.

Cornwall, G., & Stoddard, E. (Eds.). (2001). *Global multiculturalism: Comparative perspectives on ethnicity, race and nation.* New York: Rowman & Littlefield.

Cox, C. (2001). Who is responsible for the care of the elderly? A comparison of policies in the United States, the United Kingdom and Israel. In F. Ahearn (Ed.), *Issues in global aging* (pp. 33–46). New York: The Haworth Press.

Dorf, D., & Perez, G. (1995). Discrimination and the tolerance of difference: International lesbian human rights. In J. Peters & A. Wolper (Eds.), *Women's rights, human rights: International feminist perspectives* (pp. 324–333). New York: Routledge.

Filkens, D. (2002, December 1). For Kenya's Muslims: Resentments, local and international. *New York Times,* p. 28.

Ghai, A. (2001). Marginalisation and disability: Experiences from the third world. In M. Priestley (Ed.), *Disability and the life course: Global perspectives* (pp. 26–37). Cambridge: Cambridge University Press.

Hassan, G. (2006, February 7). *The road to Muslim holocaust.* Retrieved May 26, 2008, from http://www.globalresearch.ca/index.php?context=va&aid=1915.

Herdt, G. (1997). *Same sex, different cultures.* Boulder, CO: Westview Press.

Hokenstad, M., & Johansson, L. (2001). Retirement patterns and pension policy: An international perspective. In F. Ahearn (Ed.), *Issues in global aging* (pp. 25–32). New York: The Haworth Press.

Ingstad, B., & Reynolds, S. (1995). *Disability and culture.* Berkeley: University of California Press.

Kohut, A., & Stokes, B. (2006). *America against the world: How we are different and why we are disliked.* New York: Henry Holt and Company.

Marger, M. (2006). *Race and ethnic relations: American and global perspectives.* Belmont, CA: Thomson-Wadsworth.

Marsella, A. (2007). Education and training for a global psychology: Foundations, issues and actions. In M. Stevens & U. Gielen (Eds.), *Toward a global psychology: Theory, research, intervention and pedagogy* (pp. 333–361). Mahwah, New Jersey: Lawrence Erlbaum.

Mullings, L. (2005). Interrogating racism: Toward an antiracist anthropology. *Annual Review of Anthropology, 34,* 667–693.

Nakaya, A. (2005). *Does the world hate the United States?* New York: Thomson Gale.

Persaud, R., & Walker, R. (2001). Apertura: Race in international relations. *Alternatives, 26,* 373–376.

Pew Research Center. (2005, January 20). *Global opinion: The spread of anti-Americanism.* Retrieved June 10, 2008, from http://pewresearch.org/assets/files/trends2005-global.pdf.

Priestley, M. (2001). Introduction: the global context of disability. In M. Priestley (Ed.), *Disability and the life course: Global perspectives* (pp. 3–14). Cambridge: Cambridge University Press.

Roberts, D. (2001, May 23). Beijing strokes the fires of ethnic tensions. *Business Week Online.* Retrieved May 26, 2008, from Academic Search Premier database.

Schidkraut, D. (2007). Defining American identity in the twenty-first century: How much "there" is there? *The Journal of Politics, 69*(3), 597–615.

Schweitzer, G., & Schweitzer, C. (2006). *America on notice: Stemming the tide of anti-Americanism.* New York: Prometheus Books.

Silver, C. (1998). Cross-cultural perspective on attitudes toward family responsibility and well-being in later years. In J. Lomranz (Ed.), *Handbook of aging and mental health* (pp. 383–412). New York: Plenum.

Slater, D., & Taylor, P. (Eds.). (1999). *The American century: Consensus and coercion in the projection of American power.* Oxford: Blackwell.

Stevens, M. (2007). Orientation to a global psychology. In M. Stevens & U. Gielen (Eds.), *Toward a global psychology: Theory, research, intervention and pedagogy* (pp. 3–33). Mahwah, New Jersey: Lawrence Erlbaum.

Takamura, J. (2001). The future is aging. In F. Ahearn (Ed.), *Issues in global aging* (pp. 3–16). New York: The Haworth Press.

Turmusani, M. (2001). Work and adulthood: Economic survival for the majority. In M. Priestley (Ed.), *Disability and the life course: Global perspectives* (pp. 192–205). Cambridge: Cambridge University Press.

CHAPTER 12

Economic Globalization, Transnational Corporations, and the World Elite: The Threats to Diversity That Psychology in the United States Largely Ignores

Luis A. Vargas

There is an assumption that, through the efforts of psychology and other social sciences, our society in the United States[1] will enjoy an idyllic and continuing cultural plurality through the promotion of greater tolerance and acceptance. On the other hand, psychology has been progressively diverting its path into various traditional domains of other fields—for example, to neuroscience, biology, chemistry, economics, and cognitive science—using mechanistic and reductionistic theoretical models that minimize the importance of the larger contexts in which human behavior occurs. In his Honorary President's Address to the Canadian Psychological Association, Bandura (2001) stated:

Contrary to the proclamations of the divestiture oracles, psychology is the one discipline that uniquely encompasses the complex interplay between intrapersonal, biological, interpersonal, and sociostructural determinants of human functioning. . . . The field of psychology should be articulating a broad vision of human beings not a reductive fragmentary one. (p. 13)

In this insightful and forward-thinking address, Bandura noted that societies are experiencing what he calls "the growing globalization of human interconnectedness" (p. 15) through electronic technologies, vastly expanded marketplaces, and a breakdown of boundaries between life at home and life in the workplace. The effects of globalization are profound. Cultures are melding as a result of this interconnectedness. As he put it,

Transnational interdependencies and global market forces are restructuring national economies and shaping the political and social life of societies. . . . These new realities call for broadening the scope of cross-cultural analyses beyond the focus operating *within* given societies. (p. 16, emphasis added)

With the advent and growth of the "cultural competence" movement and its impact on public policy as regards health, mental health, social service, and juvenile justice systems, the future of cultural plurality would seem to be bright. However, this is in stark contrast to

- Increasing national sentiment against immigrants, which Kenneth Martinez, Psy.D., addresses in this volume,
- Unbridled American capitalism, in partnership with a world elite, that promotes, with religious-like fervor, free markets as an essential element to the dissemination of democracy, while engaging in the rapacious pursuit of economic globalization, and
- Aggressive transnational, or global, corporations that are usurping the power of national governments, particularly weaker, or "third world," governments in the deceptive guise of "the human interest."

As Bandura pointed out, the globalization forces are operating *outside* of given societies, at large contextual levels that psychology has rarely addressed. This chapter addresses threats to cultural diversity from the behavior of the American and world elite and transnational megacorporations and argues that psychology should play a greater role in examining human behavior in these much broader contexts. It begins with a definition of cultural diversity, briefly examines the guiding ideology of the United States, addresses the cultural aspects of capitalism and corporate behavior, and examines one example of how psychology might be getting co-opted into behaving much like the corporations involved in globalization. Areas where psychology could make a contribution are suggested. The chapter ends with an appeal for psychology to play a critical role in promoting cultural plurality both in the United States and the world.

CULTURAL DIVERSITY

Cultural diversity often connotes differences in readily evident elements of culture. More readily evident cultural characteristics include: language, religion, sociolinguistic and social patterns and styles of interaction and communication, patterns and styles of raising children, concepts of agency and self, and overtly expressed values such as competitiveness, entrepreneurship, independence, and assertiveness. However, elements of cultures that are not so readily evident are equally important. These include: cognitive, conceptual, and learning styles, aspects of language and religion that reflect ways of thinking, worldviews, ideologies, and epistemologies. As acculturation occurs, surface elements of the non-host culture may disappear, but those deeper elements are likely to be much more resistant to acculturative pressures. It is likely that these more subtle and ingrained aspects of culture are what buttress and cultivate more overt manifestations of culture and that, as long as these deeper aspects of culture remain, the surface manifestations of culture, which may appear to have been relinquished through acculturation, may re-surface as acculturative stress is decreased. With sufficient acculturative pressure, say, from exertion of political, military, or economic power of the dominant society, both surface and deep aspects of culture may be relinquished. When this happens, the non-host culture becomes extinct. Some may argue that cultures are melding, engaging in what are becoming hybrid cultures. This is likely to happen if the societies in which these cultures exist, or the societies that are in contact with each other, have similar power. If not, the economically and politically weaker society's culture may come to be viewed as inferior, less desirable (or even embarrassing), and dispensable by both the weaker society and the more dominant society. Thus, the direction of the acculturation turns toward the culture of the dominant society.

A DEMOCRACY CHARACTERIZED BY CULTURAL PLURALITY AND EQUALITY OR A POWERFUL ELITE PURSUING GLOBAL HEGEMONY?

For all of our pride in the United States as an exemplary democracy whose Constitution begins with "We, the People," the fact is that our Constitution was written by 55, mostly rich, men of Western European heritage, who were part of an elite group in a new country (Zinn, 1991). This is said not with the intent to decry the origins of our country (I am proud and fortunate to be a citizen of the United States), but to put our country's beginning in a broader cultural context. In an incisive article, Schwarz (1995) noted that our foreign policy experts are often misguided by the erroneously idealized view of our own national history. He contrasted the official version of U.S. history as a country accepting of cultural diversity and living in pluralistic harmony with its actual history in which an American elite of Anglo-Saxon descent has consistently imposed its culture on ethnic minorities in the United States. In this sense, the national metaphor of the United States as a melting pot emerges as a process by which to eradicate cultural and ethnic differences to produce citizens that act and, if possible, look ("unmeltable ethnics" notwithstanding) like their Anglo-Saxon superiors. Many of us culturally diverse and ethnic minority (in the political sense) professionals, who have learned to mimic, at least in surface ways, our dominant society compatriots, learn that we are tolerated until such time that we express those not-so-evident aspects of our cultures, after which our culturally rooted thoughts, beliefs, attitudes, and perspectives are often simply dismissed as misguided, uniformed, naïve, or "unscientific." But this insidious assimilatory process is extended in our foreign policy. As Schwarz (1995) commented: "Variants of the cry 'Why can't they be more like us?' have long served as a staple of American tourists and foreign-policy mandarins alike. We have made ourselves at home in the world, characteristically, by regarding it as America in the making" (p. 57).

Implicit in this process is a conceptualization of the American self as masterful, dominating, and independent.

Machiavellian Realism

Influential members of powerful societies are prone to fall victim to something that Howard Zinn (1991) calls *Machiavellian realism*. The central premise of Machiavellian realism is that idealistic aspirations for a better world are all fine and good but the "real" world does not take kindly to such puerile buffoonery. As Zinn pointed out, we can see this type of realism in our subtle or not-so-subtle encouragement that our children pick practical professions that can afford them a good living and our subtle or not-so-subtle depreciation of idealistic professions, like social work or teaching, and, worse yet, of foolhardy attempts to pursue the arts as viable professions. Zinn noted: "[Machiavellian] [r]ealism can be seductive because once you have accepted the reasonable notion that you should base your actions on reality, you are too often led to accept, without much questioning, someone else's version of what that reality is. It is a crucial act of independent thinking to be skeptical of someone else's description of reality" (p. 11). There is an irony that, while the Declaration of Independence hangs on the walls of our classrooms, proclaiming "that all men are created equal, that they are endowed by their Creator with certain unalienable Rights, that among these are Life, Liberty and the pursuit of Happiness," our foreign policy follows Machiavellian realism, as evidenced by our leaders' insistence that our country champion the cause of liberty in foreign soil for the welfare of the world (Zinn, 1991). Zinn quoted a 1980 article in *Foreign Affairs* (the official journal of the highly influential Council of Foreign Relations) by Johns Hopkins political scientist Robert W. Tucker referring to Central America, which exemplifies Machiavellian realism: "[W]e have regularly played a determining role in making and unmaking governments, and we have defined what we have considered to be acceptable behavior of governments" (Tucker, 1980, p. 270).

Has American Psychology Placed Too Much Value on Individualism?

Sampson (1988) underscored how entrenched psychology has been in a theory of the person that considers American individualism, what he called *self-contained individualism*, as not only ideal but the paradigm of psychological health. As examples, he cited the presidential addresses of two recent APA presidents. Sampson defined self-contained individualism as having firm self-other boundaries, *personal control* (what Cushman [1990] has referred to as the masterful and autonomous self that acts on and masters the environment and what Landrine [1992] referred to as the indexical self), and an exclusionary conception of self, where the self is decontextualized and is separate from others. In contrast, he defined another theory of the person that he called *ensembled individualism*. It is characterized by self-other boundaries that are fluid, *field control,* where the location of power and control extends beyond the person, and an inclusionary conception of self, in which the self is contextualized and has meaning in relation to others. Addressing the consequences of individualism in our Western political systems, sociologist Dennis Smith (2008) remarked that neoliberalism[2] has led to a political environment in which those under 40 years of age struggle to think beyond individualism.

In a subsequent article, Sampson (1989) examined the role of psychology in the context of globalization and American psychology's liberal individualist tradition. He noted that American psychology has not engaged in philosophical introspection so as to provide it with a socio-historical sense about its subject matter, as it should have done. He challenged psychology to develop a theory of the person that is reframed "in terms more suitable to resolving the issues of a global era" (p. 920). Psychology should go a step further. It should engage in inquiries about the broad vision of human beings under the pressures of globalization, as Bandura (2001) mentioned. For example, psychology might consider how individuals in the United States who value life, liberty, equality, the pursuit of happiness, and the welfare and interests of the U.S. citizenry allow our government and leaders to impose our national will on other countries, not for the sake and welfare of its citizens but for national power, control, and domination.

CAPITALISM AND THE WORLD ELITE

> Shouldn't we expect that the rich and powerful organise things in their own interests. It's called capitalism.
> —Alasdair Spark, an expert in conspiracy theories on
> the Bilderberg Group, as quoted by Duffy (2004)

The *Webster's New World College Dictionary, 4th Edition,* defines capitalism as "an economic system in which all or most of the means of production and distribution, as land, factories, communications, and transportation systems, are privately owned and operated in a relatively competitive environment through the investment of capital to produce profits: it has been characterized by a tendency toward concentration of wealth, the growth of large corporations, etc. that has led to economic inequality, which has been dealt with usually by increased government action and control" ("Capitalism," 2002, p. 217). The underlying notion in capitalism is free enterprise. We have been taught in our American educational system that capitalism is a good thing. In an ideal world in which all its inhabitants are beneficent and not motivated by power, control, and avarice, it probably is. However, this is not the case; certain historical, social, and psychological factors can operate to change and mold motivations. The father of macroeconomics,[3] John Maynard Keynes is reported to have described capitalism as "the extraordinary belief that the nastiest of men for the nastiest of motives will somehow work for the benefit of all" (quoted in Etzioni-Halevy, 1981, p. 255). It should not be surprising, then, that in 2000 the wealthiest one percent of the adult population in the world owned 40 percent of the world's assets, that 10 percent owned 85 percent, and the bottom 50 percent owned 1 percent (United Nations University—World Institute for Developmental Economics Research, 2006). The world's wealth is concentrated in North America (34%), Europe (30%), and high income Asia-Pacific (24%) (United Nations University—World Institute for Developmental Economics Research, 2006).

Monoculturalism through Global Capitalism

One view of globalization has been described as a "world-system theory" in which a world system, like capitalism, is spread worldwide (Lechner, 2001). In describing the key features of a capitalist world economy, Lechner cited Wallerstein (1974), who noted that such a world system lacks a political center and that it flourishes because it incorporates multiple political systems that allow the capitalists a structurally based freedom to maneuver and expand. Transnational corporations yield tremendous global power through their wealth. Fifty-one of the one hundred largest economies in the world are corporations (Anderson & Cavanagh, 2000). Korten (1999) views global capitalism as centrally controlled by a few powerful transnational corporations. He considers these "corporate economies" to be intended for the benefit of the richest one percent of adults in the world. He notes: "It is a triumph of privatized central planning over markets and democracy" (Korten, 1995, p. 62). In one quarter of 2005, the sales of Exxon Mobil Corporation, the world's largest publicly traded oil company, were more than the annual economic output of New Zealand (Blum, 2005). In 2006 the nation's three largest oil companies, Exxon Mobil, Chevron, and ConocoPhillips, earned almost as much as the seven other companies in the top 10 on the Fortune 500 (Hargreaves, 2007). On the other hand, independent oil and natural gas producers have had a difficult time. More than half of these independent producers reported declines in net income for 2007 (Pirog, 2008).

Wallerstein (1998) argued that the world-system of capitalism has reached its limit and that the United States as a hegemony is in decline, but what appears to be happening is that the hegemony is shifting to a world elite that emulates the established elites of the United States and Western Europe. The claims by Wallerstein (1998) and Saul (2004) that the hegemony of the United States is declining and that globalism is collapsing may be premature. I am not sure their assertions quell the concerns about the threats to cultural diversity because a conglomerate of powerful countries and a centralized elite are still joined in economic efforts that include, whether inadvertently or not, a homogenization of cultures into North American and Western European culture. One only need to look at powerful and influential organizations like the Council of Foreign Relations, the Trilateral Commission, and the Bilderberg Group to appreciate the wide-reaching mantle of influence of this group of world elite. Conspiracy theories aside, let us take a look at what these groups are.

The Council of Foreign Relations and the Bilderberg Group

In 1918 a private U.S. organization, the Council of Foreign Relations (CFR), was founded. Its 1919 handbook defined the CFR as "a board of initiation—a Board of Invention" and described its function as "one to cooperate with the U.S. government and all international agencies toward the goal of bringing them into constructive accord" (Sklar, 1980, p. 3). Some readers may be familiar with its official and influential journal, *Foreign Affairs*. The CFR has played an important role in guiding U.S. policy since World War II. Sklar noted that "a lesser-known companion institution to the CFR" was founded in 1954: the private, European-led Bilderberg Group, composed of leading national political figures, powerful international capitalists, and other influential elites from Western Europe, the United States, and Canada. It was so named because the first of its annual secret gatherings took place in the Hotel Bilderberg in Oosterbeek, Holland, in May 1954 (Thompson, 1980). According to Thompson, the group concerns itself with the immediate and long-term problems facing the nations of its membership and develops solutions through consensus, having at its immediate disposal the power and influence of national leaders, transnational corporations, and the elites of the countries that compose its membership. It is one of various vehicles of collective management for world order and of a system of transnational coordination. However, it serves the needs and wishes of its membership, which is hardly representative of the world, and it is managed by a very small number of elites from the public and private sector, who largely avoid democratic interference in the group's foreign policy, within the capitalist democracies of its members' nations, preferably by agreements of government leaders (Thompson, 1980). Thompson noted that most of the time policies developed by the Bilderberg group are "pursued with impunity."

The Trilateral Commission

A third private group deserves mention, the Trilateral Commission founded in 1973 by David Rockefeller, chairman of the Chase Manhattan Bank; Zbignew Brezinski, President Jimmy Carter's national security advisor; and about three hundred elite members from international business and banking, government, academia, media, and conservative labor (Sklar, 1980). The purpose of the commission is to develop partnerships

among the "trilateral" private and public leaders of North America,
Western Europe and Japan (which is excluded from the Bilderberg Group)
so as to formulate public policy and construct a blueprint for future international stability. The Web page for the Trilateral Commission describes
itself as formed "by private citizens of Europe, Japan, and North America
to help think through the common challenges and leadership responsibilities of these democratic industrialized areas in the wider world" (Trilateral Commission, n.d.). However, Sklar (1980) noted:

"[T]rilateralism" refers [to] the doctrine of world order advanced by the Commission . . . trilateralists are saying: (1) the people, governments, and economies of all
nations must serve the needs of multinational banks and corporations; (2) control
over economic resources spells power in modern politics . . . ; and (3) the leaders
of capitalist democracies—systems where economic control and profit, and thus
political power, rest with the few—must resist movement toward a truly popular
democracy. (pp. 2, 4)

For any proponent of cultural pluralism, it is probably evident that the
world elite of North America and Western Europe via such powerful and
influential organizations may stand in the way of preserving cultural diversity. As a psychologist, I am not ready to agree with John Maynard
Keynes's view of capitalism, although at times it is quite tempting. I believe that psychology has the expertise to examine the psychosocial and
psychohistorical processes that operate within groups like the Council of
Foreign Relations, the Bilderberg Group, and the Trilateral Commission in
order to determine under what conditions decisions about public policy
can and cannot value and promote cultural plurality.

THE INFLUENCE OF CORPORATIONS

In his book *The Devil's Dictionary*, Ambrose Bierce (1906/2007) gave this
definition of a corporation: "An ingenious device for obtaining individual
profit without individual responsibility" (p. 30). Following the logic of
Ambrose Bierce, one might argue that, psychologically, a corporation is a
mechanism for dissociating the self from personal and social consequences
of collective actions that would ordinarily run counter to individual values and beliefs about the importance of the common welfare and human
interest. Proponents of cultural diversity should recognize that one of
the greatest threats to cultural diversity is occurring through economic
globalization and a social and political system in the United States and
other elite nations that allow transnational corporations to behave like the
cultural imperialists we are telling each other to avoid being. The envi-
ronmentalist Paul Hawken (1993) noted that current corporate practices
threaten to destroy indigenous cultures, along with wildlife reserves and
wilderness areas. Korten (2001) made this observation:

Corporations have emerged as the dominant governance institutions of the planet, with the largest among them reaching into virtually every country of the world and exceeding most governments in size and power. Increasingly, it is the corporate interest more than the human interest that defines the policy agendas of states and international bodies, although this reality and its implications have gone largely unnoticed and unaddressed. (p. 60)

Like Bierce's definition, Korten noted that corporations seek to expand their corporate rights while limiting their corporate obligations. In a chilling description of corporate Machiavellian realism (or what Korten calls the "value-free objectivity of economic rationalism"), Korten (1995) cited a widely publicized memo by Lawrence Summers, chief economist of the World Bank. In this memo, Summers propounded the idea that it is in the interest of economic efficiency for wealthy countries to dispose of their toxic wastes in poor countries because those in poor countries have shorter life spans and less earning potential than those in wealthy countries. Surprisingly, this perverted logic did not go undefended. A subsequent commentary on Summers's memo in *The Economist* took the position that wealthy countries are morally obligated to export their wastes to poor countries because doing so provides their citizens with economic opportunities that they would otherwise not have (Korten, 1995).

Globalization through the Promotion of Unbridled Consumerism

Rampal (2005) distinguished between a version of cultural imperialism, in which a more powerful country forcefully imposes its ideologies, beliefs, values and attitudes (i.e., culture) on a weaker country (as exemplified in cultural dependency theory), and a more supposedly benign version in which the economic success of a dominant and powerful country makes its culture attractive to countries that are not as economically successful. Consequently, those less successful countries may come to emulate the culture of the dominant and powerful countries by choice rather than coercion or force. According to one source, there are more than 1.7 billion members of the so-called consumer class; almost half of them are in developing countries (Worldwatch Institute, 2004).

Whereas Rampal and others may see this process as more benign, I believe that this is the more dangerous and egregious type—cultural globalization through emulation of the oppressor. The irony is that the economically powerful countries tend to exploit the workforce and resources of poor countries, in part, to fatten the already fat cows. Is it any surprise that, in 1998, 20 percent of the world's people in the countries with the highest incomes accounted for 86 percent of the total private consumption expenditures, while the poorest 20 percent accounted for only 1.3 percent (Shah, 2008)? With only 5 percent of the world's population, the United

States consumes about one-fourth of the world's fossil fuels (Worldwatch Institute, 2004). North America and Western Europe account for only 12 percent of the world's population, but they account for 60 percent of private consumption; in contrast, South Asia and sub-Saharan Africa account for one-third of the world's population but only 3.2 percent of private consumption (Worldwatch Institute, 2004).

Sklar (1980) cited an article in a 1968 issue of *Forbes* magazine that quoted the president of Nabisco Corporation, Lee Bickmore, to illustrate what he believed was the goal of transnational corporations: "One world of homogeneous consumption . . . [I am] looking forward to the day when Arabs and Americans, Latinos and Scandinavians, will be munching Ritz crackers as enthusiastically as they already drink Coke or brush their teeth with Colgate" (p. 20). Sklar (1980) stressed that transnational corporations do not just advertise products, they promote lifestyles (of course, based on consumption) that are patterned after the lifestyles of the mainstream society of North American and Western Europe. These transnational corporations aspire to a time in the not-so-distant future when the social, economic, and political values of Western culture will become universal values. At the core of the values of this transnational corporate capitalism is the message: "The Western way is the good way; national culture is inferior" (Sklar, 1980, p. 23).

Mander (1992, pp. 128–137) described 11 inherent rules of corporate behavior. Among these rules were: *Amorality*, referring to the fact that corporations do not have morals or altruistic goals (although he noted that corporations try to hide their amorality under the guise of intended altruism); *dehumanization*, whereby corporations objectify the environment and community as decisions are measured against profit or public relations standards, which leads to the employees being dehumanized; *exploitation*, in which neither the workers or the raw material suppliers are compensated for the full value of their labor or materials and the owners of capital take part of the value as their profit; and *homogenization*, whereby "*all* corporations share an identical economic, cultural, and social vision and seek to accelerate society's (and individual) acceptance of that vision" (p. 135). As is obvious in the messages of Sklar and Mander, what is particularly disturbing is that the homogenization of peoples through the expansion of transnational corporate capitalism means that the image of the group in power, the United States and Western European countries, will become the universal world culture. They will *become* like us.

The implicit message in the promotion of North American and Western European goods is evident in the behavior of the denizens of third world countries and immigrants in North America and Western Europe. For example, there is a cool way to dress, and a cool way to act—it just happens to be the way North Americans and Western Europeans dress and act. In 1971, just before Nixon went to China, the U.S. table tennis team was in Nagoya, Japan, for an international competition (Wolff & Davis, 2008). The Chinese team was there for the first time in six years. One young U.S. player, Glenn Cowan, wearing a floppy hat and shoulder-length hair, flagged down a shuttle to get to a match. The shuttle turned out to be carrying the Chinese team. The Chinese players in the shuttle were taken aback by Cowan's hippie appearance, and Cowan noticed it. He told the Chinese that, while his appearance might appear strange, many youth in the United States dressed and acted just like him. We now need only look at how youth in Asian countries, including China, dress to recognize their emulation of the West.

Coca Cola helped to select torchbearers and escort runners for the Beijing Olympics and hopes to make China its largest market ("Coca-Cola to Make China its Largest Market," 2007; "Coca-Cola Seriously Marketing Olympic Push," 2007; "Coca Cola CEO Expects China to Be its Largest Market," 2007). The skyscrapers of Qingdao look like those in Chicago, Dallas, or New York. Chinese women are buying American cosmetics with the same fervor as their American counterparts. Nanjing Road in Shanghai rivals Las Vegas for neon lights and overall flamboyance. Chinese children now see Ronald McDonald as part of Chinese culture (Gluckman, n.d.). But, the cost of this insidious co-optation comes at a high price because it eventually goes beyond the relinquishment of the surface aspects of culture to the relinquishment of the deeper aspects of culture—we no longer just want to look and act American, we want to *think* like Americans.

The most recent World Health Report (Capgemini/Merrill Lynch, 2008) showed that in 2007, 0.15 percent of the world's population, the super rich, or what the report calls "ultra high net worth individuals" (Ultra HNWIs), with wealth of at least $30 million, control about a third of the $40.7 trillion, the combined wealth of the world's millionaires (what the report calls "high net worth individuals," or HNWIs). On the positive side, in 2007 the global economy increased by 5.1 percent, with the highest-growth regions being Eastern Europe, Latin America, and Asia-Pacific. However, closer scrutiny reveals that the countries with the highest percentage of Ultra HNWIs within their countries' population of HNWIs are Africa (2.0%) and Latin America (2.5%). What is important to keep in mind is that Ultra HNWIs are the very, very rich and that HNWIs hold a significant portion of their wealth in stock markets (i.e., large transnational corporations). In others words, the countries in these less developed regions are simply producing their own world elite.

Are these world elite championing the causes of their countries, improving the condition of their countries' poor, or asserting the values of their cultures? One statistic may give us a clue. In 2007, despite rising costs and considerable turmoil in the financial market, HNWIs did not give up expensive purchases, what the report calls "passion investments." *Forbes*'s Cost of Living Extremely Well Index (CLEWI), which follows the year-over-year cost of a basket of luxury goods, increased 6.2 percent from 2006 to 2007; this is more than double the rate of inflation. Private jets, yachts, high-end cars, and other luxury collectibles accounted for the

HNWIs largest passion investment, with wealthy Latin Americans over-taking North Americans in this category. HNWIs from the Middle East and Asia made their largest share of passion investments in jewelry, gems, and watches (especially men's luxury watches from Western Europe)—most of which are symbols of success in the West. In other words, the growing elite from less developed countries are *becoming just like us.*

Marketization, Urbanization, and Communication Technologies

The process of marketization has been described as producing humilia-tion through two aspects of globalization (Smith, 2008). One is what Smith terms the *imperialist impulse,* which he explained is, in modern times, "not capitalist greed but politicized fear and anger expressed in a fundamental-ist drive to dominate or destroy" (p. 374). The other is what he terms the *cosmopolitan condition,* "that anomic mixing of cultures and creeds filling the world's cities with crowds of displaced people searching for order, meaning and someone or something to blame for their discontent" (p. 374). To understand the role of urbanization in the process of globalization, it is helpful to look at some statistics from the United Nations Development Programme Human Development Report (1998). In 1970, 67.1 percent of the population of industrialized countries lived in urban areas, compared to 24.7 percent of those in developing countries and 12.7 percent of those in the least developed countries. By 2015 it is estimated that 78.7 percent of the population of industrialized countries will live in urban areas, com-pared to 49.3 percent of those in developing countries and 34.9 percent of those in the least industrialized countries. Whereas 36.8 percent of the world's population lived in urban areas in 1970, by the year 2015 it is esti-mated that 54.6 percent of the world's population will live in urban areas.

The combination of urbanization and technological advances like tele-communications, the Internet, cell phones, satellite television, alongside the expansive mesh of the U.S. film industry, together provide powerful assimilating tools through aggressive marketization. In 2002, 1.12 billion households, about three-fourths the households in the world, owned at least one television set (Worldwatch Institute, 2004). In 1990, 2 out of 1,000 people in the world subscribed to a cell phone service; in 2000, 121 out of 1,000 subscribed to a cell phone service (United Nations Develop-ment Programme Human Development Report, 2002). In 2002, there were 1.1 billion fixed phone lines and 1.1 billion mobile lines globally (World-watch Institute, 2004). From January 1996 to June 2002, the percent of internet users in the world increased from 0.73 percent to 9.57 percent (Nua Internet Surveys, n.d.). Globally, about 600 million users connect to the Internet (Worldwatch Institute, 2004).

In Singapore, one can tune in to BBC World Service on FM radio 24 hours a day. Why? Because Singapore is now one of Asia's economic powers. It values the importance of the English language in international business and wants its people to master the English language to continue and expand on its success (Rampal, 2005). The media is a both a highly seductive and a strong assimilating agent. When I watch Mexican television, I am still bothered by how many of the actors in the *telenovelas* are light-skinned, light-haired, and light-eyed and by the portrayal of characters living in middle-class houses decorated like homes in the United States. In reality, the middle class is a small group in Mexico, and most homes do not look like those shown in the *telenovelas*. Perhaps Rampal (2005) said it best, if also distressingly, as he examined the reshaping of the Asian film industry:

Asian filmmakers have adopted the Hollywood commercial success formula— predicated on the themes of sex, action, pleasure and individuality—to regain commercial success for their films, whose earlier themes of mushy love stories and family dramas have lost their appeal to an audience with access to the titillating offerings of the West through globalized television. (p. 9)

There is much psychology can currently say about the relationship of media to human development and the effects of media on beliefs, values, and attitudes. The main problem in psychology seems to be: Are we saying it to the right group? Are we stressing enough the public policy implications of our findings about the effects of the media on human development and assimilation, not just within the United States but globally?

The loss of languages is a tragic reminder how cultures are being lost. There is a close relationship between language and culture. In part, language both reveals and facilitates the way we think; in this sense, language reflects both surface and deep aspects of culture. A well-known writer in the Southwest, Sabine Ulibarri, once came to lecture at a multi-cultural seminar I co-taught. After waiting for about 10 minutes for everyone to arrive, he looked at his watch, then he glanced around the room, as if considering the diversity of the group, and said: "You know, time is an interesting thing. It works in German, it marches in French, it runs in English, and it walks in Spanish" (Sabine Ulibarri, personal communication, approximately February 19, 1987). Ulibarri's comment conveyed the importance of language in the preservation of culture and in the way we think (a deeper level of culture) about the world. As globalization continues, many languages in the world are in danger of extinction. In 2000, 59 percent of all languages in the world had less than 10,000 speakers, ranging from 93 percent of the languages in the Pacific to 30 percent of the languages in Europe (Worldwatch Institute, 2003). Surprisingly, the next two highest geographic areas with languages in danger of extinction were North America (78%) and South America (77%). But then, if we just think for a minute, it is not so surprising. We, Americans, have been eradicating indigenous cultures for centuries in the name of religion, civilization, and progress.

Migration

Migration patterns have a relationship to globalization. If the flow is toward the dominant and powerful countries, one might assume that migrants are being assimilated into the cultures of those countries. The United States, by far, hosts the largest number of migrants, almost three times more than the country that ranks second (United Nations Population Division, n.d.-a). From 1990 to 2000, there has been a substantial increase in the number of migrants residing in the more developed regions of the world but only a slight decrease in the number of migrants residing in less and least developed regions (United Nations Population Division, n.d.-b). Put another way, the net flow of migrants showed a marked increase from 1995 to 2000 in North America and Europe but a decrease in Asia, Latin America/Caribbean, and Africa (United Nations Population Division, n.d.-c). As these figures show, more migrants are residing in North America and Europe, giving them the opportunity to become more like us.

SOME EFFECTS OF ECONOMIC GLOBALIZATION

Poverty and Violence

Despite claims that economic globalization will create growth and alleviate poverty—claims from leading institutions of the Bretton Woods monetary system[4] (i.e., the World Bank and the International Monetary Fund), the World Trade Organization, and other advocates of economic globalization—the last three decades have not provided evidence of such claims; in fact, poverty and inequality are increasing (Mander, Baker, & Korten, 2001). The World Trade Organization deals with setting rules of trade between nations. According to Mander et al. (2001), the Central Intelligence Agency and the United Nations agree that globalization has brought substantial inequalities—and with those inequalities, global protest and turmoil. Up to 2.8 billion of the 6.4 billion people in the world subsist on less than $2.00 a day, and 1 billion do not have reasonable access to safe drinking water (Worldwatch Institute, 2004). Economic globalization has only led to the growth of transnational corporations and the creation of an exceptionally wealthy elite, and it has created greater poverty rather than solved it.

Mander et al. (2001) argued that these institutions, along with the U.S. government, strongly support the replacement of local farming with monocultures[5] operated by transnational corporations. Yet, almost half the world population lives off the land and grows food for their families and communities. The actions of these transnational corporations destroy the self-sustainability of local communities. A particular absurdity, they pointed out, is that an export-oriented system of agriculture tends to increase the production of high-priced luxury products, such as flowers, coffee, exotic vegetables, beef, and potted plants, which are then sent to rich countries while local populations are exploited and rendered no longer self-sustaining.

One effect of this type of imperialistic economic globalization is discontent and resentment about increased poverty and economic disparity, an effect that leads to violence both by the oppressors and the oppressed. One theory of this type of violence is offered by Pilsuk and Zazzi (2006). It posits the following: A society develops psycho-cultural beliefs and values predicated on power, domination, acquisition, and intolerance of other views. An elite network of corporate and military leaders acquire enough power to act with impunity. Natural and human resources are shunted away from local communities toward transnational corporations. Local populations, impoverished and displaced from their sources of livelihood, feel demeaned and marginalized, and may fight back. The elite creates powerful strategies and propaganda to defend its actions and responds with military action toward "enemies" fabricated by the government and media controlled or influenced by the elite. This action begins a cycle of violence, as those with power strip away any sense of agency and control that those under their economic and military domination may have. There is a cruel irony that comes with being displaced and marginalized. Those who are marginalized resort to consumerism and crime— and sometimes to rejecting the capitalist system and resorting to terrorism (Allen, 2005/2006). Thus, we see cases of impoverished youth in Mexico City beating and robbing American tourists to get their Nike shoes; we see drugged youth in Sierra Leone carrying AK-47s and wearing T-shirts with the logos of fashionable American sportswear or with pictures of American music icons, all the while languishing in an existential angst fueled by hopelessness, helplessness, and rage. We see the poor in our country and in third-world countries craving the latest Western fashions, technology, and products—some resorting to crime to get them. All this at the expense of ethnic and cultural identity and pride—factors important in developing resiliency in youth.

The Insidious Forms of Modern Racism

In a fascinating study of two important political, race-related events in New Zealand, Liu and Mills (2006) illustrated the relationship between modern racism and neoliberal globalization (what they termed *market fundamentalism*) through the use of discursive analysis. They noted that, while egalitarianism was posed as the overt discourse during these two events, the motivation to undermine the messages and efforts of a minority group (Vietnamese in the first case and Maori in the second) was an economic one. Their discursive analysis of the press coverage on these two events illustrated how criticism of the ethnic minority groups followed a pattern consistent with their theory of modern ("symbolic") racism:

(1) Minority group members are criticized for specific misdeeds that violate traditional majority group values. (2) The specific criticism against the minority group member(s) is qualified using various discursive repertoires. (3) Majority group values (e.g., some high-minded principle of morality or justice marshalled under the banner of nationality) are affirmed in the process of criticizing the minority and warranting this critique. (4) Racism or racist intent is denied. (Liu & Mills, 2006, p. 96)

This latter denial is effected by engaging in a practice of "plausible deniability" in which statements are made by majority-group members that have alternative interpretations. Liu and Mills further argued that statements made by majority-group members are either couched in traditional values of the majority group, so as to "deflect criticism and mask racism," or asserted in accord with the values of Western neoliberal globalization (e.g., equality) in order to "defend economic power and privilege" (p. 96). The analysis of Liu and Mills draws attention to the subtle and sophisticated form that racism and prejudice can take through the dynamics of economic power in a global economy. They conclude: "A challenge facing open societies today is not just racism or totalitarianism, but market fundamentalism [neoliberal globalization]" (p. 97). While this topic would seem ripe for psychological investigation, it has received little attention in the psychological literature of the United States.

Exploitation and Bullying in Global Organizations

As North American and Western European corporations expand to foreign countries, particularly third-world countries, the potential for exploiting the foreign workforce increases. Some authors argue that transnational corporations have distinct characteristics that make their behavior unique and that they should be given special attention in studies of corporate behavior (Peterson & Thomas, 2007; Roth & Kostova, 2003). Transnational corporations must deal with the cultural diversity of their employees, customers, competitors, and suppliers, alongside vastly varied economic and governmental organizations, geographic distances, and time differences that preclude face-to-face interactions (Peterson & Thomas, 2007). Peterson and Thomas (2007) provide a rich and in-depth discussion of transnational organizations as a context for organizational behavior research, and they highlight the multifaceted aspects of interactions in an organizational context, a formal institutional context, and a cultural context, as well as the nuanced and unique aspects of organizational behavior in transnational corporations (e.g., cultural differences in concepts of leadership and commitment, specialized organizational structures, and managerial roles, and the distinctive nature of expatriate roles). (Ironically, the data for this study came primarily from the most recent three years of issues of major U.S. and European management and international management journals, which raises the question about the perspective represented and the potential for unintended bias.) While most of the literature in this area of study is outside of psychology, psychology has much to offer, if only greater effort could be directed to this field of study, particularly by applying extant basic and social psychology research to the behavior of individuals in transnational corporations and the behavior of a transnational corporation as a whole.

The potential for exploitation by transnational corporations is illustrated by the use of cheap (sometimes child) labor in third-world countries and by exposure to work-related dangers and toxins in the workplace as a result of relaxed standards in third-world nations. It is also illustrated by the destruction of natural resources and extensive pollution in third-world countries, where transnational corporations often build enormous plants (e.g., the *maquiladoras* in Latin America) that take advantage of political corruption and/or the lack of laws and regulations to protect the environment in host countries. Business ethicists continue to debate whether corporations can be morally accountable and whether or how they can have a sense of collective responsibility (see Altman, 2007, who argues against the application of Kant's moral philosophy to corporate behavior, an argument that has gained popularity in business ethics). Criminologists are grappling with theories to better understand what conditions lead to corporate crime (see Piquero & Piquero, 2006, who use control balance theory to examine forms of deviance in corporations). Yet, psychology has shown limited interest in directing its efforts to the devastating consequences of such exploitation by transnational corporations and their executives.

With transnational corporations extending to third-world countries, the potential for bullying the host workforce increases as relocated expatriate managers from more dominant nations struggle to optimize productivity without fully understanding the cultural differences of the host country that is providing the employees. This is an area that has only recently begun to be explored in the business arena and one into which psychology might do well to venture, particularly because there is already a good amount of psychological literature about bullying in local venues (e.g., schools and the workplace). The dynamics of bullying within global organizations is considerably more complex than in local contexts, as has been described by Harvey, Treadway, and Heames (2007). These authors have also illustrated how a model of bullying in a global organization can guide interventions that address both the target of intervention (the bully, the bullied, the organizational culture, the organization's standard operating procedures, and the host country's legal system) and the intervening party to the global bullying activity (the individual manager, the group, the organization, and external entities like the commission of the

European Union that was established to intervene on behalf of abused employees of global organizations conducting business in the European Union).

IS AMERICAN PSYCHOLOGY JOINING THE IMPERIALIST GLOBALIZATION BANDWAGON?

At a recent psychology conference on culturally informed, evidence-based practice, a leading psychologist spoke about the globalization of evidence-based treatments. Implicit in his missive was that our profession has a moral obligation to extend the best available treatments to all people, especially those less advantaged than us. The message was noble and impassioned. Who could disagree? An insidious aspect of globalization is that those who have power and influence believe that they are acting in the interest of the world community by globalizing their products— their *cultural* products. One version of this aspect was described by Korten (2001) when he noted that a message intertwined in our political discourse about capitalism is that by promoting free markets we are, in fact, promoting democracy. I would go further and say that we are promoting *our culture.*

Kirmayer (2006) acknowledged that psychiatry is actively involved in globalization, as demonstrated by its efforts to develop an international nosology and standardized approaches to diagnosis and treatment. He noted that the World Health Organization (WHO) and the World Psychiatric Association (WPA) have attempted to negotiate (some might argue, impose) international consensus on diagnostic nosology and on what constitutes best practices in clinical intervention and prevention. He pointed out, however, that information from non-Western countries is scant. Our Western concepts of diagnosis and treatment often rely on an assumed separation of mind and body. What, then, is to happen to conceptualizations of disorders among Asian and North and South American indigenous people, who do not believe in such a separation? Kirmayer (2006) offers this insight:

Just as attempts to standardize psychiatric knowledge lead to domination of Euro-American standards, the call for evidence-based medicine invokes standards of evidence that immediately exclude most local knowledge. Since producing hard evidence depends on the costly standards of psychiatric epidemiology and randomized trials, it is not possible for clinicians or researchers in most countries to contribute to the accumulation of knowledge . . . The overall effect of the move to evidence-based psychiatry is to replace local knowledge with information obtained from large-scale studies carried out in settings where research funds, personnel and technology are readily available. (pp. 136–137)

The large-scale studies are carried out mostly in North America, Western Europe and Westernized countries like Australia and New Zealand.

Kirmayer advocates an interdisciplinary discursive approach with different methods and perspectives and with the inclusion of local knowledge.

Kirmayer's observations have relevance to what we are doing in psychology in our currently zealous promotion of evidence-based assessment, treatment, and practice. Most of our evidence-based assessments (EBAs) and treatments (EBTs) have been largely with European American participants. Some psychologists strongly advocate establishing state and federal requirements that restrict state and federal funds to implementation of only those treatments that have been designated (via decisions of an elite group of psychology scientists) as EBTs. Furthermore, we are exporting some of the designated EBAs and EBTs with little or no modifications to other countries, including less developed ones. The recent enthusiasm over culturally adapting EBAs and EBTs is, on the one hand, laudable and, on the other, concerning. Cultural adaptations are not a panacea. The solution of cultural adaptation is a compromise that ensures that EBAs and EBTs will remain faithful to the core cultural beliefs of societies (largely the United States and Western countries) that have developed them.

I believe that American psychology has to extend itself to incorporate *with equal value* the views, beliefs, and values (i.e., culture) of those on whom we might be tempted to impose our Western-based EBAs and EBTs. There is much to be learned about assessment and treatment, that is, if we can resist the temptation to discount local knowledge as "unscientific" and promote Western-based EBAs and EBTs under the guise of credible evidence legitimized by the very cultural group that developed them.

I believe that psychology also has to guard itself from being seduced by capitalist motives and the lure of economic globalization. Developing and establishing EBTs is becoming big business. For example, the Web site of Multisystemic Therapy, Inc. (www.mstservices.com) describes MST as "research proven" and as listed in the Substance Abuse and Mental Health Services Administration's (SAMHSA's) National Registry of Evidence-Based Programs and Practices. It also describes how to start up an MST program, explains the process by which an agency can obtain program licenses, sells its products, and advertises employment opportunities in the MST network worldwide. It is not difficult to see how financial motivations of MST developers and of psychologists holding the rights to these designated EBTs may sway them from their motivations as clinicians and their interests in the welfare of a distant recipient of MST in some third-world country.

CONCLUSION

The role of cultural values, beliefs, and attitudes, either as potential obstacles to or facilitators of progress has been largely ignored by dominant-world governments (Harrison, 2000). Some (Kashima, 2007; Moghaddam, 2006) posit that there are two conflicting cultural traits operating in our world: *multiculturalism*, which seeks to preserve variation and diversity, and *assimilation*, which seeks to dominate and assimilate others (to make others more like us). Moghaddam (2006) urged greater efforts, especially by cultural researchers, to develop what he calls "an integrated biocultural policy" to manage and preserve biocultural diversity and thus sustain a large supply of creative, diverse, and potentially useful ideas, worldviews, and beliefs from which people can draw upon to more effectively handle the rapid changes in our environment (see also, Kashima, 2007). He stated: "Rather than throwing up our hands and declaring that 'the solutions are political,' we cultural researchers can help to mold the discourse of politics, at both national and everyday levels" (p. 431).

I believe we, as a profession, have to assert the value of cultural plurality, to avow the importance of having different views of reality and different worldviews, and to affirm the significance of culture, in its diverse forms, in creating meaningful and strong interpersonal bonds in people's lives. We, as individuals-in-societies, have an important role to play in ensuring (1) that the many "worlds" represented by diverse cultures in the United States and global populations have equal status and (2) the recognition of the value they add to the welfare and evolution of humankind.

No civilization by itself can claim to represent all humanity or to assume full responsibility for it. Neither can one single civilization claim exclusive rights to provide a universally valid vision of how to be a good human being and how to live wisely in today's world. We may find answers to these questions only through dialogue among civilizations . . .

—Valda Adamkus, President of the Republic of Lithuania,
1998–2003 (as quoted in UNESCO, 2001)

NOTES

1. In this chapter, the term *America* is used to refer to the United States merely for the sake of convenience. The term *North America* is used to refer to the United States and Canada.

2. Neoliberalism is a political philosophy that stresses the importance of economic growth and contends that the public welfare is best ensured by minimal government interference and a free market system, which requires independence, competitiveness, and entrepreneurship.

3. Macroeconomics deals with the performance, structure, and behavior of a national or regional economy as a whole.

4. The Bretton Woods monetary system was an international reform that led to the establishment of rules for commercial and financial relations among the world's major industrial nations.

5. In this context, *monocultures* refers to a similar pattern of practices and ways of thinking imposed by global corporations on previously self-reliant, local, and diverse farming communities. These monocultures are based on the values, attitudes, and beliefs of a profit-driven, export-oriented system of agriculture that

favors the production of high-priced, high-profit luxury export items and the use of agricultural methods necessary to sustain such production rather than the production of food items and the use of agricultural methods aimed at the self-sufficiency of the local communities.

REFERENCES

Allen, M. (2005/2006). Human motivations and political action: Transforming responses to the challenge of globalisation. *International Journal of the Humanities, 3*(7), 139–144.

Altman, M. C. (2007). The decomposition of the corporate body: What Kant cannot contribute to business ethics. *Journal of Business Ethics, 7,* 253–266.

Anderson, S., & Cavanagh, J. (2000, December 4). *Top 200: The rise of corporate global power.* Retrieved February 3, 2009, from http://www.corpwatch.org/article.php?id=377.

Bandura, A. (2001). The changing face of psychology at the dawning of a globalization era. *Canadian Psychology/Psychologie Canadienne, 42*(1), 12–24.

Bierce, A. (1906/2007). *The devil's dictionary.* Sioux Falls, SD: NuVision Publications.

Blum, J. (2005, April 29). Oil major's 1st quarter earnings shoot up. *Washington Post.* Retrieved June 19, 2008, from http://washingtonpost.com/wp-dyn/content/article/2005/04/28/AR20054281906_pf.html.

Capgemini/Merrill Lynch. (2008). *World wealth report 2008.* Capgemini. Retrieved June 24, 2008, from http://www.us.capgemini.com/worldwealthreport08/.

Capitalism. (2002). *Webster's new world college dictionary* (4th ed.). Hoboken, NJ: Wiley.

Coca Cola CEO expects China to be its largest market. (2007, September 17). NEWSSGD.com. Retrieved February 2, 2009, from http://www.newsgd.com/business/enterprise/content/2007-09/17/content_4246362.htm.

Coca-Cola to make China its largest market. (2007, September 16). *China Daily.* Retrieved June 25, 2008, from http://www.chinadaily.com.cn/bizchina/2007-09/16/content_6110146.htm#.

Coca-Cola seriously marketing Olympic push. (2007, September 20). *China Economic Review.* Retrieved June 25, 2008, from http://www.chinaeconomicreview.com/olympics/2007/09/20/coca-cola-seriously-marketing-olympics-push/.

Cushman, P. (1990). Why the self is empty: Toward a historically situated psychology. *American Psychologist, 45*(5), 599–611.

Duffy, J. (2004, June 6). *Bilderberg: The ultimate conspiracy theory.* BBC News. Retrieved June 19, 2008, from http://newsvote.bbc.co.uk/'mpapps/pagetools/print/news/bbc.co.uk/1/hi/magazine/377301.

Etzioni-Halevy, E. (1981). *Social change: The advent and maturation of modern society.* London: Routledge.

Gluckman, R. (n.d.). *The Americanization of China.* Gluckman.com. Retrieved June 25, 2008, from http://www.gluckman.com/Americanization.html.

Hargreaves, S. (2007, April 24). *Big oil's money machine.* CNN Money. Retrieved June 25, 2008, from http://money.cnn.com/2007/04/24/news/companies/oil_profits/index.htm.

Harrison, L. E. (2000). Why culture matters. In L. E. Harrison & S. P. Huntington (Eds.), *Culture matters* (pp. xvii–xxxiv). New York: Basic Books.

Harvey, M., Treadway, D. C., & Heames, J. T. (2007). The occurrence of bullying in global organizations: A model and issues associated with social/emotional contagion. *Journal of Applied Social Psychology, 37*(11), 2576–2599.

Hawken, P. (1993). *The ecology of commerce: A declaration of sustainability.* New York: HarperCollins.

Kashima, Y. (2007). Globalization, diversity, and universal Darwinism. *Culture & Psychology, 13*(1), 129–139.

Kirmayer, L. J. (2006). Beyond the "new cross-cultural psychiatry": Cultural biology, discursive psychology and the ironies of globalization. *Transcultural Psychiatry, 43*(1), 126–144.

Korten, D. C. (1995). *When corporations rule the world* (1st ed.). San Francisco: Kumarian Press.

Korten, D. C. (1999). *The post-corporate world: Life after capitalism.* San Francisco: Berrett-Koehler Publishers.

Korten, D. C. (2001). *When corporations rule the world* (2nd ed.). San Francisco: Berret-Koehler Publishers.

Landrine, H. (1992). Clinical implications of cultural differences: The referential versus the indexical self. *Clinical Psychology Review, 12*(4), 401–415.

Lechner, F. (2001). *Globalization theories.* Retrieved June 19, 2008, from http://www.sociology.emory.edu/globalization/theories.html.

Liu, J. H., & Mills, D. (2006). Modern racism and neo-liberal globalization: The discourses of plausible deniability and their multiple functions. *Journal of Community and Applied Social Psychology, 16*, 83–99.

Mander, J. (1992). *In the absence of the sacred: The failure of technology and the survival of the Indian nations.* San Francisco: Sierra Club Books.

Mander, J. B., Baker, D., & Korten, D. (2001). Does globalization help the poor? Third World Traveler. *IFG Bulletin, 1*(3). Retrieved June 17, 2008, from http://www.thirdworldtraveler.com/Globalization/DoesGlobaliz_HelpPoor.html.

Moghaddam, F. M. (2006). Catastrophic evolution, culture, and diversity management policy. *Culture & Psychology, 12*(4), 415–434.

Nua Internet Surveys. (n.d.). *Internet users 1996–2002.* Global Policy Forum. Retrieved June 19, 2008, from http://www.globalpolicy.org/globaliz/charts/internettable.htm.

Peterson, M. F., & Thomas, D. C. (2007). Organizational behavior in multinational organizations. *Journal of Organizational Behavior, 28*, 261–279.

Pilsuk, M., & Zazzi, J. (2006). Toward a psychosocial theory of military and economic violence in the era of globalization. *Journal of Social Issues, 62*(1), 41–62.

Piquero, N. L., & Piquero, A. R. (2006). Control balance and exploitative corporate crime. *Criminology, 44*(2), 397–430.

Pirog, R. (2008). *Oil industry profit review 2007* (Order Code RL34437). Washington, DC: Congressional Report Service.

Rampal, K. (2005, February–March). *Cultural imperialism or economic necessity: The Hollywood factor in the reshaping of the Asian film industry.* Razon y Palabra: Primera Revista Electronica especialiazada en Communicacion. Retrieved June 17, 2008, from http://www.razonypalabra.org.mx/anteriores/n43/krampal/html.

Roth, K., & Kostova, T. (2003). The use of the multinational corporation as a research context. *Journal of Management, 29*, 883–902.

Sampson, E. E. (1989). The challenge of social change for psychology. *American Psychologist, 44*(6), 914–921.

Sampson, E. E. (1988). The debate on individualism: Indigenous psychologies of the individual and their role in personal and societal functioning. *American Psychologist, 43*(1), 15–22.

Saul, J. R. (2004, March). The collapse of globalism: And the rebirth of nationalism. *Harper's Magazine, 308*(1846), 33–43.

Schwarz, B. (1995, May). The diversity myth: America's leading export. *The Atlantic Monthly, 275*, 57–67.

Shah, A. (2008, January). *Behind consumption and consumerism.* Global Issues. Retrieved June 19, 2008, from http://www.globalissues.org/TradeRelated/Consumption.asp.

Sklar, H. (1980). Trilateralism: An overview. In H. Sklar (Ed.), *The Trilateral Commission and elite planning for world management* (pp. 1–58). Cambridge, MA: South End Press.

Smith, D. (2008). Globalization, degradation, and the dynamics of humiliation. *Current Sociology, 56*(3), 371–379.

Thompson, P. (1980). Bilderberg and the West. In H. Sklar (Ed.), *The Trilateral Commission and elite planning for world management* (pp. 157–189). Cambridge, MA: South End Press.

Trilateral Commission. (n.d.). The Trilateral Commission. Retrieved February 5, 2009, from http://www.trilateral.org.

Tucker, R. W. (1980). The purposes of American power. *Foreign Affairs, 59*(2), 241–274.

UNESCO. (2001, April 23–26). *Globalization and cultural diversity.* UNESCO. Retrieved June 24, 2008, from http://portal.unesco.org/en/ev.php-URL_ID=18219&URL_DO=DO_PRINTPAGE&URL_SECTION=201.html.

United Nations Development Programme Human Development Report. (1998). *Growing urbanization.* Global Policy Forum. Retrieved June 19, 2008, from http://www.globalpolicy.org/globaliz/charts/urbaniz1.htm.

United Nations Development Programme Human Development Report. (2002). *Cellular phone subscribers by region.* Global Policy Forum. Retrieved June 19, 2008, from http://www.globalpolicy.org/globaliz/charts/celltable.htm.

United Nations Population Division. (n.d.-a). *Countries hosting largest number of migrants, 2000.* Global Policy Forum. Retrieved June 19, 2008, from http://www.globalpolicy.org/globaliz/charts/migtotalcounttable.htm.

United Nations Population Division. (n.d.-b). *Number of migrants residing in major regions, 1990 and 2000.* Global Policy Forum. Retrieved June 19, 2008, from http://www.globalpolicy.org/globaliz/charts/migtotaltable.htm.

United Nations Population Division. (n.d.-c). *Net migration flow per region, 1995–2000.* Global Policy Forum. Retrieved June 19, 2008, from http://www.globalpolicy.org/globaliz/charts/mignettable.htm.

United Nations University—World Institute for Developmental Economics Research. (2006). Pioneering study shows richest two percent own half world wealth. Retrieved February 2009, from http://www.wider.unu.edu/events/past-events/2006-events/en_GB/05-12-2006/.

Wallerstein, I. (1974). The rise and future demise of the world-capitalist system: Concepts for comparative analysis. *Comparative Studies in Society and History, 16*, 387–415.

Wallerstein, I. (1998). *Utopistics: Or, historical choices of the twenty-first century.* New York: New Press.

Wolff, A., & Davis, D. (2008, June 16). Opening volley. *Sports Illustrated, 108*(24), 58–66.

Worldwatch Institute. (2003). World languages in danger of extinction, 2000. Global Policy Forum. Retrieved June 19, 2008, from http://www.global policy.org/globaliz/charts/language.htm

Worldwatch Institute. (2004). State of consumption today. Retrieved July 5, 2008, from http://www.worldwatch.org/node/810#7.

Zinn, H. (1991). *Declarations of independence: Cross-examining American idealology.* New York: HarperPerennial.

Appendix: Key Questions

CHAPTER 1

What is the significance of the early segregation of and discrimination against racial and ethnic minorities to the current educational and economic progress of these minorities?

CHAPTER 2

What are the differences and similarities between African Americans and black immigrants?

CHAPTER 3

What are major challenges in changing the current workforce?

CHAPTER 4

How do health beliefs influence health, health care utilization, and compliance?

CHAPTER 5

How should diversity be represented within academic curricula? What principles should guide our decisions?

CHAPTER 6

Human diversity issues are important to both academic learning and school climate. Develop an organizational and policy framework to help faculty and administrators with program and curriculum development and with campus activities. Then, describe strategies that you develop from your framework.

CHAPTER 7

For mental health professionals to bring about culturally informed social change, what essential constructs should they be prepared to integrate into their work?

CHAPTER 8

How can we better understand and respond to the needs of graduate students of color in multicultural courses?

CHAPTER 9

After having been a strong proponent of diversity throughout your career, you are appointed as an administrator at a college. As you begin your new position, how would you go about ensuring that diversity is central to your administrative role?

CHAPTER 10

What are racial microaggressions, and how do they create disparities in employment, education and health?

CHAPTER 11

Consider how an identity as an American influences a person's ability to understand various types of oppression worldwide (including racism, sexism, classism, heterosexism, etc.).

CHAPTER 12

What role(s) do you think psychology should play in addressing globalization and its effects on cultural diversity?

About the Editor and Contributors

JEAN LAU CHIN, EDD, ABPP, is professor and dean of the Derner Institute for Advanced Psychological Studies at Adelphi University in Garden City, New York. Prior to her current position, she held executive management positions as Systemwide Dean of the California School of Professional Psychology at Alliant International University; president, CEO Services; regional director, Massachusetts Behavioral Health Partnership; executive director, South Cove Community Health Center; and co-director, Thom Child Guidance Clinic. She is a licensed psychologist with over 35 years of experience in education, health, and mental health services. Her prior faculty appointments included: associate professor at Boston University School of Medicine and assistant professor at Tufts University School of Medicine. Dr. Chin is an educator, administrator, clinician, and scholar. She has published extensively, with 10 books, many chapters and articles, and over 200 presentations in the areas of diversity and cultural competence; ethnic minority, Asian American, and women's issues in health and mental health; and leadership. Her most recent books are: *Women and Leadership: Transforming Visions and Diverse Voices* (2007) and *Learning from My Mother's Voice: Family Legend and the Chinese American Experience* (2005). She serves on many national and local boards including: the Advisory Committee for Women's Services and the Eliminating Mental Health Disparities Committee for Substance Abuse Mental Health Services Administration, U.S. Dept of Health and Human Services; Board for the Advancement of Psychology in the Public Interest of the American Psychological Association; board member of the National Asian Pacific American Families Against Substance Abuse; and president of the National Council of Schools and Programs of Professional Psychology.

JEFFERY B. ALLEN, PhD, ABPP, is a professor at the Wright State University School of Professional Psychology. He has professional experience that includes an internship at Brown University, a postdoctoral fellowship at the Rehabilitation Institute of Michigan in Detroit, and employment as a clinical neuropsychologist in a medical rehabilitation facility in Lexington, Kentucky. He is a diplomate in clinical neuropsychology through the American Board of Professional Psychology. He is widely published in neuropsychology, head injuries, and memory in sources such as *Neuropsychologia, Brain Injuries*, and *Archives of Clinical Neuropsychology and Assessment*. He has also published a number of clinical texts, including the *Innovations Series* through Professional Resource Press and *Treating Patients with Neuropsychological Disorders: A Clinician's Guide to Assessment and Referral*, through APA books. His areas of teaching include physiological psychology and clinical neuropsychology and integrative assessment. Dr. Allen has also had the opportunity to co-teach the Multicultural Lab at the School of Professional Psychology. His interests include neurobehavioral disorders, quality of life in medical populations, cognitive and neuropsychological assessment, and outcome measurement in rehabilitation. Presently, he is director of the Community Memory Clinic in Dayton, Ohio, which offers neuropsychological assessment services to underserved populations. The clinic strives to improve accessibility and cultural sensitivity in working with African Americans and other diverse populations.

ROSIE PHILLIPS BINGHAM, PhD, received her doctorate from The Ohio State University and is vice president for student affairs and a professor in counseling, educational psychology, and research at The University of Memphis. She has served as chair of the Women's Foundation for a Greater Memphis, an organization that seeks to improve the lives of women and children in the Memphis community. She holds a diplomate (ABPP) in counseling psychology and has served as president of the Association of University and College Counseling Center Directors, the International Association of Counseling Services, and the Society of Counseling Psychology of the American Psychological Association. Bingham is a founder and organizer, along with Drs. Lisa Porche-Burke, Derald Wing Sue, and Melba Vasquez, of the National Multicultural Conference and Summit of the American Psychological Association, and was the summit's keynote speaker in 2007. She serves on the editorial boards of *In Session* for the *Journal of Clinical Psychology* and *Journal of Career Assessment*; is a past member of the editorial boards of the *Journal of College Student Development*, the *Journal of Counseling and Development*, and *The Counseling Psychologist*; and is co-editor of the book *Career Counseling and African Americans* (2001). Her primary scholarly focus is on multicultural vocational psychology, and she actively purses advocacy in the area of inclusion. Bingham is the recipient of numerous awards, including the Woman of the Year Award from the Society of Counseling Psychology-Section for the Advancement of Women, the Society for the Psychological Study of Ethnic Minority Issues Charles and Shirley Thomas Award, the National Multicultural Conference and Summit Dalmas A. Taylor Award, the American Psychological Association Society of Counseling Psychology Lifetime Achievement in Mentoring Presidential Citation, and the Teachers College Winter Roundtable Janet E. Helms Award for Mentoring. Bingham also holds fellowship status in the American Psychological Association's Society of Counseling Psychology-Division 17, the Society for General Psychology-Division 1, and the Society for the Psychology of Women-Division 35.

ELAINE A. BURKE, PhD, has been a full-time faculty member at the California School of Professional Psychology at Alliant International University, for the past 14 years. She received her doctorate in clinical psychology from the University of Denver, School of Professional Psychology, in 1990 and completed fellowship training in neuropsychology. She has many years of clinical experience, and her clinical work has focused on work with children and adults who have difficulties with learning, medical or neurological problems. The patient populations have included a number of different cultural populations, including individuals who were economically disadvantaged. Her clinical work includes administrative roles and private practice. She has also provided clinical consultation and education to the community, such as work with Senior Companions. Her clinical and research interests are sex roles/gender and culture, assessment and culture, health and culture, diversity training, and international issues. She is also very interested in neuropsychology, particularly with children and the elderly population. She has taught numerous multicultural classes related to her interests and has had faculty leadership/administrative roles as the coordinator of the Multicultural and Community Emphasis area, the class coordinator for the Intercultural and Diversity Processes class, and chairperson for International and Multicultural Initiatives. In addition, she has had a number of publications and has presented on many topics related to multicultural and internationalism in continuing education classes, including presentations at the National Multicultural Conference and Summit and the American Psychological Association (APA) Annual Conferences. She has been active in APA and is currently membership chair for Section IV (Women) of Division 12 (Society of Clinical Psychologists). Her research and teaching interests have led to a passion for multicultural and international issues. Her extensive traveling has emphasized culture, including an intensive six-week course on International and Community Health in South Africa, a tour of Ghana on the African Diaspora, a tour of Southeast Asia focusing on ethnic minority populations and a class on the Learning Potential Assessment Device in Israel. During her sabbatical, she taught at the United States International University-Kenya campus and assisted them in developing a program to train counselors to work with patients who had HIV/AIDS and their families. She also did research on attitudes toward HIV/AIDS, health beliefs, and gender roles while in Kenya. These experiences have enabled her to incorporate global issues as well as multicultural issues into her classroom teaching and the campus curriculum.

MELANIE E. L. BUSH, PhD, is the author of *Breaking the Code of Good Intentions: Everyday Forms of Whiteness* (2004), published by Rowman and Littlefield Publishers, Inc. She is currently an assistant professor of sociology and anthropology at Adelphi University (Garden City, NY) and has published numerous articles in scholarly journals including: *Sage Race Relations Abstracts*; *Tsantsa: Revue de la Societe Suisse d'Ethnologie* (special issue on "School–Society–Globalization"); "International and Comparative Literature on Whiteness" in *Towards a Discipline Specific Bibliography of Critical Whiteness Studies* (Center on Democracy in a Multiracial Society, University of Illinois at Urbana-Champaign); and "Everyday Whiteness" in *SOULS: A Critical Journal of Black Politics, Culture and Society* (Institute for Research in African American Studies at Columbia University, New York). She is a contributor to *1000 Peace Women Across the Globe* (Scalo, 2005), produced by The Association 1000 Peace Women for the Nobel Peace Prize 2005. Forthcoming works include a book entitled *Tensions in the "American" Dream: The Imperial Nation Confronts the Liberation of Nations*, co-authored with R. D. Bush, St. John's University (Temple University Press); "Whiteness Matters: National Belonging in the United States" in *Athanor. Semiotica, Filosofia, Arte, Letteratura* (special issue on White Matters/ Il Bianco al Centro Della Questione, Serie annuale del Dipartimento di Pratiche Linguistiche e Analisi di Testi dell'Università di Bari); a "Case Study: United States Nationalism and Nationalism Post World War II" for *Nations and Nationalisms in Global Perspective: An Encyclopedia of Origins, Development, and Contemporary Transitions* (edited by David H. Kaplan and Guntram H. Herb, Oxford, UK, ABC-CLIO); and the book chapter "United Statesians: the Nationalism of Empire" for the *Handbook of the Sociology of Racial and Ethnic Relations* (edited by Hernan Vera and Joseph Feagin, Springer Science and Business Media, Inc.). She served as guest editor for a special issue on "Multiculturalism and Higher Education" of the *Electronic Magazine for Multicultural Education*, Fall 2006. Dr. Bush has presented at a range of national and international conferences, universities, libraries, community and faith-based organizations related to issues of racial and social justice and equality, U.S. nationalism, academic freedom and education, and the common good. She serves on the American Sociological Association Task Force on Academic Freedom and Scientific Integrity and is involved with numerous academic association and university committees.

JOHN C. CAREY, PhD, is the director of the National Center for School Counseling Outcome Research and professor of school counseling at the University of Massachusetts. He is actively involved in evaluating effective school counseling interventions and in developing the research base to support effective practice. He has published extensively in the school counseling and counselor education literatures, co-edited the first book on *Multicultural Counseling in Schools* (1994) and co-authored a recent book on *Evidence-Based School Counseling* (2007).

DANA L. CARUSO, PsyD, received her doctorate in clinical psychology from Antioch University, New England, her master's degree from Goddard College, and her bachelor's degree from Skidmore College. Her dissertation title was *Multiculturalism in Climate and Curriculum: Students' Perspectives in one New England Independent School.* Dr. Caruso is currently doing postdoctoral work towards licensure.

ANGELA M. DESILVA, MA, is a doctoral candidate at Boston College in the developmental, educational, and counseling psychology program. She earned her master's degree in mental health counseling at Boston College as well. Angela's areas of research include social supports and mental health among immigrant groups as well as the intersections of risk-taking behaviors, spirituality, and mental health among adolescents and young adults. Her clinical work includes providing outpatient therapy to and consultation services for diverse groups of children and adolescents in school and community settings.

JAMES E. DOBBINS, PhD, ABPP, is a graduate of the University of Pittsburgh, where he received his PhD in clinical psychology. Dr. Dobbins is currently a professor and the director of Postdoctoral Training for the School of Professional Psychology at Wright State University. He is a teacher and a scholar whose professional experiences are oriented toward social responsibility and social change. His professional experience includes research in health attitudes and beliefs among underserved populations, multicultural, organizational and higher education consultation, as well as child, adult, and family therapy. He holds the distinction of Board Certification in Family Psychology from the American Board of Professional Psychology. He has been an officer of that board and holds several national positions including immediate past president of the National Council of Schools and Programs of Professional Psychology and the current vice president for diversity, Division of Family Psychology, in the American Psychological Association. Dr. Dobbins is a life member of the Association of Black Psychologists and served as chair of the National Convention Committee from 1985 to 1988 and historian from 1988 to 1989. During this same period he was also appointed by Governor Richard Celeste to serve two terms as commissioner for minority health in the State of Ohio. From 1997 to 1999 he served as member of the Board of Directors for the American Orthopsychiatric Association. He has been a consultant for the Dayton Urban League for over 20 years. In this capacity he has developed model programs that serve families and youth. Dr. Dobbins has lectured nationally and locally. In his practice he provides clinical services, including psychotherapy services, management consultation, program development and evaluation, to a broad range of organizations and institutions. He has received numerous teaching awards for his contributions to education, the community, and the profession. He remains productive as a writer who has authored over thirty papers, grants and book chapters related to his professional interests and specialties.

MILDRED GARCÍA, EdD, is the seventh president of California State University, Dominguez Hills, and the first Latina president in the California State University System. CSU Dominguez Hills is a comprehensive urban university located in Los Angeles County. Over 12,000 enrolled students choose from 45 baccalaureate degrees and 21 master's degrees offered by the university's six constituent colleges. Having assumed the presidency on August 1, 2007, Dr. García is a good fit for one of the most ethnically and culturally diverse universities in the western United States. Named to *Hispanic Business* magazine's 100 Most Influential Hispanics list for 2007, President García brought with her a commitment to multicultural alliances and a belief that these coalitions strengthen students' self-development and opportunities, as well as strengthen institutions and communities. García came to Dominguez Hills after serving, from 2001 to 2007, as president of Berkeley College in New York and New Jersey, where she championed the cause of access with success—the obligation to make the attainment of a college degree a realistic goal for all who strive to succeed. Under her leadership, the college began offering full academic programs in an online format, and over 28 bachelor's and associate's degrees were approved. Prior to Berkeley, she was at Arizona State University (1997–2001), Montclair State University (1986–1996), and Hostos Community College of the City University of New York (1979–1986). Foremost an educator, García is a scholar in the field of higher education. Her research has concentrated on equity in higher education and its impact on policy and practice. She has written extensively and is a much sought-after speaker at national and international conferences. Among the books she has authored are *Succeeding in an Academic Career, Assessing Campus Diversity Initiatives* (co-published), and *Transforming the First Year of College for Students of Color* (with Laura I. Rendón and Dawn Person). Most recently, she was a keynote speaker at the Association of American Colleges and Universities' Annual Meeting, and presented at the American Council on Education's Third Summit for Women of Color Administrators in Higher Education. García received a EdD and MA in higher education administration from Teachers College, Columbia University; an MA in business education/higher education from New York University; a BS in business education from Bernard Baruch College of City University of New York (CUNY); and an AAS in legal secretarial sciences in business from New York City Community College of CUNY.

D. J. IDA, PhD, is frequently asked to speak on the issues of cultural competence and workforce development. She has helped author the subcommittee reports on *Eliminating Disparities* for the President's New Freedom Commission on Mental Health, as well as the Annapolis Coalition for Workforce Development's *Action Plan for Behavioral Health Workforce Development*. She has also served as peer reviewer for the U.S. Surgeon General's report on mental health, *Culture Race and Ethnicity*. She is executive director of the National Asian American Pacific Islander Mental Health Association (NAAPIMHA) and served as the principal investigator for Growing Our Own, a federally funded project that developed the first national cross-disciplinary curriculum to train clinicians on providing culturally and linguistically competent services to AAPIs. She worked with the National Latino Behavioral Health Association to develop a curriculum to train interpreters to work specifically in a mental health setting. She is also working with the Khmer Health Advocates, Inc., to develop training on a blended care model to address the health crisis in the Cambodian community. Dr. Ida serves on numerous boards and commissions, including the U.S. Department of Health and Human Services, SAMHSA, Center for Mental Health Services National Advisory Council and the national Board of Mental Health America.

ANNIE I. LIN, MA, is a doctoral student in the Department of Counseling and Clinical Psychology, Teachers College, Columbia University. She is also an adjunct faculty member at LaGuardia Community College, where she is involved in teaching and advising internship/career development. Her research interests include racism, acculturation, and Asian American issues.

KATHLEEN A. MALLOY, PhD, ABPP, is a graduate of Ohio University, where she received her PhD in clinical psychology. She is currently a professor at Wright State University's School of Professional Psychology. She has a Board Certification in Clinical Psychology from the American Board of Professional Psychology. Dr. Malloy has numerous publications and national presentations in the areas of graduate training in diversity issues, intimate partner violence, and feminist therapy. She has developed and, for 15 years, directed a domestic violence program designed to offer both culturally sensitive treatments for perpetrators and victims of intimate partner violence and training for graduate students in providing those services. Dr. Malloy has taught graduate courses on diversity issues for 20 years and helped to develop the series of diversity courses now being offered at Wright State University's School of Professional Psychology. She is a member of the Association of Women in Psychology and, in 2006, served as program chair for their national conference. She is currently serving as secretary/treasurer of the National Council of Schools and Programs of Professional Psychology. She is a past president of Ohio Women in Psychology and a former board member of the Ohio Psychological Association.

GUERDA NICOLAS is a licensed clinical psychologist and the assistant director of the Institute for the Study and Promotion of Race and Culture (ISPRC) along with Dr. Janet E. Helms. She is also an associate professor at University of Miami, Florida, School of Education, Department of Educational and Psychological Services. She obtained her doctoral degree in clinical psychology from Boston University. She completed her predoctoral training at Columbia University Medical Center and her postdoctoral training the New York State Psychiatric Institute/Columbia University, Department of Child Psychiatry. As a multicultural (Haitian American) and multilingual psychologist (Spanish, French, and Haitian Creole), her research is reflective of her background and interests. Her current research projects focus on developing spirituality across the lifespan among ethnic minorities, culturally effective mental health intervention for ethnic minority adolescents, with a specific focus on Immigrant children, adolescents, and families. In addition, she conducts research on social support networks of Carribeans with a specific focus on Haitians. She has published several articles and book chapters and delivered numerous invited presentations at the national and international conferences in the areas of women issues, depression and intervention among Haitians, social support networks of ethnic minorities, and spirituality.

KIMBERLY A. PRATER, BA, is a doctoral student at Fordham University in the clinical psychology program. She earned her bachelor's degree in human development at Boston College. Kimberly's areas of research include mental health among immigrant groups and treatment outcomes at residential treatment centers servicing children and adolescents. Kimberly provides outpatient therapeutic services to diverse groups of children and adolescents in community mental health centers.

DAVID P. RIVERA, MS, is a doctoral student in counseling psychology at Teachers College, Columbia University. He earned a BS in psychology from the University of Wyoming, where he was a McNair Scholar, and an MS in clinical community counseling from Johns Hopkins University. The bulk of his professional experience is in higher education administration, including multicultural affairs, academic/career advising, and counseling center work. Areas of research and clinical interest include racism/anti-racism, microaggressions, Latina/o issues, sexual orientation identity development, and college student development.

GARGI ROYSIRCAR, PhD, received her doctorate in educational and counseling psychology at Texas Tech University. She is the founding director of the Multicultural Center for Research and Practice at Antioch University, New England, and a professor of clinical psychology. She conducts research on social justice community outreach, the interface of acculturation and ethnic identity with the mental health of immigrants and ethnic minorities, worldview differences, multicultural counseling competencies, training of graduate students in multicultural competencies, and multicultural assessment and instrumentation. She has authored 65 journal articles and chapters on these topics.

KUMEA SHORTER-GOODEN, PhD, is a professor and director of International-Multicultural Initiatives at Alliant International University (AIU). She served for several years as the coordinator of the Multicultural Community-Clinical Psychology (MCCP) Emphasis Area (Los Angeles Campus) of the California School of Professional Psychology (CSPP) of AIU. Prior to joining CSPP, Dr. Shorter-Gooden was the director of the student counseling center at The Claremont Colleges and clinical director of the Community Mental Health Council in Chicago. She is the co-author, with Charisse Jones, of *Shifting: The Double Lives of Black Women in America* (HarperCollins, 2003), winner of a 2004 American Book Award. Dr. Shorter-Gooden has numerous published articles in journals such as *Journal of Black Psychology, Cultural Diversity and Mental Health, Journal of Adolescence, Psychological Foundations*, and *Psychotherapy*. In addition, she has contributed chapters to the following books: *Psychotherapy with African American Women: Innovations in Psychodynamic Perspectives and Practice* (edited by L. C. Jackson & B. Greene, 2000), *The California School of Professional Psychology Handbook of Multicultural Education, Research, Intervention, and Training* (edited by E. Davis-Russell, 2002), and *Handbook of African American Psychology* (edited by H. A. Neville, B. M. Tynes, & S. O. Utsey, in press). Dr. Shorter-Gooden is currently a consulting editor for *Professional Psychology: Research and Practice* and for *Cultural Diversity and Ethnic Minority Psychology*, and she has served as an ad hoc reviewer for *American Journal of Community Psychology, Clinical Psychology: Science and Practice, Journal of Adolescence, Journal of Black Psychology, Journal of Marriage and Family, Psychology of Women Quarterly*, and *Sex Roles*. A licensed psychologist, Dr. Shorter-Gooden has a private psychotherapy and consultation practice in Pasadena, California, where she works with adults and couples as well as organizations. She is an active presenter and workshop leader around issues related to African American mental health, women's issues, and multiculturalism and diversity. She was a "Master Lecturer" at the 2007 California Psychological Association Convention and has appeared on *The Today Show*.

JOSEPH E. TRIMBLE (PhD, University of Oklahoma, Institute of Group Relations, 1969), formerly a fellow at Harvard University's Radcliffe Institute for Advanced Study, is professor of psychology at Western Washington University, a senior scholar at the Tri-Ethnic Center for Prevention Research at Colorado State University, and a research associate for the National Center for American Indian and Alaska Native Mental Health Research at the University of Colorado Health Sciences Center. He has held numerous offices in the International Association for Cross-Cultural

Psychology and the American Psychological Association (APA). He holds fellow status in three APA divisions: 9, 27, and 45. He is past-president of the Society for the Psychological Study of Ethnic Minority Issues and a former council member for the Society for the Psychological Study of Social Issues. Since 1972, he has served as a member of scientific review committees and research panels for the following federal agencies: NIAAA; NIDA; NIA; NIMH; National Heart, Lung and Blood Institute; NICHD; NCI; National Center for Research Resources; Risk, Prevention, and Health Behavior, NIH; Center for Substance Abuse Prevention; National Academy of Sciences; NSF; NIDA's Subcommittee on Epidemiology and Prevention Research; and NIDA's Risk, Prevention, and Health Behavior Initial Review Group. Currently, he is a member of NIDA's Health Services Research Subcommittee. Dr. Trimble has generated over 130 publications on cross-cultural and ethnic topics in psychology, including 16 edited, co-edited, and co-authored books; his co-edited *Handbook of Racial and Ethnic Minority Psychology* was selected as one of *CHOICE* magazine's Outstanding Academic Titles for 2004. His recent books include (with Celia Fisher) the *Handbook of Ethical Research with Ethnocultural Populations and Communities*, and (with Paul Pedersen, Juris Draguns, and Walt Lonner) *Counseling Across Cultures, 6th Edition*. He has received numerous excellence in teaching and mentoring awards for his work in the field of ethnic and cultural psychology, including: the Excellence in Teaching Award and the Paul J. Olscamp Outstanding Faculty Research Award from Western Washington University; APA's Division 45 Lifetime Achievement Award; the Janet E. Helms Award for Mentoring and Scholarship in Professional Psychology at Teachers College, Columbia University; the Washington State Psychological Association Distinguished Psychologist Award for 2002; the Peace and Social Justice Award from APA's Division 48; and the Distinguished Elder Award from the National Multicultural Conference and Summit in 2007.

LUIS A. VARGAS, PhD, is an associate professor at the University of New Mexico School of Medicine. He was previously the director of the clinical psychology internship program for 14 years. He served six years as chair of the New Mexico Board of Psychologist Examiners. He is a past president of Div. 37 (Society for Child and Family Policy and Practice), an Association of State and Provincial Psychology Boards Fellow, and an APA Fellow of Divisions 37, 12, and 45. Professor Vargas's clinical and scholarly work has focused on providing culturally responsive services to diverse children and adolescents, particularly in Latino communities. He is co-editor, with Joan D. Koss-Chioino, of *Working with Culture: Psychotherapeutic Interventions with Ethnic Minority Children and Adolescents* and a co-author, with Joan D. Koss-Chioino, of *Working with Latino Youth: Culture, Development, and Context*, both published by Jossey-Bass.

JANEECE R. WARFIELD, PsyD, is associate professor at the School of Professional Psychology at Wright State University and the program co-ordinator for the Center for Child and Adolescent Violence Prevention. Dr. Warfield completed her doctorate at Wright State University and a postdoctoral fellowship at Georgetown University Hospital, specializing in infants, developmental disabilities, and children with chronic illness. Her professional interests include multicultural and diversity training, violence prevention, infant mental health, mental health consultation to Early Head Start and Head Start, developmental disabilities, treating children exposed to trauma, and parent-child relationships.

JULIE L. WILLIAMS, PsyD, CRC, is a graduate of the Wright State University School of Professional Psychology, where she received her PsyD. She is currently an assistant professor in the same program. Her professional experience includes an internship and postdoctoral fellowship in rehabilitation psychology/research and neuropsychology at Mt. Sinai School of Medicine in New York. She has also worked as a clinical psychologist at Mt. Sinai Medical Center, specializing in rehabilitation psychology and neuropsychology. Dr. Williams has presented nationally on the psychological aspects of disability, including the ways in which disability interacts with a variety of issues, such as suicide, sexuality and other diversity variables. She has also presented on the identification of psychological issues in medical settings and how to intervene when working with patients with disabilities and their families. Dr. Williams's clinical and training interests focus primarily on disability issues, rehabilitation psychology, health psychology, and neuropsychology. She has endeavored to provide strong mentorship in her work with students in psychology who have disabilities, an effort that led to her being awarded the 2007 Disability Mentorship Award from the Committee on Disability Issues in Psychology of the American Psychological Association.

DERALD WING SUE, PhD, is professor of psychology and education in the Department of Counseling and Clinical Psychology at Teachers College, Columbia University. He has served as a training faculty member with the Institute for Management Studies and Columbia University Executive Training Programs. He was the co-founder and first president of the Asian American Psychological Association, past president of the Society for the Psychological Study of Ethnic Minority Issues, and past president of the Society of Counseling Psychology.

Index